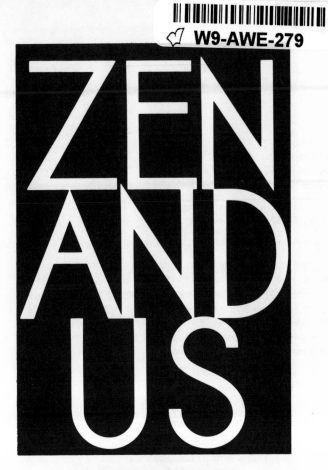

ZEN AND US

KARLFRIED GRAF DÜRCKHEIM

Translated from the German by Vincent Nash

E. P. DUTTON   NEW YORK

Published in the United States by
E. P. Dutton, a division of NAL Penguin Inc.,
2 Park Avenue, New York, N.Y. 10016.

Published simultaneously in Canada
by Fitzhenry and Whiteside, Limited, Toronto.

Originally published in West Germany under the title Zen und Wir.

Library of Congress Cataloging-in-Publication Data

Dürckheim, Karlfried, Graf, 1896–
Zen and us.
Translation of: Zen und wir.
1. Zen Buddhism. I. Title
BQ9265.4.D8313   1987   294.3'927   87-6895

ISBN: 0-525-48331-4

W

Designed by Michele Aldin

10 9 8 7 6 5 4 3 2 1

First American Edition

For Maria Hippius

Editor's Note

Quotations from Buddhist texts, as for example the section from the *Shin Jin Mei* on page 63 and the hymn attributed to Buddha on page 67, have been translated from the author's German in an effort to preserve a unity of tone and the author's interpretative intent. There exist, however, some very notable translations of these same texts by such figures as D. T. Suzuki, R. H. Blythe, and others.

Contents

Preface   xi

STARTING POINTS   1

    What Has Zen Got to Do with Us in the
    West?   3
    The Light from the East?   5
    What Zen Is Essentially About   6
    Zen's Answer to the Problem of Living   9

WESTERN HUMANITY—ANGUISH AND AN END
TO ANGUISH   13

    SUFFERING AND PROMISE—THE SOURCES OF THE
    QUEST   15

THE SHACKLES OF OBJECTIVE CONSCIOUSNESS   18

     What Objective Consciousness Is—Why It Is
     Dangerous   20
     The Pain of Living   24
     Depersonalization of the Individual   26
     The Decline of Community   30

PORTENTS OF CHANGE   32

     From Natural to Supernatural Experience   32
     New Wine in Old Bottles   37
     From Knowledge to Insight   39

ZEN'S ANSWER   45

     THE SUBLIME MESSAGE OF ZEN   47

     Everyone, in His True Nature, Is Buddha   47
     The Experience of Being   49
     The Experience of Being and Dualism   52
     The Doctrine of Not-Two   56
     Non-attachment to "Being"   63
     The Opening of the Inner Eye   65
     What Zen Looks Like in Practice   70
     Passing on the Message   72

     LIVING ZEN   74

     Masters and Students   74
     Heart to Heart   77
     Stillness and Silence   79
     The Discipline of Silence   82
     Paradox   84

     PRACTICING ZEN   86

     The Meaning of Exercise   86
     Dismantling the Ego   89

The Purpose of Technique   92
Zazen   97
The Three Stages of Consciousness and the Five
Steps on the Way   109

THE TALE OF THE WONDERFUL ART OF A
CAT   114

ZEN FOR THE WEST—WESTERN ZEN   123

Preface

What was said in the first German edition of this book regarding the significance of Zen for people in the West has proved true. The waves of Zen have beaten powerfully in upon the Western mind since then. But taking up Zen in the West can mean two things: becoming a Buddhist or opening oneself to the general, human significance of Zen's message. The second aspect is the only one that concerns me here. I know it is sometimes thought that Zen cannot be divorced from its Buddhist origins, and that Zen is Buddhism or nothing. This may be true for the theorist who, having no personal experience of the doctrine that true nature (Buddha-nature) is present in all of us, sees Zen as a purely Eastern vision of the human condition, or knows it only from books or as a tourist. Anyone, however, who is not deaf to the Absolute or who has spent some time on one of the Zen exercises—zazen, for example— soon finds that Zen is concerned with the basis of all genuine religious feeling, and indeed of all human growth and maturity. Zen enables us to do two things: first, to become one with our "true nature," in which the Absolute is present within us; and, second, to fulfill our human destiny by transforming ourselves and becoming a transparent medium, so that the Absolute within us can shine through. Zazen—seated meditation, in which meditation is not "contemplation," but a way of change—is a sober, stern, and rigorous exercise. It provides a healthy antidote to the ecstasy-seeking so popular today, and its emphasis on physical discipline brings it close both to the Western concern with personal form and the Christian conception of spirit becoming flesh. Its truth is universal and rooted in experience, and the encounter with it will help us to rediscover that truth and that experience in our own tradition—and revitalize our own spiritual life.

Starting Points

What Has Zen Got to Do with Us in the West?

What has Zen got to do with us in the West? Everyone, everywhere, is talking about Zen. Everything published on Zen at once finds eager readers. Where does this strange attraction come from? Is it a passing fashion? Is it the lure of the exotic? Is it a way out of our own problems and into another, faraway world? All of this may be partly true—but the fascination really comes from something else.

People today are aware that there is something basically wrong with current social values. Deep down, they know that the ways of thinking and acting that are supposed to enable them to cope with "outside" life are really undermining their own inner life—and they suffer increasingly from this knowledge. With no beliefs left to sustain them, they run from themselves, from this growing inner emptiness, and seek refuge in outside distractions. They lose contact with themselves, and their inner breathing falters. Feelings of guilt and fear take over. Bewildered and rudderless, they look around desperately for a way out. If, at this point, they happen on a text by one of the Zen masters, something deeper speaks to them immediately. They seem to breathe a new freedom. They feel as if a spring breeze had suddenly melted the icebound crust of their existence, as if a new liberty were being promised and a hidden life called into being. This is what makes Zen, in all its forms, attractive: it promises to free our real life, our real being, from the falsehoods and confusion that stifle it.

Zen speaks with vital force, and whenever it speaks, it breaks through the crust of what is and shows that it can become something else. It smashes through the tidy ideas, concepts, and images that prop us up and help to keep us going, but also shut us off from the real life within us—a life that expresses itself in a never-ending process of renewal. Zen touches the reality within us—Life, which transforms, redeems, and creates without ceasing, which is always on the way to becoming something else and which cannot be pinned down to any fixed form. Zen throws the door wide and points the way into the open. This is why it shakes the orderly citizen in all of us, with our fondness for well-worn daily routines; why it threatens the guardians of accepted values; why it enrages all those who rely on "systems" to keep their little worlds running smoothly; why it is also deeply disturbing for all of us who feel that nothing is "real" unless we can understand it rationally. Zen offers us something that lies wholly beyond that kind of understanding. But this is precisely what makes it so attractive and so promising for all of us who are sick of leading lives deadened by indolence, set ideas, and easy comfort, and who are looking for new horizons, thirsting for real life—real life that catches fire only when we make the leap from the safe and relative into the perilous and absolute.

The Light from the East?

Zen promises us something radically new—but why should this come from the East? Surely the mysterious spring flows in the West as well? It does indeed, but only in secret—hidden or discredited by the thrust of the Western mentality's development. In the East, everyone has always known where to find it, and its waters were guided long ago into a complex system of canals that kept them flowing. But is the East still what it was? Surely westernization has left it with nothing of its own to tell us? This is a question that people are constantly asking today. But just as the significance of ancient Greek culture for us in the West is in no way diminished by what may have happened to the Greeks in the meantime, so the significance of the Oriental spirit and its achievements is in no way affected by the political, economic, or even intellectual development of the peoples of Japan, China, and India. This development often seems to threaten the surviving manifestations of the ancient Oriental outlook—but it may in fact be bringing the spirit of the East home to us fully for the first time. This becomes clearer if we realize that the avidity with which the peoples of the East are seizing on Western ideas and life-styles reflects not only the need for Western products and technology as keys to survival and power, but also the deeper need to develop, at long last, a side of the human spirit that they have so far neglected and that human beings need in order to be complete: the rational side, which helps us to explain the world about us and cope with it in practice.

Conversely, the more we are led by an obscure attraction to explore the manifestations of the ancient Oriental mind, the clearer it can and should become that the tension we feel between the Eastern and the Western mentalities ultimately has nothing to do with cultural differences, but expresses a basic human dilemma. Depth psychology has shown that a man cannot be a complete human being, and thus a complete man, unless he recognizes the feminine side of his nature, takes it seriously, and tries to develop it. In the same way, we Westerners cannot be complete human beings and fulfill our destinies as complete Westerners unless we recognize and develop something that at first seems Oriental, but is actually waiting in every one of us to be noticed and acknowledged.

In a specifically Eastern form, the Eastern spirit embodies human qualities and possibilities that the Western mentality has obscured and prevented from developing properly, even though human beings are incomplete without them. To this extent, the experience and wisdom of Buddhism, and particularly of Zen, are not simply Eastern, but of universal human significance—indeed of very special significance in an age that has given us such frightening proofs of the dangers of developing our capabilities in one direction only.

What Zen Is Essentially About

Zen is essentially about rebirth from the experience of Being.

Zen teaches us to discover the transcendental core of our own selves in an immediate and practical sense, to "taste" divine Being in the here-and-now. It has nothing to do with analytical logic, dogmatic belief, or even speculative metaphysics, but points the way to an experience we can have and, indeed, are meant to have. Once we have had it, we come to see that our earthly existence, between the twin poles of life and death, is rooted in a transcendental state of Being, which forms the hidden ground of our own nature and which we, as human beings, can and must bring to consciousness. But to have this experience and have it validly, we must first discard the old consciousness, which has hardened into habit and determines the way we think and act. What this means as possibility, challenge, path, and consequence, Zen teaches in a manner that is valid not only for the East, but for us Westerners as well. And Zen is particularly important for us today because we, too, must now cross over—assuming we realize that we have reached the crossing point. The Eastern master uses rigorous practice to bring his student to a point beyond which something wholly different and unexampled beckons, and this is where the general development of the Western spirit has left many of us today. Increasingly, people are coming to an extreme point where they are filled with anger and despair at what they themselves and the world around them have become—but are also aware of something new in themselves, holding the promise of freedom.

As soon as the true self awakes, however, inertia exerts its dead weight, protecting things as they are and preventing us from making the breakthrough—and so the forces of darkness and delay are again at work today, using the sacrosanct traditions of science and religion as a pretext to impede the progress of the new. As usual, the reactionaries' efforts, both overt and covert, are finding support in the huckstering tactics of those who "sell" the new, without understanding it or at too low a price—spreading ideas and practices that are positively harmful and prevent the forces of good, which are breaking through on all sides, from achieving final victory.

The concepts of nothingness and Being, the boundary and the breakthrough, Tao and Zen, are already being bandied about on all sides. The whole thing is discussed, dissected—and above all distorted, since we are given to understand that we can grasp Zen intellectually and make it a part of ourselves without effort or change on our part. This is one way of turning something that is meaningful only when fully lived and practiced into a kind of intellectual parlor game. Generally speaking, we are only too inclined to surrender to the spell of abstract ideas and high-sounding concepts without noticing the highly practical demands they make on us, or in any way relating them to ourselves. This is also the danger if we approach Zen in the wrong way. We must be clear on one point: Zen may look like a speculative system, its ideas and concepts may seem purely abstract to the ignorant or uninitiated—but it is actually concerned, in a real and burning sense, with our own experience in the here-and-now. It touches our lives, with our sufferings and the everlasting cycle

7

of death and rebirth, on the deepest level and penetrates to our real nature, which is only waiting to be discovered and acknowledged. This discovery, if we make it, is the one decisive event in our human existence—the event that breaks all the molds and makes everything over. It is with this event and nothing else that Zen is concerned—with satori, the "great experience," in which Life, which brings us forth and shapes us, which cherishes and everlastingly gives birth to us anew, and which we ourselves are, reveals itself to us and enters our consciousness.

Anyone who has worked hard enough on himself, or whom personal need has left open to receive it, can hope to know satori, which has nothing to do with existing religious beliefs—although its nature undoubtedly places it at the heart of all true religious feeling and so makes it the key to every renewal of religious life. This has always been true, and it holds true today for those who have lost their first, instinctive contact with the basic truths of human life, have shed the beliefs once rooted in those truths and later distorted by theology, and have failed in their efforts to penetrate the mysteries of life by merely rational means.

When it leads us into the truth of life, Zen may take the form of a blossom on the Eastern branch of life's tree—but the experience, wisdom, and practices that it offers are offered to all.

Thus, Zen has universal significance and is not a special religion or *Weltanschauung*. Nor does it try to force alien forms on people who come from other traditions. On the contrary, Zen is a light shining through all of the multicolored windows through which the people and peoples of the earth all try, as their various natures and traditions direct them, to see what lies outside. It is like rain; it lets every seed grow in its own way, but without it every plant dies. It is the earth in which life has all its roots, and in which we must all sink our roots afresh if we want to find the way to ourselves and be renewed. It is the air that every human creature breathes and without which all human life ultimately suffocates.

Zen's Answer to the Problem of Living

In the form in which it reaches us from the East, Zen is often incomprehensible. If it is to help us, we must be able to peel off the alien externals and to separate its general human values, which are what count for us in the West, from the trappings of the East—of Buddhism, Mahayana Buddhism, and even Eastern Zen—all of which may mask its universal truth from us to start with. Even then, we will be able to hear what Zen has to tell us only if we try to approach it not in a spirit of theoretical inquiry, but at the urging of our own vital needs. We shall never understand what Zen is about if we try to break it down into a theory—in other words, if we stand back and try to be objective. From a distance, there is no such thing as Zen.

A loved woman exists fully and has meaning only for the man who loves her, an enemy only for those who fear him, a friend only for those whom his understanding warms, and a healer only for those who seek a cure. In the same way, Zen exists only as a living answer to real-life problems, to the sufferings and longings of individual human beings. If we try to take Zen objectively and to judge it by the standards of logic, ethics, or aesthetics, then we shall simply miss what it has to say, or misunderstand its message completely and reject the whole thing as obscure and abstruse. Whenever we try to force the inexplicable into an image or a concept, we are really trying to tame it and make it familiar—and there is always a danger that its real and vital meaning will be lost.

Westerners tend to be the prisoners of their own rationality, and there is something grotesque and naïve about the way in which they boldly pass judgment on religions—including their own—in terms that strip them of any real meaning. All that is left is the shell—images, observances, words, and empty concepts—reflecting something that was felt and thought long ago, but is now parted from its living source and has become lifeless and misleading. A living religion (and a religion is only real when it lives) is always an answer to the vital needs and longings of mankind. Religion can neither exist nor be understood in any other way. But today one has the feeling that many of the guardians of religion—the churches and churchmen—are themselves deeply alienated from the real meaning of the "doctrines" they profess. Otherwise, they would hardly see the unearthing of a link between the revelation imprisoned in dogma and conventional practice and the vital foundations of belief in personal feeling and experience as a dangerous attempt to subjectivize something objective—as if the superhuman and transcendental elements in religion had no roots and counterparts in human beings themselves.

To remain a force for action in the human heart, religion must be directly relevant to life, and to the sufferings and aspirations that give life its shape, for this is the only area in which religion is meaningful, valid, and vital. When revelation no longer speaks to the human heart, it becomes a doctrine and depends on the leap of faith for credibility—or it becomes a worldview and holds true only as long as reason accepts it. How else could millions of our own contemporaries have lost their so-called faith because they can no longer reconcile things that have happened to themselves or others with their rational-ethical notions of divine order and the justice of God?

There are plenty of wrongheaded ideas about faith, and most of them are rooted in the assumption that religion is objectively true and universally valid, has nothing to do with the way people really feel, think, and react, and needs to be protected against the "merely subjective" element in individual experience. But all of this misses the point on three counts:

1. We need the distinction between the objective (conceptually definable) and the subjective (colored by personal feelings and desires) as long as we are dealing with verifiable facts—but here we are shifting into an area where there are no objective or scientific facts, where the "real" is only real insofar as it exists in an individual consciousness and provokes an individual reaction.

2. If we reject all religious experience as merely subjective, we are forgetting that religious experience—like every other personal experience—falls into two basic categories: the relative and purely individual experience of a particular person in a particular time and place; and personal experience that comes from the individual's real center, from his inmost nature, where time and place do not apply. This kind of experience is not psychologically determined—though the images we use to convey it and the words we use to interpret it may be—and it is not, therefore, "merely subjective." Essentially, it bears witness to humanity's transcendental nature, which, since humanity consists of individuals, can speak only through a particular person in a particular time and place. Whenever humanity's true nature—i.e., the mode in which divine Being is present in all of us—speaks out like this from the depths, its words have a validity beyond time. How else could the sayings of the sages and great mystics, all the way back to Lao-tse, continue to touch the hearts of those wise enough to hear them with their timeless truths?

3. There is a third reason why the idea that individual experience can reflect a supernatural, transcendent reality is not taken seriously or is even discounted altogether. Christian theology has always kept the terms *supernatural* and *transcendent* for a divine reality totally beyond human ken—and this means that they are not available to describe even the most profound of human experiences, which are thought of as being "intrapsychic" and thus at a vast remove from the transcendent. Without entering into theological argument, it must still be said that human experience undoubtedly can encompass something that wholly outstrips natural reason and its power to comprehend. This kind of experience feels entirely different and floods us with a mysterious energy; indeed, the whole thing is so overwhelmingly unlike even the most striking of our everyday experiences that if we call the one physical, natural, human, and worldly, we have no choice but to call the other metaphysical, supernatural, otherworldly, and transcendent. We shall leave it an open question whether these

experiences are pre-theological (the product of natural piety and thus of less value than theological truth) or whether theology, which has the duality of all verbal systems (logos), is not surpassed utterly by the realities revealed to us in mystical experience. One thing, however, is sure: we can only make contact with the transcendental truths of Zen if our own experience, our own anguish, leaves us open to receive it, and if we can see it as an answer to that anguish—or as the fulfillment of an inner promise. If Zen is to work for us, the first question is, "What is the anguish and what are the longings of people in the West to which Zen today holds the answer?"

Western Humanity—
Anguish and
an End to Anguish

Suffering and Promise—
the Sources of the Quest

It is suffering, above all, that gives human beings no rest, keeps them on the move, and drives them on unceasingly. "Mark it well, all you who ponder and are given to reflection, your swiftest steed on the path to perfection is suffering," said Meister Eckhart.

If suffering sets people searching, then relief from suffering is what they are looking for, and there is a clear implication that this goal can be reached, the cause of suffering found, and suffering itself eliminated.

There are three basic things that make people suffer. The first is the constant threat of annihilation, the terrifying uncertainty of life and its transience, which makes them long for permanence, security, something solid to hold on to. The second is despair at life's meaninglessness, which makes them look for a permanent meaning. The third is a sense of the fearful insecurity of life, which makes them look for a place of permanent safety. At first, people rely on their own strength and try to find stability, meaning, and security in the world around them. But they are bound to fail, and when they do, they turn for peace to the stillness of divine Being, where fear, despair, and sorrow are healed from another direction.

But if people are tormented by the impermanence, meaninglessness, and desolation of the everyday world, and look outside it for a cure, this surely suggests that there is some deep-seated intuition promising them something else, something that they can experience directly and that eliminates uncertainty, senselessness, and insecurity by offering them permanence, meaning, and safety from another source— something that is not, in fact, of this world. The truth is that to be human is not simply to be an ego, to be rooted in this world and depend on it; it is also to operate on a far deeper level as the medium through which Being seeks to manifest itself in the world, and thus to have a share in Being oneself. This is why the suffering inflicted by the world and the longing to be free of it are not the only cause of human anguish. Another is loss of the ability to serve as a medium for Being, i.e., loss of contact and union with the Absolute in ourselves. But suffering is not the only thing that drives human beings on into the divine haven where wanderings cease, a home anchor beckons, and fear, despair, and sorrow are at last laid to rest. If we respond to the suffering that cries out within us for relief, we respond even more profoundly to the divine life that animates our innermost being and is constantly seeking to manifest itself in us as fullness, form, and unity, in a never-ending process of change and creation. This is the source of the wholly new energy that drives us forward—the energy that springs from the promise felt within, and the longing for ultimate fulfillment it generates.

If it is true that a promise provides our real impetus, then our goal is not redemption, but fulfillment of that promise—a fulfillment in which vitality, beauty, and unity are all perfected: not redemption from a life filled with sorrow, but awakening to a new life; not existence fading into the stasis of Being, but Being creatively manifest in the multiple forms and order of existence. It is true that this is a Western, not an Eastern, a Christian, not a Buddhist way of looking at things. But the way to this fulfillment leads across a common threshold: satori, the great experience.

The three components of human happiness are vitality, beauty, and a sheltering sense of community. We always start by relying on ourselves and looking for these three things in power, order, and fellowship as the world understands them. Failing to find them there, we eventually seek them in the only way that makes sense—in Being, which transforms, fulfills, and brings us to new life.

Turning to Being is turning inward, but turning inward for fulfillment would surely be a futile exercise unless what we found there was, in some sense, absolute and totally divorced from the agonizing ego-world complex in which we are entangled to start with.

And so people today, bitterly conscious of the imperfections of existence, are driven on by two factors in their search for something better: an overpowering sense of the world's relativity and the sense of a hidden absolute—a promise deep within themselves.

The way forward leads from the anguish rooted in the old self to the experience of what we really are, and from the experience of what we really are to fulfillment in a new self; it leads through the death of the old self to the birth of a new self from what we truly are—i.e., to the true self.

Zen knows about redemptive Being and the life that springs from it. Zen knows about our inner nature, in which Being is present within us, offering us salvation and the genuine hope of a new life that will transform and remake us. Zen knows about the wall that cuts us off from Being, and it knows how we can tear it down. But we shall understand Zen only if we can hear within ourselves what Zen, in its own way, is saying. To receive the gift that Zen offers us, we must first ask ourselves, What is the anguish, the human anguish, that afflicts us today? And what are the signs that promise us that it will end?

17

The Shackles of
Objective Consciousness

Our problems in the West begin when one particular form of consciousness—itself a necessary stage in human development—takes complete hold and dominates all others. This is *objective consciousness,* which makes us see reality as something "objective," that is, something existing without reference to ourselves, and makes us apply the yardstick of "objectivity" to everything we do. Bravely setting out to understand, control, or shape the world around us, we discount our own aspirations and desires as "merely subjective." But succeeding or failing only in terms of an "objective" reality is precisely what human life is not about. Indeed, human life is primarily a matter of experiencing, transforming, and fulfilling—or failing to fulfill—ourselves subjectively, and joy and pain tell us if, and where, we are living in or out of line with our deeper nature's promise and potential. Where and how is that deeper nature, our innermost core, to become real if not in our *subjective* selves and *subjective* experience? If we sacrifice the claims not only of our puny egos, but also of our true nature to those of a supposedly "objective" world, and deny and repress our subjective selves in the name of a life that can manifest and fulfill itself only in "objective" systems, then we ultimately fail to make contact with ourselves and plunge into a kind of pain that is particularly and peculiarly human. Failure to grasp the meaning of Buddhism, and indeed Oriental wisdom in general, is synonymous with a failure to grasp the nature of this pain and to recognize the danger that threatens us all if we let this type of consciousness, which objectivizes everything, take over. The saving doctrines of Buddhism and of Zen see this danger for what it is and know how to save us from the anguish it causes.

Objective consciousness and its systems and values have a far firmer hold on the Western than on the Eastern mind, and this is why the manifestations of the Eastern spirit often strike the Westerner as alien and diffuse. But as soon as the Westerner starts to realize that his ways of thinking and perceiving are incomplete, and to be made uncomfortable by that fact, the promise latent in the Eastern spirit begins to cast its spell.

The universal truth embodied in Zen is no less accessible to the Westerner rooted in Christian belief than it is to the Easterner—but we are genuinely receptive to it only when we personally feel the anguish and danger that Zen sets out to remove. This is why we cannot make fruitful contact with Zen until we understand what objective consciousness is, why it is dangerous, and why it makes us suffer.

Asked to say what reality is, a Westerner automatically responds from the part of his subjective nature that is rooted in the objective, defining ego, using concepts belonging to a consciousness conditioned by Kant's space-time categories and also rooted in the ego. This is completely natural for us, but by no means completely natural for everyone. An educated Easterner—even a scientist who has just spoken of reality in terms dictated by that ego—will instantly "think again" if asked to say what reality *really* is and attempt to answer from the part of his subjective being that is rooted not in the ego, but in Tao- or Buddha-nature, i.e., in his "true" nature. And what will he say? He may simply smile and say nothing, or he may reply in symbols, images, and paradoxes that mean nothing to us. If he has to say something, however, he will surprise us by saying, first of all, that the reality perceived by the reflective ego is itself an illusion, masking the "true nature" of all reality, which can never be grasped conceptually. Our surprise results from the fact that we Westerners identify in-

19

stinctively and utterly with the self of everyday consciousness and no longer realize that the image of reality imprinted on that consciousness is extremely limited, that it misses the reality of Being and is transcended by it. It is at this point that we must turn to epistemology for a clearer picture of what objective consciousness is.

What Objective Consciousness Is—Why It Is Dangerous

The objective vision of life is grounded in the *ego*—the ego that is meant when we say "I am I." The *principle of identity* thus lies at the heart of objective consciousness and its vision of reality. When a person thinks of himself, he thinks of something he identifies with himself—something standing fast amid the flux of events. This self-anchored ego provides the standpoint from which he sees the world around him, and its consciousness defines what he sees by asking, "What is that?" and replying, "It is such-and-such," thus congealing life into *facts,* which are fixed and to which he must cling. Everything perceived and experienced is seen from the standpoint of the self and related to the self—and becomes, as it were, the anti-self. The world is something that can be—or has been—defined and understood objectively, and things are "real" only to the extent that they are rooted in this objective reality, which is itself pinned down in *concepts.* This means that nothing is real unless it has been—or can be—integrated within a conceptual system. If it cannot be integrated within such a system, it is either not real yet or has stopped being real. It is merely "subjective"—the stuff of images, fancies, beliefs, feelings, and desires.

The person who is identified with his defining ego and anchored in objective consciousness is affected in two ways: first, he has a special way of seeing, a "theory" concerning what is to be regarded as real and assumed to be so; and, second, he takes a special, pragmatic view of the world, sorting it into what counts and does not count for him. Looking at it, he accepts as real only things that he sees as having a definite existence "outside" himself. In the same way, the only thing that makes him real himself is having a definite *standpoint* and sticking to it—and this standpoint determines the positive or negative significance of everything else.

Objectivity in general has nothing to do with physical objects, but is one of the ways in which things are brought to consciousness and anchored in it. It has its own type of consciousness, and this is governed by the ego, the self that defines the anti-self and registers objects ("objects of consciousness") only in counterpoint to itself. This is why *antitheses* are another feature of this consciousness. Seeing itself as something that it equates with itself, the ego sees everything else as something that it contrasts with itself, generating the typical *subject/object duality* of objective consciousness. Similarly, whenever the ego sees something as having a definite existence, it also marks it off from other things around it (it is "this" and not "that"), thus immediately breaking the whole of perceived reality down not simply into objects, but into antithetical objects. Antitheses, like objectivity, are a basic feature of the reality constructed by the defining ego. The consciousness that perceives objectively and operates with antitheses or dualisms stands and falls—like the reality in which it deals—with the self-anchored ego. "Here/there," "before/after," "above/below" exist only in relation to the fixed ego at the heart of consciousness and the reality perceived by that ego. And so we see that space and time are the natural ordering principles of the self-defining, all-defining ego's worldview, and pertain solely to the way in which life is brought to consciousness in relation to that ego. But what happens if this ego disappears?

The person identified with his ego naturally sees the reality presented to him by that ego as the whole of reality, and dismisses as unreal anything that has not been made, or cannot be made, to fit in with it. Anything that affects him and cannot be objectively defined—feelings, beliefs, experiences too deeply felt for words—must be labeled and made to fit the system before it can be acknowledged. At best, it constitutes a kind of preliminary form of objective consciousness, the only consciousness with the authority to process reality "as it is." Similarly, the only licensed subject of perception is the perceiving ego embodied in that consciousness. There is nothing outside the ego, and if the ego goes, he assumes that the whole of reality—and he himself—will go with it. This view of life offers no escape from the pain of imprisonment in objective consciousness. It is the way people think when they have no subjective existence outside the ego; but they are wrong, and the spiritual anguish of even educated Westerners is only deepened by their "natural" tendency to think in these terms. Recognition of this error is one of the basic features of all Eastern wisdom. Eliminating it and teaching the way that leads out of anguish are the central and universally significant concern of Zen.

The West says, If this ego ceases to be, then meaningful reality disappears with it. But the East says, It is not until this ego and the reality it has shaped cease to be that humanity's "true nature" is released and true reality dawns—and only from this reality can the essential, the greater, the true self emerge.

Zen says that, far from "nothing" being left when a person drops his normal ego—and he can drop it—the whole of life is present in a different way, that is, it is *really* present for the first time. The individual ceases to be a subject perceiving the world solely as a multiplicity of defined objects, and becomes a subject in whom life comes internally to consciousness as something transcending objects and antitheses. This new vision depends on a widening of the consciousness, a qualitative leap that everyone must make at a certain point in his development—the leap that takes us from life writ small into Life writ large, from the relative into the Absolute, from what we naturally are into what enlightenment can make us—people whose lives are rooted in a new knowledge. Enlightenment opens the door to the secret. What secret? Our own inner nature, hidden at first from the worldly ego's gaze, in which supra-worldly Being dwells within us. It is with this leap into Being that Zen is concerned.

The time to make the leap has come when Being, which is present within us to start with, sustaining and nurturing us without any effort on our part, has been wholly dominated and obscured by objective consciousness. This is precisely the point many of us have reached today, but it is also the point where we in the West have one major problem and challenge to confront: to free our true nature, we must question a way of seeing that not only colors and shapes our whole awareness of the world, but has also given us our finest achievements, the outstanding achievements of Western science and technology. How can we resolve this dilemma?

Long ago, our medieval ancestors had to break through the fog of hallowed images of reality constructed by the pre-rational mind, which prevented the rational mind from seeing that reality plainly. The breakthrough brought into existence the new human being, self-reliant, unprejudiced, observing nature at a distance and using rational concepts to measure it objectively, ultimately bringing it under his control. And now the time has come to open another new era by dispelling the fog of another fixed system and striking forward into the open, for the new world before us today is partly hidden by the very energies that produced the last era and made it great—but have now hardened into a straitjacket. Today, the rational mind is the barrier. Science plumbing the depths of nature, technology literally storming the heavens, our universal organizing talents, and all the other things of which we in the West are justly proud—all of this has left us with a blinkered regard for the rational consciousness to which we owe it all, so that anything that consciousness cannot grasp immediately seems dubious. But now the new values that hold the key to the future are bursting from the other side of human nature, the side that reason cannot penetrate. There are more signs than we suspect that the new era is dawning. More people than we realize are having experiences in which their true nature speaks to them, experiences that disturb and gladden them by suddenly bringing them the sense of a new reality outside the one they know—a reality charged with saving energy, filled with promise and making new demands on them. It is no longer understanding and controlling the objective, tangible world that counts here, but seeing the truth of transcendent nature, which is present in us and in the world around us and, once it comes to consciousness, transforms our lives and gives them wholly new horizons. But who can teach us Westerners to pay attention, before it is too late, to the experiences in which this nature speaks to us?

Here lies the significance of Zen. Everything Zen says breathes the air of the other, greater reality that opens out before us when we throw off the shackles of objective consciousness. Everything Zen does centers on taking these experiences seriously. They themselves are never the product of abstract speculation, but burst unexpectedly from the darkness of existential anguish or the glimmering dawn of existential promise, on the outermost edge of what can still be rationally grasped. All of Zen's practical exercises are meant to prepare us for these experiences, which transcend the old boundaries, but to see what they are really aiming at, we must take a closer look at the ways in which the objective view of reality actually affects human life.

The Pain of Living

When objective consciousness rules a person's thinking, his chief aim in life is to assert himself by acquiring wealth, prestige, and power. It is vital—and not only for the purpose of understanding Zen—to realize that self-assertive practice and "objective" theory have the same starting point: the ego constantly concerned with ensuring its own survival and defending its own position.

If this ego *is* the individual, the individual not only sees

24

the world around him as a fixed system of facts, giving him something to hold on to and steer by; he also sees himself as the natural center of existence as he lives it, i.e., as an ego with a right to be—and remain—what it is.

If this ego *is* the individual, the individual not only says "I am I," but adds "I shall remain I." Basically, he sees everything else in counterpoint to that "I," either confirming or contesting its will to remain what it is, either prepared to go along with it or willfully standing apart. He never says yes to anything—however much he stands to gain in a personal, developmental sense from doing so—without first making it clear that his will to remain what he is must not be tampered with.

The greatest threat to the ego is constant change, the apparent impermanence of everything, and, finally, death. The ground-notes of existence—the constant threat of extinction, meaninglessness, and vulnerability—fundamentally center on one thing: the individual's determination to preserve himself in circumstances that are safe, make sense, and allow him to live in security with others. Existence is acceptable only if every danger has been removed from it, meaningful only if it runs its course among secure meaning and value systems. Above all, he wants things to be definite—and he wants to keep what he has. This is why he clings to his attitudes, resists external change, holds on to his possessions, and, even in the realm of thought and knowledge, hangs on to his opinions once he has arrived at them. Enmeshed in fixed concepts, he wants life to be a cross between a cottage and a castle, combining security with comfort and allowing him to bask in the esteem of others like himself and quietly give himself up to the enjoyment of his own company and anything else that keeps him happy. Even when he takes up a cause and sacrifices his purely selfish ego for a thing, project, or community, he assumes that something lasting—a cause, a community, or even a value system—is at stake. Objective consciousness can indeed produce selfless effort as well as naked self-assertion—as long as that effort serves something "objective." At the center of this physically safe, intellectually meaningful, and spiritually reassuring vision of life, the individual identified with his world-ego can hold out indefinitely.

So far, so good, but the bill refuses to add up, because this is not what life is like and because the main item is missing. The main item in human life is never the ego circling a fixed point, but an inner nature from and through which a greater life seeks to manifest itself in constant change, extending to everything and including the ego. A person imprisoned in his ego is like a caterpillar dreaming of heaven—not just a heaven without feet to trample it, but a heaven without butterflies either, although the butterfly is the caterpillar's hidden meaning and is fated to explode its present form. Inner nature can manifest itself only in constant change, but the ego and its will to remain what it is make change impossible, always circling a fixed point—even when the fixed point is nothing more than the code that determines how people in a given community behave. This is how one specific type of human anguish starts. And this anguish increases as the individual inexorably falls victim to a world he himself has willed into being: the rationally ordered, ethically determined, and technically regulated world in which we live today, the world that has exhausted our inner resources and now threatens to crush us.

Depersonalization of the Individual

Being is the animating force in everything that lives, and it provides a threefold impetus: every living thing seeks to live; every living thing seeks not merely to live, but to become fully and uniquely itself; and every living thing seeks to fulfill itself in transcendent totality. This threefold urge is innate and universal, and in it we sense the vital plenitude of Being that generates, sustains, and renews everything that is. In it we see the regularity and order of inherent form underlying the full spectrum of individual phenomena. In it we feel the unity of Being in which everything is ultimately one—the unity from which everything sprang and to which it is constantly striving to return.

When Being enters consciousness and while it remains, it gives us a basic strength and confidence in life, it bears witness to our true nature, it expresses faith in a universal order matching that nature, and it lends us the security that comes from feeling part of a wider whole and from peace of heart. But as the ego gradually asserts itself and weakens our contact with Being, the unconscious forces that so far have supported, shielded, and given meaning to existence are transformed into conscious intentions and desires, for example, the desire for security in an existence where we respond to the world as we see it by relying on what we ourselves know, own, and can do; the desire to shape and order things in patterns that make sense to us; and the desire for human fellowship and the comfort it offers. The Absolute was our first home, but we now move into a new, relative structure that we have built ourselves and that makes us feel secure because we know how it works and why it works the way it does.

By living exclusively in this new system and accepting only what squares with it, however, we start to push Being even further away, and our true nature increasingly drops out of consciousness. As we identify with, become enslaved by, and hide behind artifacts and systems of our own devising, we are increasingly in danger of being devoured by them. Today this process is affecting people in three ways: victimized by impersonal systems of their own creation, they are turning into objects themselves; they are being forced to repress their individuality; they are no longer allowed to take their own transcendental dimension seriously.

There is less and less room today for individuals with their own sufferings and aspirations toward happiness and meaning—individuals who run their own lives and demand the freedom to do so; for as life is depersonalized, the individual himself is turned into a thing, a component, an object. He is seen as a thing and treated like a thing, and must live like a thing. Even the sciences that study him, such as conventional medicine and psychology, narrow their focus to what can be rationally defined and grasped, to what can be turned into a thing. Wherever he is, and particularly at work, he is at the mercy of the organized world around him—a minor cog in the meshes of a machine that is omnipotent and omnipresent and cares only for output and order. All his functions are measurable, and he himself is reduced to simple functioning, like another machine. The fact that he is not a thing, but a human being, with his own life, his own sufferings, his own aspirations, and his own claim to be fully himself, matters nothing to the objective systems and the people who run them—or matters only when his personal problems threaten to upset the smoothly running system that he is expected to serve, and serve productively.

A person's humanity is enormously reduced when he becomes a mere object of rational knowledge, part of a fixed system, the source of an output that can be objectively measured. To get ahead, he must let his "soul" go; to serve as an interchangeable spare part, he must sacrifice his own individuality. In short, he must "adjust" to the needs of a totally organized world in which everything is expected to run without a hitch. Deep down, however, he can only "adjust" if a life without problems has genuinely become his own supreme ambition. Once this happens, once a superficially trouble-free existence becomes the main target, running away from pain and suffering seems entirely reasonable, and anything that drowns out and screens the suffering inherent in human life becomes acceptable. But to live like this is to miss the truth of life, and living a lie can lead to sickness and anguish. Even sickness and anguish, however, are rapidly relieved in a civilization that increasingly resembles an enormous factory churning out remedies to enable people to keep going wrong—painlessly. Their pain is there to tell them that they have gone wrong, but instead of reading the symptoms and changing direction, they surrender their freedom to shape their own lives, and chase the mirage of a life that seems serene, but is totally lacking in transcendental depth. The person who strikes this kind of bargain with the world and lives out his life without a care has no further need of God and ultimately feels free—but only because he is no longer aware of his chains. The claims of his own true nature and his roots in transcendent Being are forgotten. But in spite of everything, his true nature is still there, as his real center and the medium through which the Absolute is striving to manifest itself in him. He is dimly conscious of an inner struggle, and his life—unless he realizes what is happening and rises to the challenge—is governed by a lie. If this makes him suffer and if any of his childhood beliefs have survived, he asks God for the strength to continue living in this lie—and thinks that he is showing humility when he is really only running away from himself.

To get rid of personal values, and particularly personal aspirations, to objectify everything, to lose individuality and to deny transcendent Being—this is to strike at the wholeness and essence of the human condition. This is what happens when existence becomes completely worldly or "secularized," and we lose sight of supra-worldly Being, which holds the key to real existence, which we are meant to manifest, and whose transforming, gladdening, and mandatory inner presence is the only thing that can save us.

But it is only the sight of it that we lose, for basically every human being always remains what he is, a personal, individual subject, rooted in transcendence. This is why his true nature, if constantly repressed, still makes its presence felt and ultimately raises the standard of revolt. Everything that is done to turn a person into a thing only brings him closer to the day when he inevitably realizes that real life starts when he opens the door to personal values. Only constant denial of his individuality really makes him start to sense its rightful claims. He sees that the rationalization of life has sacrificed the feminine to the masculine element in the human makeup and that this feminine element must be restored—and he also sees that human individuality has an absolute right to fulfillment. When this right is denied, the individual sickens; he is tormented by feelings of fear, shame, and desolation for which he can find no obvious cause. The suppressed forces of his deeper nature erupt and turn against him without his realizing it, finding a variety of self-destructive, self-damaging outlets. Angst is a common symptom today, and is always a sign that a person's inner nature is choking for air. As the transcendental roots of their humanity slip from consciousness, and as the secret but unchanging claims of that dimension cease to find satisfaction in forms of belief that have also been turned into things, people increasingly become the victims of the unholy world they themselves have created. At last, when the pain grows unbearable, when they can no longer run from themselves, they must listen to the voice from within, look closely at inner experiences that they have previously ignored, and search for paths leading to a new system of belief. In the fullest sense, this process brings people back to themselves. It is powerfully under way today—and gaining added momentum from the fact that the emphasis on things and organization has also robbed the communities in which people live and the jobs they do of the central, hallowed element that once gave them something solid, meaningful, and safe to hold on to.

The Decline of Community

The individual claims of a person's inner nature pass unnoticed as long as he remains part of a privileged whole, an organic community that supports him, gives his life meaning, and offers him security. His deeper aspirations are subsumed in the aspirations of the whole community, and his personal nature is not denied, even if the community ignores his purely personal concerns. When he is truly a part of the community, the community lives subjectively in him. What it is determines how he behaves, and the ways in which he interrelates and coexists with others have value and meaning for him and for them in terms of the life they share within it. By identifying with it, he knows—even when he is forced to repress his own wishes—that he is fulfilling himself in a way that, if not yet personal, is still entirely human. It is only when the community breaks up and is replaced by an impersonal "collective," when the organic becomes the organized, and when objective, pragmatic values are the only ones that count, that everything changes. Rated solely in terms of output and efficiency and ignored as a "person," the individual no longer has any references outside himself, and the basic meaning of his life—now a matter of concern to him alone—becomes a problem he must confront and solve for himself. As society increasingly moves in this direction, educating people solely to take their places as productive components in objective systems, their inner natures are driven into contradiction and rebellion while they are still young. Young people—and even children—find themselves facing inner problems that simply do not exist as long as family life remains vigorous and stable. Self-fulfillment becomes a matter of vital importance at a very early age, and the young are thrown into hopeless confusion.

Painless integration within the community and gradual absorption of its values, ethics, and rules of conduct used to be the norm—but this is now being replaced by rigid conformity and the forced acceptance of ideals, standards, and conventions that seem less and less convincing and can no longer be lived by as a matter of course. If a person is still instinctively referring to the things told him in childhood and to the old standards and beliefs, serious inner conflicts develop when he eventually has to fend for himself. He senses that the time has come to strike out on his own and to give his insistent true nature its head, but feels guilty—either because he is betraying the standards originally dinned into him or, if he sticks to them, because he is betraying himself. When this point is reached—and countless people have reached it today—there is no going back. The only way is forward, bravely forward to the one true source of personal existence and personal decision. This source is nothing other than the *realm of personal experience* and the unmistakable voice of humanity's true nature that speaks from it. Obviously, when objective values that have lost credibility are rejected, instincts and urges normally

31

checked in organic communities are likely to break through. It goes without saying that they must be subordinated to the community's code, consideration for others, and spiritual obligations—although the real conflict now is no longer between instinctive egoism and altruism, but between loyalty to the community and fulfillment of the individual's true nature. The rebellion of the young already prefigures the rebellion of true nature—the new self that has come to maturity and insists on being acknowledged and seen for what it is. The first, decisive step toward this maturity is taken by turning to *supernatural experience,* as people today are doing—paying attention to those experiences in which true nature, the medium in which the Absolute is present and seeks to manifest itself in us, speaks as challenge and as promise.

This experience comes as the climax of a maturing process in which we first go astray and lose contact with our true nature, but eventually find our way back to it and hear once again the voice of wisdom from our own inner depths. It is Zen's purpose to bring these depths to consciousness.

Portents of Change

From Natural to Supernatural Experience

The suppression of our true nature is the surest path to the deepest pit of human suffering—and out of this suffering is suddenly born the longing to find a way back to a life infused with that true nature. Yesterday we still took it for granted that our business in life was to master the world and find our place in it; today this aim is no longer enough. It seems too narrow, too superficial, once we have sensed the presence of something deeper within: the true, the supra-worldly life, inexorably forcing its way toward the light. This life never stands still, but is changing all the time, and any fixed system deflects its vital impulse. Whenever this happens, a strange unrest takes hold, inexplicable feelings of fear, guilt, and emptiness, which none of the everyday remedies can cure. We may be secure, but the fear persists. We may be living virtuously, but the guilt is still there. We may be rich, but the emptiness remains. The real problem lies in another direction.

The sense of longing felt by people today conceals the hidden knowledge of a fullness that flows from humanity's true nature, which itself depends on nothing and can break our own dependence on all the things placed within the worldly ego's grasp by wealth, position, and power. It is the knowledge of a meaning beyond meaning or unmeaning, justice or injustice, as the ego understands those terms; knowledge of the inner self, ceaselessly revealing itself in an ever-changing pattern of forms that merge into and flow from one another; knowledge of security born of a love that has nothing to do with human love and breaks our dependence on that love—a love that takes all the heartache out of solitude. This hidden knowledge underlies the great longing, and in it our *true nature* is at work. In it, Being is present within us in a way that makes us strangely independent of all the things clung to by the world-centered, world-dependent ego. It is a knowledge that has nothing to do with the ordinary logic of objective consciousness, and makes nonsense of that logic's smug claim to be the only logic that counts. We first sense it dimly on the outer rim of consciousness. Later, we feel it as a promise. Later still, we hear it as a voice; and this voice grows steadily clearer, more hopeful, and more challenging. We are filled with a new sense of purpose and at last start to see the importance of the times when this knowledge first flickered within us or—even more powerfully—was briefly present as a certainty. It is only at this point that we can recognize the real turning points in our lives, the glorious moments when Being speaks to us, but that we dismiss as unreal, as long as we cling to tangibles. It is only at this point that we are willing to listen to those who have had these sensations before us, have recognized their importance, and have made them the first step on a way where this momentary experience is progressively revealed as the one true reality. At this point we are also ready for the wisdom of the East, which has never stopped listening for the voice of hidden knowledge—and obeying it as an infallible guide to the inner way.

This is the central difference between the culture of the East and the civilization of the West: the keynote in the West is *form*—the form that a person imposes on the world (objective systems) and on himself (personality); the keynote in the East is *maturity*—maturity reached by following the way that every human being must take to become a person in the fullest sense. This way is the way of inner experience—of *transcendence present within us*—and the new era is heralding itself by focusing on that experience.

The Western mind has thus far rested on two pillars: rational knowledge derived from natural sense-data, and a belief in supernatural revelation. The East, which has nothing equivalent to Christian belief and has never looked to pure reason for an explanation of life's meaning and purpose, finds true knowledge and the key to human nature as it really is in something else: supernatural experience and natural revelation. This insight comes only when we have gone beyond the limits of our natural powers, and helps us only if we are prepared to take inner experience seriously and let the inner voice guide us. It has two components, the conviction that there is a higher reality that commands belief, and the conviction that we can already sense this reality as something present within us in the here-and-now. It was long regarded as the private property either of the East or of a privileged few in the West, but is now coming slowly to general awareness and has even—in moments of shattering illumination—become for many people a personal certainty. Westerners, no less than Easterners, have fateful moments when Being comes to life within them—but Westerners have not thus far been taught to

34

understand what is happening and see its importance. This is where Zen can help them—can help *us*.

What are these fateful moments? They are the times when something deeper unexpectedly touches us and lifts us suddenly into another reality. This experience can come, like an all-transforming light, when our world is darkened by suffering, and it can come, suddenly casting an otherworldly radiance over everything, when we have reached a peak of worldly happiness. It can come when our strength, wisdom, and spiritual endurance are exhausted and we despair—if we accept that despair and see that the new self that emerges when the old one collapses is what we really are. It sometimes comes when annihilation threatens, when we can suddenly look death in the face without flinching and feel a new, unknown life within us—giving us the inexplicable conviction that we cannot be harmed, that we can do anything. It sometimes comes when we are filled with despair at life's meaninglessness or with a crushing sense of our own guilt. If we can accept the unacceptable, if we can endure the unendurable, then—as we accept, as we endure, and as our strength burns lower—we may suddenly experience an inner light that illuminates us utterly, that has nothing to do with understanding a particular thing, but that shifts the whole basis of our understanding. Sometimes it also comes when we accept loneliness or helplessness of an intensity that threatens our very survival; even as it gnaws at our vital substance, we may have a sudden sense of being cherished and protected on a deeper level, of being rooted in an intimate relationship with something we cannot define. This is the age-old experience of the essential *unity* of all things in Being, in which every person has a share. This sudden, inexplicable sense of being firmly anchored in power, clarity, and love is an expression of the mystery that is being revealed in humanity itself—the mystery of Being, in whose fullness, order, and unity the whole of existence is rooted and is constantly renewing itself as life, meaning, and security.

Who can tell how often the horrors of battlefield, air raid, prison, and death camp—in short, the darkest moments—have brought people face to face with the divine power within themselves, suddenly flooding them with light at the moment of ultimate disaster? This is modern humanity's hidden treasure: the experience of something "utterly different," which has enabled countless men and women not only to endure the unendurable, but also to bear witness to true nature, which is only waiting to be recognized, heard, and let in. How many people have felt the strength that comes when death seems certain—and is humbly accepted? How many have seen understanding dawn from despair when they have stopped looking for reasons and accepted what they cannot comprehend? How many have felt the inexplicable security into which ultimate loneliness can turn when the unbearable is borne? But how few have known what all this meant— although many have been left with a new hope, a new faith, and a new determination to search out the way to the life and the truth that are humanity's true heritage. Zen knows what all this means, and Zen knows about this way.

Thus we see that there are three factors driving Westerners into themselves and helping them to see the treasures of inner experience: the anguish caused by depersonalization in an object-centered society, the destruction of the community that once sheltered and supported the individual, and the horrors we have all lived through in recent decades. Out of all this comes the feeling—and for some the certainty—that there is another dimension we can experience and that can give life in this world a more-than-worldly meaning.

A person thrown back on himself encounters an inner reality that remains hidden as long as he believes that leading a full life is merely a matter of getting on and getting through. It is only when the crisis comes, when life leads him to the edge of the abyss, plunges him into misery and despair, and leaves him more alone than he has ever been before, that he really starts to think about himself and to notice that, deep inside, something new is struggling into consciousness. Coming face to face with his true nature, he experiences something that is not of this world and yet makes him what he is—and its coming to consciousness carries absolute conviction. All of these signs mark the threshold that today's generation is preparing to cross—if it knows which way the future lies.

There are many different areas in which this new experience is reflected: existentialism, abstract art, psychotherapy, modern literature, and, above all, the widespread interest in meditation exercises and the inner way (an interest that has nothing to do with restoring or improving practical performance). It is the young, with their new ideas and new ways of doing things, who are most obviously breaking away from patterns of thought, creativity, behavior, and community living that are fossilized and obsolete. People everywhere are starting to find Being in everyday existence—and releasing their own creative energies in the process. New art forms give us the visible evidence, but on a far deeper level, we can sense that contemporary anguish is finding a positive outlet in people themselves and sending them out in search of something new.

New Wine in Old Bottles

People always approach the unfamiliar in traditional ways. But new wine is always spoiled by old bottles, and so the meaning of the new something toward which people are groping—often without knowing exactly what it is—is being travestied. Many of them are genuinely weary of the world, but the spirit in which they turn to exercise to unlock inner experience is still ruled by the world and the ego.

Small groups and associations are mushrooming on all sides under leaders of varying wisdom and ability, who claim that their exercises will release the adept from his old consciousness and give his life a new meaning. Exercises of all kinds are being urged on the public under respectable names: yoga, meditation, self-exploration, and relaxation therapy. But all too often these activities are more likely to cut people off from the very thing they are passionately seeking than to help them find it. Stress-relieving exercises often degenerate into a cult of "letting go." In the same way, exercises used to shed the old self and find a new one are easily perverted into mere pleasure in release—which does no good and may actually do harm. For example, many people find today that certain "exercises" give them a temporary sense of release from their old identities, but never go beyond this first sensation. Of course, contact with the saving ground of true unity may be a part of this experience, but nothing comes of it unless the new spiritual energies are channeled and consciously centered on a new life and wholehearted practice; otherwise the only result is a cult of experience that is actually incompatible with Being. The exercise becomes a damaging passport to pleasure. Used like a drug to procure the same agreeable sensations over and over again, it substitutes for—and wastes—something that can only come slowly, from bedrock experience and painful, unremitting practice.

Equally dangerous are those relaxation exercises that lull a person into false, unproductive, slothful repose—practically anesthetizing him in the process. These have nothing to do with genuine tranquility of spirit or with the dynamic stillness we register as life-source and challenge, that links us with the divine. They generate a lifeless calm, which certainly makes a pleasant change from angst and agitation, but which distorts instead of releasing the creative energies of life.

A third danger comes when the presence of Being is first sensed, if the meaning of those first contacts—release from the old ego—is reversed and that ego is allowed to batten on the new experience. Filled with a new inner strength, the neophyte easily forgets that this comes as a gift from outside, and is not meant simply to increase his worldly powers. He takes the credit himself, and something that should make him humble inflates his pride instead. What is gained in such cases is not merely wasted, but dangerously feeds the power instinct as well. Nor are others the only ones to get hurt; whenever something is given to serve the cause of Being and is used to achieve worldly ends, it rebounds disastrously on the user. This is why it is generally dangerous to use "initiation" exercises (which help Being to manifest itself in existence) for purely practical purposes, thus distorting them completely. This is what happens, for example, when a person treats yoga—a group of practices whose name originally meant "to yoke to Being"—like gymnastics and uses it to increase his fitness and efficiency, instead of to help him on the inner way.

Sensuous release, experience for its own sake, indolence, pride, the secular misuse of the energies of Being, and the pragmatic dilution and distortion of initiation exercises—these are the dangers that face anyone starting on the quest lightly or without proper guidance.

From Knowledge to Insight

The task that faces us all today is that of renewing ourselves by transcending objective consciousness and overcoming the dangerous limitations of the defining ego. This necessarily takes us into the realm of supernatural experience, and we must find the path that leads to—and beyond—that experience. The ways of thinking and behaving that we need here are totally different from those dictated by the defining ego, and the implications are both theoretical and practical. Thought that deals solely in opposites and dualities must yield to a vision of life rooted in supra-worldly experience, and a way of life of which insight is the keynote must grow out of that vision.

Like the term *mysticism,* the word *insight* is still an instant irritant to many "enlightened" (i.e., half-educated) Westerners—particularly when they are used to thinking in purely scientific terms. It is surely odd that a profound distrust of mysticism should often unite the loudest champions of reason, which claims to know all there is to know about reality, and the loudest champions of organized religion, which claims to know all there is to know about "higher" reality. How can

39

this happen? Perhaps because each side feels that the mere possibility of supernatural experience, in which Being—transcending all reason, but directly felt as absolute energy, order, and unity—is revealed, threatens the seamless consistency and universal validity of the reality it has made its own.

But supernatural experience is not the whole story: also necessary is a conscious and careful process of spiritual training and development that overcomes the restrictions of dualistic thought and builds on each experience as it comes, gradually shaping the individual and making him mature in such a way that everything he experiences and does is rooted in the truth of Being, beyond all antitheses. Insight (as opposed to pragmatic knowledge) gained in this way is always the product of experiences in which Life enters us entire, because it has not been turned into a "thing"—that is, it has not been filtered through the various categories and concepts that manufacture "things," and so has not been robbed of its basic reality. Only if it is real in this sense does the relative form that it assumes in us match the absolute form embedded in our true nature.

To gain insight, we must turn inward; but merely turning from the outside world to our own inner world is not enough. The inner world, too, can be turned into a thing—as the self-analysis practiced in conventional psychology shows us. It becomes a thing, for example, whenever we "think about" ourselves or try to say exactly who and what we are. As long as consciousness remains unchanged, the difference between insight and ordinary knowledge is not a matter of looking in or out; it is a matter of turning objective into subjective consciousness.

When I once asked the great Zen teacher Daisetz T. Suzuki, "What is Eastern wisdom?" he told me: "Western knowledge looks out, Eastern wisdom looks in. But when we look in as if looking out, we turn 'in' into 'out.' " This, then, is the problem: we are constantly turning "in" into "out," i.e., turning it into a thing. But how can we stop ourselves from doing this? In other words, when we look in, how can we prevent objective consciousness from distorting our deepest experience? Surely inner experience is bound to express itself in images and concepts with objective meanings? Indeed it is—and every religion operates like this, using a consistent system of images and concepts to convey the nature and effects of a fundamental experience. But we must remember that these images and concepts are "interpreted experience" from the outset, and need to be related back to the original experience before they can be understood. Buddhism is no exception to this rule.

Just as there is no Christianity without Christ, there is no Buddhism without Gautama Buddha and without an understanding of what he suffered, experienced, and taught. And just as the mystery of Christianity is revealed only to the believer, so the mystery reveals itself in Buddhism only to a very special type of consciousness.

The starting point of Buddha's life and teaching was the question of suffering—its nature, its origin, and the possibility of finding release from it. The doctrine of the non-self, which is central to Buddhist thought, seems to follow naturally from the impermanence of everything. Similarly, human suffering seems to follow logically from an error, an illusion, a clinging to something that has no lasting reality, but dangles like a mirage before the consciousness that registers the evanescent only, and prevents us from seeing the truth. There is often a hard logic about Buddhist writings, particularly the early ones, that attracts the Western reader by its seeming clarity. But if everything the Buddhist scriptures say is so easy to understand, why was Buddha's great enlightenment needed to discover it? This question brings us to something that is often forgotten when Buddhism and other religions are being discussed: in the great religions, the truth seems to be stated in an open, accessible form, but is actually encoded. Basically, what all of them, including Buddhism, are giving us is not ordinary, instantly digestible knowledge, but an illuminated, inner, secret, insightful knowledge. One of the more sweeping and naïve distortions of Eastern wisdom is made by people who describe and interpret the supernatural meaning of Bud-

41

dhist doctrine from the standpoint of ordinary, objective consciousness—and then belittle it with patronizing praise (it is "noble" and "humane") or condemn it as hybrid and misleading (it preaches "self-salvation").

The reality from which insight comes is the primal reality, with which we are always fundamentally one. We can only find this reality, however, by following a tortuous path and passing through various stages—objective consciousness taking us further from it, anguish at loss of contact with it, and final victory over that anguish—before we come back to and achieve awareness of it on the basis of a new and broader consciousness. Buddhism speaks to us of a reality that has nothing to do with the reality that our ordinary notions of life have taught us to see, the reality of everyday thought and speech. But this is not true of Buddhism only; the transcendent truth of any religious experience is obscured and distorted when we see, define, and express it with our normal, worldly understanding, or try to grasp its images and symbols in that way. This is why the great religious teachers constantly remind us that they are speaking of a truth that only the inner ear can hear and only the inner eye can see. The opening of the inner eye is a central concept in Zen. It means waking to a new and wholly different level of the self—to new strength rooted in a new consciousness. Only a new consciousness, which has nothing in common with objective consciousness, can put us in touch with the truth that really counts, and this implies a spiritual revolution. Once we have grasped this, the great adventure beckons. Are we going to meet the challenge?

Of course, a person may be happy with his old view of things, and there is nothing wrong with this—if somewhere, deep down in his feeling for life, his links with true nature have never been severed. Unconscious of his share in Being, he takes a naïvely realistic view of the world, and this need never change, unless he again experiences the unity of Being, normally concealed from him by his natural ego. But the situation changes, and changes radically, when he leaves the ego and antitheses behind, hears the call of Being, and knows that the only way to seize this new experience fully is to drop the old outlook that confines his vision to things and tangibles. If, at this point, he still claims that the divisive ego's vision and values are the only ones, he is allowing prejudice to rule his conscience and throwing away his chance of becoming an integrated, mature, and rounded human being, fully in tune with his own real nature.

Obviously, even when we have experienced Being and seen into the real heart of life, we are still free to reject all of this and opt instead for "natural" experience, objective reality, and the objective view of life's meaning. But we must know what we are doing and accept responsibility for it. Surely, having gone as far as our natural capacities will take us and come to a point where the supernatural can reveal itself to us, we should spare no effort to break the hold of the defining ego and thing-centered outlook that have given us the wonders of technology, but—as long as they dominate the scene—stop Being from coming to consciousness within us, and stop us from fulfilling ourselves in true nature.

Westerners cling to this ego and its consciousness with a stubborn pride that leaves little room for the higher consciousness in which Being is tasted through senses beyond normal sense and manifests itself in a new spirituality and a new physicality. Most of us who stand in the Western tradition still want to think that reason is preeminent, still use objective images and concepts to shore up once-for-all beliefs, and are still afraid to face up to our deepest experiences—although these are the experiences in which Being comes home to us and gives us a new and deeper knowledge. This knowledge is neither objective nor tangible, but it carries total conviction. It enables us to think about and deal with the world on a new basis and allows us to see the world's inner workings—and it breathes the truth of divine life back into our beliefs at the very point where we have fallen prey to worldly understanding with its hunger for "proofs."

The Westerner feels the anguish his native outlook has brought him, but he also feels the futility of trying to relieve it by the very means that have caused it. If the easy way out—running from himself into apathy, conformity, and resignation—is no longer enough, he must listen to the voice of his innermost nature, which can never be objectively grasped. This, too, is a part of Zen's message. If we approach it with open, questing minds, we may find that, far from being merely Eastern, it is actually saying, in its own way, something that the great thinkers of the West have also known and taught, and which has always been the creative, renewing wellspring of life. When a person hears the inescapable, unmistakable call of his true nature, there can no longer be any question of not answering it. When he has an experience in which the Absolute touches and summons him, and fails to respond, he is missing the way he was meant to follow, and will pay the price for doing so.

Zen's Answer

Woe to this degenerate age
Of consummate unbelief!
Empty of virtue, people
Are scarcely now to be bettered.
Too long have they been
By holiness deserted,
And wrong thinking
Has eaten deep into them.
Since truth is so weak,
The devil rules them,
And evildoers and enemies of truth
Are not few in number.
Now it angers them that they too,
Powerless to destroy or rend it in pieces,
Must listen face-to-face to the teaching
Of him who is come.

—SHODOKA

("The Song of the Experience of Truth,"
by Master Yoka, c. 800.)

The Sublime
Message of Zen

Everyone, in His True Nature, Is Buddha

Deep in their true nature, people are Buddha,
As water is ice. And as without water
There is no ice, so without Buddha
There is no one.
Woe to those who seek afar off
And know not what is close at hand!
They are like people standing in water
And shouting for water nonetheless.
Born noble and rich beyond counting,
They wander their way as if poor, wretched
And unsolaced.

—SONG OF THE ZEN
MASTER HAKUIN

On my travels in Japan, I once met a Christian missionary who had worked in a small village, way out in the country, for eighteen years. He had had his share of problems, but had made the occasional genuine conversion. "The only thing," he said, "is that, when their time comes, these people die as Japanese and not as Christians." I asked him what he meant, and he explained: "When they come into the world, it's as if they put only one foot on this shore, and never forget that they really belong on the other. And so 'dying' is simply a question of pulling back the foot that they've put in this life—they do it naturally, cheerfully, and without a trace of fear."

This is the old Oriental feeling about life. But must it be Oriental only? Surely we should be able to have it, as well? Or do we regard it as the kind of primitive belief that only a childish and undeveloped mind can come up with? If we do, we are responding only to that part of the fundamental insight which has found its way into a rational system of thought—and lost its truth in the process.

In practice, our readiness to accept the truth of human experience and wisdom still usually stops at the point where we can no longer "classify" what we hear. This is our Western reluctance to go beyond objective facts, that is, facts that are not colored by personal experience—although it is only beyond these facts that transcendent reality reveals itself and can be "tasted." Even when it has not explicitly entered our consciousness, however, the reality of Being still lives in our true nature, in what we fundamentally are. For Buddhists, this true nature is Buddha-nature; thus all of us, deep within ourselves, are Buddha. But we are not aware of this—although all our "vague longings" are unconsciously expressing the secret power of this true nature, drawing us into itself.

"Surely," I once asked D. T. Suzuki, "a person looking for the truth is like a fish looking for water?" "Yes," the old teacher answered, "but even more like water looking for water!" This sums it all up, humanity's problem and Zen's answer—which also holds true for us in the West! There is another Oriental saying: "The drop of water may know that the ocean contains it—but does it also know that it contains the ocean?"

We often say that someone is "trying to find himself." But no one can ever find himself unless the self that seeks is the same as the self that is sought. If this is true, and if the self that is found is the same as the self that finds it, then who seeks and who is sought? We are touching here on an ultimate mystery. A mystery for whom? Possibly only for people whose consciousness is solely of the classifying and dissecting type. It is only by overcoming this consciousness that we can live the mystery as Life become conscious of itself—Life, which we ourselves are.

The Experience of Being

Zen is the doctrine of Being, of the experience of Being and of life rooted in Being. This doctrine is not a philosophical theory of being, and has nothing to do with metaphysical inquiry, but expresses an inner *experience*—the experience of Being, which we ourselves *are,* in our true nature. This experience is the consequence, content, and medium of a certain *consciousness;* indeed, it is itself the consciousness in which Life achieves awareness of itself in human beings.

When we experience our true nature, we experience Being, since our true nature is the mode in which Being is present within us. Thus, Zen does not offer us a supernatural revelation or ask us, who live in the ego and its world, to believe in an otherworldly redeemer. Zen expresses a supernatural experience and shows us an otherworldly something in which we *are* redeemed, and in which, in a certain sense, we have never been anything else. Of course, when this experience suddenly comes to a normal person leading a normal life, it may seem like a supernatural revelation. In Buddhism, this supra-worldly something is known as Buddha-nature. It is the light within us, and when we wake to it and see that it is there, it illuminates us and changes us utterly.

49

To experience Being for the first time is always to experience a promise as well—the promise that we can break through from what we *have* (the worldly ego's province) to what we *are* (the supra-worldly come to consciousness in our true nature). In this case, "knowing" what we are does not mean "having" it as an "object" of consciousness; it means experiencing in the self what the self truly is.

Zen is experience and experience only: experience sought, experience found, experience affirmed, experience heeded, experience made fruitful, experience borne witness to. And so Zen knowledge is never knowledge *of* something *(savoir),* but direct personal knowing *(connaissance),* and Zen itself vanishes the moment this personal knowing is reduced to objective knowledge. Entangled in the ego and befogged by the so-called facts conjured up before us by objective consciousness, we have no contact with this experience and live out our lives in error and anguish, until what we *are* bursts into what we merely *have,* and everything is suddenly flooded with light and instantly, totally *is.* It is at this moment that the divine arrow at last hits its mark, wounding us with a great longing and inexorably drawing us home. Following its pull, we become seekers of the way, and "not knowing the way, we move forward on the way, with hands outstretched, with hands outstretched. . . ."[1] And then we meet someone who senses at once that we are looking for the way and in whom we recognize ourselves as seekers, someone who happens to cross our path at that very moment—or perhaps only the master in ourselves. If we choose to follow him, the great light may suddenly shine out in us. Taking fire and rising, we find the *way* stretching before us, and for the first time it is the great *way to total change*—change that is both purpose and never-ending process.

But what exactly is this watershed experience, this experience that underlies the whole of Zen and on which the whole of Zen centers, this experience that Zen exercises pre-

1. Ancient Indian saying.

pare us for, and that takes on form in other exercises that remake us, this experience that is expressed in conflict, creativity, and love? This question will not go away, and we have to answer it anew whenever our understanding and insight deepen. To have the Zen experience is to experience our true nature and Being coming to consciousness within it. It is to experience Being in and through our true nature. It is to experience Being as what we are, beyond all the concepts and images of "having." It is to experience Being as a universal brotherhood in which we all share and that gives us the key to every language and religion—allowing us to see one another as we are, in the same fullness, light, and love.

We cannot experience Being in the way that we experience a tree, a thing, another person—as objects distinct and apart from ourselves. Being and true nature can be sensed only as an indwelling presence. But how can we experience this presence without its becoming an "object" of consciousness—since all experience depends on consciousness? Obviously, we are talking of a special type of experience and of a wholly new type of consciousness. It is only in this new consciousness that Life can become an inner presence, and only in this experience that Life—which we ourselves are—can fulfill itself by becoming what it truly is. "Life cannot be fulfilled unless it return to its plain source, in which life is Being, which the soul receives when it dies to itself, so that we may live in that life in which life is Being," wrote Meister Eckhart. This, then, is the Zen experience—the experience of Life as Being, before the two have been estranged by the consciousness that sorts the unity of "being" into the multiplicity of "having." This consciousness is itself a natural part of being human, and so we cannot rid ourselves of it; but if we are entirely ruled by it, the illusions of possession and attachment ensnare us and prevent us from making the breakthrough.

The consciousness that separates us from the animals also separates us from God—when it claims to be absolute. Prevented by it from seeing the truth ourselves, we immediately denounce as "mad" anyone who sees and behaves in a wholly new manner after his first encounter with Being—until he returns to what we wrongly regard as normalcy or finds Being *in* having, and successfully preserves its inner presence in his everyday existence. To have the Zen experience is thus to wake from the illusion that objective, dualistic consciousness is the only one that counts, and to shed both its deadening systems and the habit of thinking in things and antitheses—not only in sorting and dealing with the world, but in dealing with and searching for the living truth. To break the illusion is to break the spell of objective thought, and thus the hold of dualism. The essential step on the path to this freedom is taken by silencing discursive thought and listening to the voice that speaks in and out of the silence that follows when dualistic thinking has been left behind.

The Experience of Being and Dualism

Stubbornly to seek the truth's deepest meaning
Is to wear yourself out in idle cogitation.
Put your thinking to silence—
That is what matters!
Do not linger in thought
Upon antitheses;
To chase after and seek them—
Beware of so doing!
For one breath of antithesis
Hands your spirit over to confusion.

—From the Shin Jin Mei (Seal of Belief)
　　by the Third Patriarch, Sosan

Zen is the doctrine of Being transcending all antitheses, Being in which there is no before and after, no here and there, no this and that, no Peter and Paul. This is the problem Zen sets the thinker—particularly the Westerner, who naturally thinks in antitheses, and the Christian believer, who naturally feels that he cannot survive without dualism. A Christian priest once said to me, "You can write what you like—as long as you keep dualism." Why did he say that? Because, for him, dropping dualism meant accepting "monism," and that ultimately meant denying the distance between human beings and God, fusing the two—and seriously shaking one of the main pillars of Christian belief. But is this really what it means? It is—if we take the unity of nonobjective experience, reinterpret it in objective terms, and equate it with identity. If we do this, we are turning non-dualism into an objective "one," in which all human beings are one—and in which God and mankind are also one. This "one" is perceived as "something," in which all distinctions are resolved and everything becomes identical— certainly a blasphemous notion when applied to the man/God relationship.

If we go on and attribute this blasphemy to Zen, we are missing Zen's decisive message, and will continue to miss it until we can break the hold of objective consciousness. The experience of Being is the experience of opposites that coincide. The objective, dualistic view of reality that objective consciousness gives us is an illusion, and when it falls away, Being reveals itself to us as fullness, order, and unity transcending all antitheses. In Zen, all of this is experienced, tasted, sensed in a way that leaves no room for doubt. To describe it is not to state a theory of being, but to recount a deeply personal experience, one in which we experience our true nature as one of this unity's modes, and experience this unity in our true nature's language. Every antithesis between person and thing, between "I" and "you"—and thus between the self and God—is superseded and resolved when we experience this unity, in which there is no "two." Afterward, although we still live in the dualistic ego and "see" through its dualistic consciousness, dualism itself is lifted onto a higher plane. The image of God fashioned by the old consciousness, which had turned God into an external "thing," recedes, and the very fact of having experienced divine unity—and ourselves as a part of that unity—as the ultimate reality makes us feel the contrast between ourselves and God, the All-One, all the more keenly once we have left that unity behind and are back in the ego; but we also have a powerful sense of being intimately connected with God in a way that confining Him within a mere external image makes impossible. God now lies beyond imaginings and concepts. Doubt, which pertains to ego-vision only, no longer has anything to fasten on, and unity experienced *within* the incomprehensible generates the true belief that doubt—which is sparked only *by* the incomprehensible—cannot touch.

This kind of belief is only possessed a priori by people who, living in the ego, have retained a basic contact with unity. But unity is lost from view as objective consciousness tightens its grip—and belief goes with it. The Zen experience holds the answer here; it can lead all those who have irrevocably lost their old beliefs to true belief—including true Christian belief. (Obviously, Buddhists are not the only ones who can have this experience.)

The basic realization is always the same—that the stream of life divides in two when it hits the ego-centered consciousness; its pure light is refracted by the ego's prism and split into antitheses. Once this happens and the primal life-consciousness divides into a self/object consciousness, life necessarily presents itself in dualisms: before/after, here/there, transient/permanent, relative/absolute, spirit/matter, etc. A person who identifies entirely with this ego naturally shrinks from anything that threatens his individual permanence. And he naturally thinks of Being—experienced as the antithesis of contingent, perishable, here-and-now existence and as a challenge to the ego's stability and logic—as absolute, everlasting, and unlimited. But this conception of the Absolute is rooted in the ego's thinking and is valid only from the ego's standpoint. It imposes the basic pattern of egocentric thought on the Absolute and projects it outside the individual, turning it, like anything else experienced and thought, into a "thing," an object of consciousness. Here again, the static ego and its consciousness interpose and cut us off from the truth.

When we identify with the defining ego and accept the reality it gives us as an object of consciousness, we are robbed of divine reality, which is never an object of consciousness and can never be represented objectively. And so we fall into doubt, always a sign that true unity—the unity that becomes an inner presence in satori—has been lost.

What makes us sacrifice something we have experienced in that unity, with total, unquestioning clarity, to a vision of reality that is rooted in the defining, divisive ego? Only our inability to shake off that ego's spell. What, when we have experienced satori, makes us bow to the stubborn misconceptions of people who have either never experienced it or have lacked the courage to follow it up? Only the fear that comes from confusing what we have actually experienced ourselves with what others mistakenly believe we have experienced. If, having had the mystical experience of unity, we look back on it objectively, mistake it for everlasting sameness, and run from it in horror, then we have simply failed to understand the grace we have received. We are setting the reality we imagine, a reality engendered by reason and subject to its laws, above the reality we experience.

Of course, even when we have experienced the unity that transcends all antitheses, we remain tied to the old ego with its antithetical thought patterns. But when Being enters us, everything—even the things we see objectively through the old ego—is transfigured. This is because we can now see antitheses—including the man/God antithesis—as the way in which ultimate unity is reflected in the ego. We can also experience for ourselves how the gap between us and the objectively "other" disappears when we encounter a "you" in whom absolute *unity* is present and active. When God is truly, intimately present to a person, the sense of oneness with God that he has experienced in his true nature will persist—even when his ego insists that God is infinitely far away. Neither the objective ego nor belief that insists on an absolute distance can bridge the gap between God and mankind—but the Zen experience can.

The Doctrine of Not-Two

Believing is not-two.
Not-two is believing
In that which cannot be uttered.
Are not
Past and future
An everlasting now?

—From the Shin Jin Mei

Speaking of the "One" undoubtedly causes serious misunder-standings—and this is why Zen speaks of the "not-two" in-stead.

When it says "not-two," it is saying that the One that it means is not "something" different from "not-one." Thus, if we try to describe the Being experienced in satori by saying that Zen is the doctrine of the One, and that this One is something that transcends all antitheses, we are missing the real point of Zen—because Being cannot be described.

The first glorious experience of a non-dualistic absolute beyond time and space can lead to another misunderstanding: the conviction that this is in itself the experience of truth transcending antitheses. This is not so. It is true that the first experience of Being beyond space and time, which shatters the spell of ego-based reality, always has a bright, happy, "heavenly" feeling. But transcendence experienced as other-worldly brightness is followed at once by transcendence ex-perienced as darkness—as if hell showed its face only to those who had seen heaven and only the experience of absolute good could steel them to encounter absolute evil. The One that really transcends antitheses is revealed only in the experi-ence of Light beyond light and darkness—which follows the experience of darkness. When we first experience Being, we experience the absence of antitheses, but we immediately con-trast this experience with ego-reality, which is ruled by anti-theses, thus showing that the defining, divisive consciousness is still with us. And so we fall short of ultimate knowledge, which stays out of reach while we remain rooted in the old consciousness or, having overcome it briefly, relapse and cling to it again as the only one that counts. Absence of antitheses, perceived through this consciousness, is still not transcendence of antitheses, which comes in the real Zen experience: satori.

The Being that is talked about in Zen does not reveal itself to us until we realize that non-antithetical and antithetical reality are fundamentally one—or, to put it more accurately, not-two. But this is surely as far as thought can take us? Certainly, and this is precisely the point: the truly supra-antithetical cannot come to inner consciousness until thinking stops, is suspended, or is neutralized. In other words, when Zen speaks of not-two, it is not asking us to follow a chain of reasoning that leads by logical steps to a logically impossible conclusion; it is speaking of an experience that we can have as human beings, but that lies beyond the reach of logic.

The ultimate negation of dualism is precisely what satori is not. What we experience in satori is the reconciliation of non-dualistic and dualistic thought—and this reconciliation comes when satori itself makes us see that the ego, with its divisive consciousness and its system of antitheses, is not merely disruptive of unity, but is actually also the medium through which ultimate unity reveals itself inwardly for the first time. We come to see that dualism is in fact the mode in which Being, which transcends it utterly, must manifest itself to us as long as we identify with the ego and its consciousness. It is only clinging to dualism that is fatal. In fact, anyone who knows anything about satori sees the defining ego's worldview as a divine gift to humanity, for it is only against the background of this worldview that redemptive Being and redeemed existence come to consciousness.

The doctrine of the One—which is not *the* One because it is not something, but not-two—is central to Zen. Zen repeatedly tells us that this true One has not been properly revealed to us as long as we continue to see it as the opposite of something else that is *not* the One. This means that we can never ask "What is it?" since the question alone shows that we are on the wrong track. If we see it as the "supra-antithetical," the "supra-worldly," "Being," or "void" in opposition to the antithetical, the worldly, existence, or plenitude—or even contrast it mentally with these—not-two at once disappears. We are forced to use words in referring to it, but the moment we use a word and thus define something, misunderstanding threatens. We always start by contrasting our own experience of non-antithesis with such everyday antitheses as many/few, poor/rich, strong/weak, light/dark, good/evil, something/nothing—and then try to overcome this obvious inconsistency by calling it "the void." Immediately, however—and although we are applying it to an experience beyond antitheses—the word *void* itself acquires antithetical significance. Zen is always alive to this fatal property of words, and this is why it treats them with caution.

The void that we define as void—and we can do so only by contrasting it with the non-void—is still not the true Void. The true Void does not come to inner consciousness until this antithesis, too, has been eliminated. When we then use the word *void* to denote the void revealed to us in our true nature, we mean something entirely different, and so we shift into upper case—Void—to make the distinction. This, of course, is confusing and a constant source of misunderstandings of the kind we face when Meister Eckhart speaks of "God," and we are left wondering whether he means the Godhead, "which is as far above God as the heaven is above the earth" (i.e., the Godhead that transcends all antitheses, including the ego/God antithesis), or the God who "passes out of being when the ego passes out of being." Similarly, when we read Zen texts, we must always try hard to work out what they are really saying. As used in Zen texts, however, the term *void* nearly always means Void.

What is true of Void is also true of Love beyond love and hate, Justice beyond justice and injustice, Life beyond life and death, Being beyond being and nonbeing, Form beyond

58

form and formlessness, Light beyond light and darkness, and so on. But Void, Love, Justice, Being, Form, and Light reveal themselves to us in the Zen sense only when objective, antithetical consciousness has been wholly replaced by subjective consciousness.

There is, of course, another love beyond love and hate, namely "Christian" love, which is bestowed, regardless of liking or disliking, on enemies no less than friends. But although it transcends these antitheses, this love is still itself the antithesis of a condition in which we are torn between love and non-love. The Love that really lies beyond antitheses is at the heart of non-love no less than love—and also at the heart of fluctuation between the two. Only that which speaks from this Love is not-two, or Being, to which we can no longer attach the definite article (*the* One), since it is not a definite thing, but Being—the inexpressible beginning and end, the alpha and omega, the *true nature* of all things.

Whenever Being "emerges" as an inner presence, it wears a different face—revealing itself as love, void, life, truth, reality, depending on the particular antithesis from which the individual starts. This is the ultimate mystery, and it comes to us only in the void and remains with us only in silence. But it is always *the same not-two* that is revealed—*the same One* that is sensed in all of life's manifestations by those who experience it. Basically, there is nothing that can be said about it, and yet people are constantly asking what they are to "understand" by it—only to realize at last that silence is the final answer to their question.

Then Vimalakirti also turned to all the assembled bodhisattvas and asked: "My lords, how may a bodhisattva enter the realm of not-two?"

In the assembly of the bodhisattvas, there was one Dharmesvara, who began: "My lords, coming into being and ceasing to be are two—but things have never really come into being and so cannot cease to be. To penetrate the truth of this law of not-coming-into-being is to enter the realm of not-two."

59

The Bodhisattva Gunagupta said: " 'I' and 'mine' are two. Because there is an 'I,' there is also a 'mine.' If there were no 'I,' there would be no 'mine,' either. To realize this is to enter the realm of not-two."

The Bodhisattva Gunasiras said: "Purity and impurity are two; whoever grasps the true nature of impurity sees that neither purity nor impurity exists—and so follows the purity of nirvana. To realize this is to enter the realm of not-two."

The Bodhisattva Sunetra said: "Form and formlessness are two. To discern formlessness in form is to enter the oneness of things without clinging to formlessness. To realize this is to enter the realm of not-two."

The Bodhisattva Pusya said: "Good and not-good are two. To think neither good nor not-good is to arrive at nondiscrimination and to recognize the truth. To realize this is to enter the realm of not-two."

The Bodhisattva Simha said: "Sin and virtue are two. To understand the nature of sin completely is also to understand that it does not differ from virtue. To realize this is to enter the realm of not-two."

The Bodhisattva Narayana spoke as follows: "Worldliness and supra-worldliness are two. To see that the nature of worldliness is futility is to discover the nature of supra-worldliness, in which there is neither entering nor leaving, neither overflowing nor dispersal. To realize this is to enter the realm of not-two."

The Bodhisattva Sadhumati said: "Samsara [the cycle of rebirth] and nirvana are two. To understand the nature of samsara is to know that there is neither samsara nor attachment nor liberation nor extinction. To realize this is to enter the realm of not-two."

The Bodhisattva Pratyaksa said: "Annihilation and non-annihilation are two. If, in their true natures, all things are neither destroyed nor not-destroyed, there is no form of destruction, and if there is no form of destruction, this is the void—and the void has the form of neither destruction nor nondestruction. To attain this sphere of truth is to enter the realm of not-two."

The Bodhisattva Vidyuddeva said: "Knowing and not-knowing [enlightenment and error] are two. The true nature of not-knowing, however, is knowing. Knowing cannot be grasped, since it

60

lies beyond all distinctions. To persist in this belief and be free of the thought of duality is to enter the realm of not-two."

The Bodhisattva Punyaksetra said: *"Virtuous and sinful conduct, and conduct that is neither sinful nor virtuous, are two. In itself, the nature of these three types of conduct is empty; if it is empty, there is ultimately neither virtuous nor sinful nor indifferent conduct. To realize this is to enter the realm of not-two."*

The Bodhisattva Puspavyuha said: *"Duality arises from the ego; a person who understands the true nature of the ego is not ruled by dualistic thought; a person who clings to neither of these opposites has neither a subject nor an object of consciousness, and enters the realm of not-two."*

The Bodhisattva Srigarbha said: *"Attachment and non-attachment to things are two; if there is no attachment to things, things are neither taken nor relinquished. To realize this is to enter the realm of not-two."*

The Bodhisattva Ratnamudrahasta said: *"Longing for the world and longing for nirvana are two; if a person does not long for nirvana and is not weary of the world, then duality ceases. Why? Because if there is attachment, there is also liberation—but if there is no attachment to start with, there can surely be no point in longing for release. If there is neither attachment nor release, then there is no joy [in nirvana] and no weariness [of the world]. To realize this is to enter the realm of not-two."*

The Bodhisattva Manicudaraja answered: *"Honesty and dishonesty are two. The person who is truly honest makes no distinction between honesty and dishonesty. To be free of this duality is to enter the realm of not-two."*

The Bodhisattva Satyapriha said: *"Reality and non-reality are two. When reality is understood, it is not seen—and how much more is non-reality not seen. Why is this? Reality cannot be seen with the eye of the body, but only with the eye of wisdom—and in the eye of wisdom there is no seeing which is the opposite of not-seeing. To realize this is to enter the realm of not-two."*

When all the bodhisattvas had spoken their minds in this fashion, they asked Manjusri: *"What does it mean when a bodhisattva enters the realm of not-two?"* Manjusri answered: *"My view*

*is that nothing can be said or explained, described or understood in
this matter, and that the whole question cannot even be discussed. To
realize this is to enter the realm of not-two."*

*Then Manjusri said to Vimalakirti: "Each of us has now
had his say—and I would ask you, Lord, also to tell us your opinion
as to how a bodhisattva enters the realm of not-two."*

> *Vimalakirti entered the circle,
> knelt—and said nothing.
> This is known as "the thunderous silence of Vimalakirti."*

And they took their answer from this mighty silence.[2]

How many of us know how to listen properly—to listen so that silence speaks? The wisdom of the East is born of
silence, and so is the wisdom of Zen. Zen teaches us how to
listen to and hear the silence of Being, which—amid all the
noises of the world—is calling us into the truth.

> *There is no grasping the nature of true nature
> And no casting it aside.
> Only so can the center
> Of the unattainable
> Be attained.
> It is silent when it speaks
> And speaks when it is silent.
> Wide open stands the mighty door
> Of the giver
> Truth.*

—SHODOKA

2. Adapted from the ninth chapter of the Vimalakirti Sutra.

Non-attachment to "Being"

Every two depends upon the One
But with this alone you must not rest content.
Do not chase Being, the ever-active,
And do not stop at non-Being, the empty.
When you find the One
And are freed into serenity,
All of this will fall
Effortlessly from you.
If, wanting motion to be stilled,
You return to this one thing, hoping to find stillness,
You only drive stillness
Further into movement.
For how can you grasp the One
While you still hesitate
Between One and Other?
If you do not understand
The One,
You lose even what the two
Has brought you.
Being recedes
When you pursue it;
Nothingness turns its back
When you run after it.
A thousand words and
A thousand thoughts
Take you only further from it.
Thought seizes nothing
But shells without substance.
If thought guides you,
Even for a moment,
You lose yourself
In the void of the not-something
Whose mutability and transience
Are born entirely of your error.

—from SHIN JIN MEI

When a person has gone as far as his natural strength and wisdom can take him, and finds himself able to accept death, meaninglessness, and absolute loneliness, forgetting the terror and despair they once caused him, he is doing something that his ego alone cannot do. It is at this very moment that he may receive the grace of that experience in which he senses the strength, meaning, and unity of Being, and suddenly feels himself redeemed and liberated into new life. His joy is indescribable. Fear, despair, and desolation vanish. He feels filled with power, flooded with light, utterly sheltered, and totally at peace. Radiantly, he tastes the power that has freed him into himself. Small wonder that, having sought the ultimate experience, he believes that he has found it at last—but the blow soon falls and he finds that he is wrong.

The happiness fades, and so does the strength that made him feel immortal, the meaning that carried him far beyond unmeaning, and the love that filled his solitude. All of this fades, and he feels the world's threatening presence more sharply than before. The very experience that seemed to free him from anguish forever now plunges him into the anguish of an even deeper despair. For now, having actually tasted what he had only believed in, hoped for, and dimly sensed before—limitless, absolute, supra-worldly Being—he is fully aware for the first time how relative, restricted, and narrow the world really is. Now that he has glimpsed the great light, the darkness seems even darker. A tormented exile from a lost paradise, he wants only to find once again the unutterably wonderful thing he has experienced, and, having found it, to dwell in it forever. How natural this longing is—but how clearly it shows that dualism still clings to him and that his experience of Being is still not satori, the experience promised in Zen. His own experience has registered as "something" immeasurably different from the world to which he has returned—and he wants to have it again and possess it forever. But this is chasing a mirage, for, by trying to *have* the experience again, he actually drives it away, because there is nothing to "have." Transformation in Being is what it is all about.

Even plumbing the depths of our own soul may do us no good, if a pleasant sensation of emptiness is all we get out of it.

"When you find yourself plunged in reverie so delightful that you would choose to remain in it forever, tear yourself free," said Meister Eckhart, "and seize on the task next to hand, for these are melting sensations and nothing else!" Melting sensations! And this is also the temptation permanently involved in looking for release through artificial means. A drug-induced "high" merely cries out to be repeated and rarely engenders the new sense of moral purpose that every true experience of Being brings with it—the stern inner call to self-transformation and unremitting practice—so that we can at last become permanently anchored in what we have experienced. Lacking this power to transform and mold conscience, the drug experience is an illicit experience. If it is repeated and becomes addictive, it ushers in a process of regression that actually bars the path to higher development.

A person called to the *way* always finds the world he lives in as a "natural human being" too narrow, but the only way of overcoming this world is to push boldly on and grow beyond it. We cannot shake off the burden of world-being by turning our backs on the world and trying to steal away from it, but only by facing up to it and smashing straight through to its inner immensities. To do this, however, we need another kind of experience, an experience we can have only if, having once known supra-worldly unity, we find it again in and with the world. We *understand* only if, in this experience, we see what divides us from unity, and if we succeed in bearing witness through this dividing element.

The Opening of the Inner Eye

If we use the words *Being, Void,* and *not-two* in an effort to understand Zen, and if we think of these ideas as something definite, the great danger is always that the new consciousness, which understands, may be basically the same as the old one, which prevented us from understanding. Ultimately, we are dealing with something that cannot be understood, and yet there always seem to be ways of hinting at it that can themselves be understood. Any attempt to provide a comprehensible account of Zen—including the present one—puts everything at risk; it invariably classifies something that cannot be classified, or at least connects it with a system of thought, even if that system is a broadened one.

The most that thought, pushed to its furthest limits, can give us is the rind of a fruit—the rind we must crush to reach the fruit itself. And so we must accept what is so hard to accept: that a higher reality cannot emerge in satori as long as our consciousness remains unchanged, but only when the old consciousness has been destroyed and a new one forged. And since consciousness determines the subjective self, we can also say that enlightenment depends upon the subject's having a new stance—or, more accurately, that it coincides with our birth as a new subject.

It is a common mistake to assume that "enlightenment" means the dawning of a new light that allows us to see something new, while we ourselves remain the same. Of course, this can happen too—when suddenly we see a problem, thing, or person in a new light and all our uncertainties are instantly dispelled, or when we unexpectedly see something we had failed to see only a moment before. This experience—when a whole series of seemingly unconnected elements suddenly falls into place and forms a pattern—can be a powerful one. And people can indeed be enlightened concerning the way in which everything fits together; they suddenly have a new worldview, giving them a new security and firing them with new energy. But this has nothing whatsoever to do with the enlightenment, the *awakening,* that is central to Zen. In Zen, it is less a matter of the old eye's showing us a new world than of a new eye's remaking the old world for us. This new eye is not simply the old one enlightened. Enlightenment does not mean that the ice around us melts, but that our own substance is changed; it means that we transform both ourselves and our way of seeing and, becoming new, see new things in a new way.

However powerful it may be, the experience of Being as something "utterly different" is still not enlightenment, still not awakening, still not the opening of the inner eye—still not satori. However great our joy may be when we experience Being as something beyond all objective antitheses, this experience is merely a foretaste of the experience of ultimate truth. *Dissolution of the ego in true nature* is only the first step, and leads to nothing unless it is followed by the second: *true nature's unfolding in the ego.* The inner eye, as Zen understands it, opens only when the experience of Being reveals unity to us in and with the world, showing us that the world is both the barrier that divides us from Being *and* the medium through which Being, the world's hidden true nature, manifests itself and forces its way toward the light.

When a person "wakes," Being not only becomes an inner presence, but the cause that obscured it, the "root of evil," is seen *from within.* The opening of the inner eye is also—and chiefly—the unmasking of the ego.

> *Seeking the builder of this dwelling,*
> *I vainly passed through the cycle*
> *Of many births—*
> *Births, like all births, freighted with sorrow.*
> *But now, builder of the tent, you are known*
> *And shall build it no more.*
> *Your rafters are broken,*
> *Your cross-ties all shattered.*
> *Free of all bonds, redeemed,*
> *The spirit has come, where all desires cease.*

This hymn is attributed to Buddha, who is said to have composed it at the time of his enlightenment. D. T. Suzuki glosses it like this: "The monster, the house-builder, the constructor of the prison-house, being known, being seen, being caught, ceases at last to weave his entrapping network around Buddha."[3]

This realization comes in satori as a shattering personal experience, and is much more than an abstract grasping of the fact that the defining ego and its consciousness conceal Being from us, in that recognition of the ego *experienced* in satori actually breaks its hold on us. This is not to say that we no longer have to *live* under the restrictions and conditions imposed on us by the ego once we have had this experience, but we *exist* from another source. We are no longer enslaved by the ego and its way of seeing, and no longer at the mercy of the anguish it causes.

At the same time, the unmasking of the ego as the great sinner and separator, and liberation from it, is only one side of the knowledge that comes in satori.

The inner eye looks in two directions. It sees both the world-self and the true self, and once it opens, we see the world-self not only as a constant threat to Being's inner presence, but also as the medium through which Being reveals itself in here-and-now existence. We know that the ego, with its static concepts and its fixed images and attitudes, is constantly barring the path to true life, but we also know that Being manifests itself only in the anguish caused us by the ego's concealment of it and the ego's limitations. Being transcends all antitheses, but it can come to consciousness only against the background of something that contradicts it—and static ego-reality serves a positive function by providing that background. The opening of the inner eye, looking in two directions, lets us see that the dualistic world renders us one inestimable service in that it manifests the One to us in this very dualism, and constantly prepares us for the One in the anguish caused us by this same dualism. And so we really "see" only if we experience Being without trying to hang on to it, if we recognize it without seeing it as "something," if we

3. D. T. Suzuki, *Mysticism: Christian and Buddhist* (Westport, Conn.: Greenwood Press, 1976).

surrender to it without losing ourselves in it, if we can go back to the world no longer the same but transformed, preserving the undiminished experience within us and henceforth able to see and interpret the world only in terms of Being. Born to ourselves from our true nature, we live as changed beings in a world of change. As D. T. Suzuki explains, it is the relative, empirical ego that has been unmasked, and the spirit freed of that ego's restrictions is the absolute ego. "Enlightenment consists in seeing into the meaning of life as the interplay of the relative ego with the absolute ego. In other words, enlightenment is seeing the absolute ego as reflected in the relative ego and acting through it. Or we may express the idea in this way: the absolute ego creates the relative ego in order to see itself reflected in it, that is, in the relative ego. The absolute ego, as long as it remains absolute, has no means whereby to assert itself, to manifest itself, to work out all its possibilities. It requires a relative ego to execute its biddings."[4]

Recognition of the right relationship between Being and existence, between the reality of the absolute ego and the objective world of the empirical ego, lies at the heart of enlightenment; thus enlightenment itself is not merely a redeeming vision, but makes positive demands on us. It is true that the objective world has become "transparent" once and for all, allowing Being to show through—but the real task now is to bring Being into everything we see and do, to make existence fully real in terms of Being. It is this new sense of responsibility toward a new world, and not merely the breaking of the old one's spell, that really makes the Zen experience satori.

If ultimate unity genuinely has us in its grip, we have a sense of being deeply at one with the world and all humanity, connected with them in the true nature that we share; and we also share a common destiny: that of becoming what we are in our true natures. What we feel for one another expresses what our true nature makes us, what we aspire to be and what

4. Ibid.

69

we should be: brothers and sisters in Being, born to go through life together and to help one another toward awareness of what we really are, transforming ourselves in the process, so that the Absolute can shine through the form we wear in this contingent world. This is where compassion and companionship really begin, in the urge to help others to tear from their eyes the veil of the ego, the ego that sees antitheses only and deludes us into thinking that these antitheses are the true reality. D. T. Suzuki reminds us that enlightenment is not fleeing from the world and sitting cross-legged on a mountaintop, calmly watching while people bomb other people down below; there are more tears to it than we like to think.[5]

And so satori is not blissfully dissolving in All/One/Being; it means constantly seeing, creating, and bearing witness to Being in existence, to the true self in the ego, to the Absolute in the relative, to the divine in the world.

In satori, the world is suddenly given to us afresh, with a new meaning and a new radiance, as promise and as obligation. The fields are still green, but the green is a deeper green. Humanity is still human, but human in a higher sense and called to a new life. Is there anything here to set Zen at odds with Christian thought?

What Zen Looks Like in Practice

> *The moon pours light*
> *Across the stream abundantly.*
> *The pines breathe softly.*
> *Who is leading this sacred evening*
> *Toward everlasting night?*
> *Deep in his heart he wears the seal,*
> *The flawless pearl of Buddha-nature.*

5. D. T. Suzuki, *Introduction to Zen Buddhism* (New York: Grove Press, 1964).

Whenever a person has the Zen experience, life becomes Life, penetrates the essence of his human life, and becomes that essence. Within it, he continues to live his physical life in the here-and-now, like everyone else, but he himself is different, lives his life differently, and lives it with a different purpose.

"To be ordinary is Zen, and to be contrary is not Zen; your daily life, however much you have Zen, is not to deviate from that of your neighbors. If there is any deviation, it must be in your inner life." But daily life is now rooted in Life become conscious of itself. "This is not, however, that dark consciousness of the brute or child which is waiting for development and clarification. It is, on the contrary, that form of consciousness which we can attain only after years of hard seeking and hard thinking."[6] When his inner eye has been opened, a person continues to live normally in the here-and-now, but transcendence enters the here-and-now. Having awakened to Being, he lives from his true nature, as a self poised between past and future, in an everlasting now. And because he lives in this everlasting now, space and time are transformed. He suffers like anyone else, but somewhere he suffers as if he did not suffer, and—whatever pain the world causes him—he never loses the radiant good humor that comes from deep within. So what does Zen look like in practice?

Laughter, perhaps—uncontrollable laughter, exploding all the certainties of a moment back. Anger, perhaps—erupting selfless and uncaused. Movement as natural and flowing as the flight of a bird winging effortlessly higher. Action rapid and precise: essentials only—nothing else! Fetch water when there's a fire, and do that only. Eat when you're hungry, and do that only. Sleep when you sleep, and do that only. Write when you write, and do that only. Everything conscious, alive, and direct, with never a breath between thinking and doing. No holding back, just letting life flow

6. Both quotations are from D. T. Suzuki, *Living by Zen,* ed. Christmas Humphreys (New York: S. Weiser, 1976).

from the center—as free and light as a wingbeat, as true as an arrow flying to its mark, as weightless as a dance step, as devastating as a sword blow, as precise as a sculptor's chisel, as liberating as the breath of spring, and always suffused with love. No clinging, no cleaving to anything. Stillness in the very heart of tumult. Every moment as fresh as dew, and as deep as a well reflecting the stars and all eternity with them. Sharing all the world's sufferings and never questioning the role we have to play in it. Merciless to ourselves and unsparing of others—as the love that bears witness to a higher law commands us. And always the strong serenity that a kind of dying has taught us, the clarity and cheerfulness that come of sensing a meaning that embraces unmeaning, and the happiness that comes of feeling safe, whatever the world may inflict on us.

> *Walking is Zen,*
> *Sitting, too, is Zen.*
> *If I speak or am silent,*
> *Tarry or hasten:*
> *Everything, in its true nature,*
> *Is stillness.*

—SHODOKA

Passing on the Message

A famous Zen master was asked to define the true nature of Zen, but refused to say anything. Pressed for an answer, he said that he did not know what Zen was, and that, furthermore, no one could say what it was. When someone suggested that a teacher with so many students must surely know, if anyone did, he stuck to what he had said, but finally added: "Saying what Zen 'is' is as different from real Zen as saying what it feels like to put one's finger into boiling water is from actually doing it." What does this story mean? It means that

Zen can only be experienced personally and directly. And yet the message must still be passed on.

The way in which that message is presented—or can be presented—always depends on the level of consciousness of the actual or intended audience. There is no experience so private that it cannot stand up to everyday language, familiar images, and healthy common sense, and no mystery that cannot be conveyed to outsiders if their religious roots are still intact and if, ideally, the charismatic origins of the religion are still effective. Even a simple account of a post-mental experience of Being can strike an answering chord when it touches the pre-mental presence of Being in people who have reached the "mental" stage of human development, but have not entirely lost contact with Being. Today we have reached the mental stage in the West, but Being still touches us directly if we respond to it from the primal depths of our consciousness. If we rely on objective consciousness when we look at a religious doctrine, its logic may well convince us and its ethic attract us—but its real meaning will elude us. The more deeply our perception of reality is colored by the systems and restrictions of rational consciousness, the surer we are to miss the hidden meaning when it comes to us in a form that we can "understand."

This is why talking and writing "about" Zen is always a risky business. As Alan Watts rightly says: "In writing about Zen there are two extremes to be avoided: the one to define and explain so little that the reader is completely bewildered, and the other to define and explain so much that the reader thinks he understands Zen!"[7] And yet, as long as Zen exists, people will carry on trying to gain an insight into the nature of the Zen experience and to pass this insight on to others. The only question is—how?

We can understand the teachings of Zen only by keeping our eyes firmly fixed on the experience that is its starting point and its destination. By any standards, the Zen experi-

7. Alan Watts, *The Spirit of Zen* (New York: Grove Press, 1960).

ence is immensely worth having, and Zen teaching does us a genuine service by giving us an insight into this experience, into how we can have it and how it affects us. If, however, the insight is divorced from the experience, it sinks back into the realm of abstract theory and philosophical debate.

We are having *experiences* all the time, but unless they lead to insight, they do nothing for us. Zen turns humanity's deepest experience into insight, and presents that insight in its teaching. But even this is not enough; *exercise* is still needed to make insight a living reality. Only exercise—the hard, unremitting exercise in which a person sets out to draw practical conclusions from his insight into the Zen experience and its causes—holds the key to progress. And so Zen is three things: *experience whose importance is recognized; insight that illuminates;* and *constant exercise.* Only these three things together are Zen, and without them there is no Zen. For Zen is not a matter of theory, but of *practice*—practice based on a certain type of experience and leading back to that experience. Zen is not a theory of life, but a *living practice.*

Living Zen

Masters and Students

What does Zen set out to do for us? To wake us to our Buddha-nature, our true nature. And so we perform certain exercises to achieve a state of mind and being in which we can see ourselves in our true nature and manifest that true nature in and through ourselves to others. Our aim is to allow the Absolute within us to shine through; Zen's aim is to remove all the obstacles and help this to happen.

To practice Zen we need three kinds of knowledge: (1)

we must know that satori—the experience that subsumes a person in his true nature—is possible; (2) we must know what it is that separates us from our true nature; (3) we must know the way that leads from concealment of true nature to experience and manifestation of it.

Any practice that sets out to remake us depends for success on one thing: our knowing what it is that stands in the way of awakening and renewal. And what is that obstacle? The defining ego, whose consciousness and life-system shape our thoughts, feelings, and actions when we identify with it. Thus, Zen's central purpose is to stop us identifying with the ego, to shatter the ego and its carapace and to overthrow its value-system.

All Zen exercises share the same initial aim: to subvert the objective ego and its values and, by doing so, to pull from underneath our feet the ground that prevents us from making contact with the true ground of existence. This is where masters come in. Zen without masters is unthinkable. All Zen texts tell us how masters embody and transmit the meaning and purpose of Zen, and all Eastern wisdom is the wisdom of the masters, showing their students the way—the way that redeems them from the ego and frees them into their true nature. In the West today, there is a burning need to find this way, and as it grows sharper, so the call for masters grows louder.

Zen masters are unrelenting and harsh. If anything is fixed, it must be overthrown. If we lay claim to anything, that claim is rejected. If we cling to anything, it is torn from us. If we are proud of anything, it is held up to ridicule. Our illusions regarding ourselves are stripped bare. When we think we know something, it is made to seem absurd. And there are no lengths—no lengths whatsoever—to which a master will not go. He says and does things that we cannot begin to understand until we have grasped the lofty purpose that justifies it all: the senseless answer, the sudden onslaught, the well-aimed blow, the jarring shock, the punch in the face, the thump on the ear, the grating insult, the mocking laugh, the terrifying scream, the things that the ego cannot accept and yet must accept, the things that make the gorge rise and yet must be swallowed, the things that take us by surprise and knock us sideways, demolishing everything on which our normal picture of the world and ourselves has taught us to rely for support, uplift, and security. It is precisely when the ground is pulled away and we plummet that we may suddenly sense a truth outside our normal way of seeing, and realize that the fixed values that used to be the whole story and formerly defined our own position are simply the objective correlative of a subjective stance that our own finite understanding has determined, and that has therefore cut us off from something that can never be determined.

But to do all of this a master still needs one thing, without which he cannot function: a student. And when can a person call himself a student?

A person can call himself a student only when he is consumed with longing, when anguish has brought him to the ultimate barrier and he feels that he must break through it or die.

He can call himself a student only when restlessness of heart holds him fast and will not let him go until he finds a way of stilling it.

He can call himself a student only when he has set foot on the way, knows that he cannot turn back, and is willing to be led forward and obey.

He can call himself a student only when he is capable of unquestioning faith, can follow without understanding, and is ready to face and endure any trial.

He can call himself a student only when he can be hard with himself and is prepared to leave everything for the sake of the One, which is forcing its way within him toward the light.

It is only when the unconditional has seized him that he can accept every condition and endure all the hardships of the way on which the master leads him.

ALL OR NOTHING is written in large characters above

the door through which the student passes on his way to the exercise room. He must leave everything behind, but can take one certainty with him: it is not caprice that awaits him, but the clearsighted wisdom of the master, who focuses unwaveringly on what he really is and spares no effort to bring it to life; a kind of dying is expected of him, but its meaning is not death, but Life beyond life and death; not the destruction of existence, but Being that irradiates it. This is the meaning of the way that the master shows his student.

Heart to Heart

What to say, what to do, how to behave when one wishes to reveal Being to another person, who "naturally" thinks and lives in ways that conceal it from him? This is the question that has always confronted the prophets of Being, and to which the Zen masters have found their own answers. And it is precisely the finding of constant new solutions to this problem that is Zen's most typical feature. How does the Zen master set about leading his student toward the experience of Being? Formal instruction is not the most important part of the process. Overall, what really counts is communication from heart to heart, from true nature to true nature—from Being, which I *am* in my true nature, to Being, which every other person also *is* in his true nature.

A Zen teacher in the East cares nothing about his student's past. He ignores complexes and dreams. He is not a psychoanalyst, and he does not behave like a teacher. He does not probe, correct, or advise. He is filled with the One and focuses solely on the One. He looks only at what his student really is, feels his way toward it from what he really is himself, loves it, tries to make contact with it, and drives unwaveringly forward in search of it. For him, everything that blocks the student's true nature is summed up in one fatal error: a clinging to things that the student regards as unchanging and that stop him from changing himself. This is the root of the evil, and it must be torn out completely. Everything the master says and does thus bursts spontaneously and directly from the realm of the "undetermined" and sets out to liberate the undetermined in his students too. This is a matter of instant, here-and-now contact, for this is the only type of contact that reflects the everlasting *now* and in which the student can receive the lightning-stroke of revelation, smashing through the system that has thus far held him prisoner. Every familiar image, every well-worn concept, every merely conventional description of evil is dangerous. Only speech or silence, action or inaction, which comes here and now, once and unrepeatably, from the heart—from direct contact with the One—can get through to the student, touch on the presence of Being within him, wake it, and bring it to the light.

I remember what my own master said when I expressed the fear that his concepts and images might not help me much with Europeans: "You've got it wrong! Either you understand or you don't. If you don't, every concept, every image you use will be meaningless. If you do, you will always find your own way—find the word, gesture, or even silence that will touch the other person at that moment, break through his wall, reach his true nature, and, depending on his temperament and maturity, enable him to take the next step." This is what Zen is! Every word, every action has meaning and value only at a particular moment, in a specific situation. The fixed concepts and images of conventional religious practice and teaching often dam the living spring, so we should not be shocked when we hear that countless Zen students, after a lifetime of studying the scriptures and kneeling before the Buddha's image, have burned those scriptures and smashed that image once satori has brought them the direct experience of Being.

Stillness and Silence

The first means that a Zen master uses to prepare and open his student to the experience of Being is *silence.*

Silence as the path to experience in which a person senses the presence of Being in himself is practiced in the art of meditation, i.e., silent concentration in zazen. This exercise has its roots in an entire culture of stillness, which is typical of the East in general and Zen in particular.

Silent contemplation is the central element in the life of monks, but sitting in silence is not practiced only in monasteries. It is, on the contrary, a natural part of life in the East, whenever it respects the old traditions. But even in the East, only those who know what they are looking for find the greatest treasure it has to offer: contact with what we really are.

All the masters tell us that the reality of life—which our noisy waking consciousness prevents us from hearing—speaks to us chiefly in silence. "In the working of the Eastern mind," says Suzuki, "there is something calm, quiet, silent, undisturbable, which appears as if always looking into eternity. This quietude and silence, however, does not point to mere idleness or inactivity. . . . It is the silence of an 'eternal abyss' in which all contrasts and conditions are buried; it is the silence of God who, deeply absorbed in contemplation of his works past, present, and future, sits calmly on his throne of absolute oneness and allness. . . . Woe unto those who take it for decadence and death, for they will be overwhelmed by an overwhelming outburst of activity out of the eternal silence."[8] This stillness is also the stillness of Zen. It is the stillness of the unfathomable fountainhead and source of all belief, which can never be obscured because it is the point at which life, transcending all concepts and images, originates, and this is also why no concept, image, or question can penetrate it.[9]

There is hardly anything that Westerners have more

8. Suzuki, *Introduction to Zen Buddhism.*
9. Karlfried Graf Dürckheim, *The Japanese Cult of Tranquillity* (London: Rider, 1974).

trouble in finding or more difficulty in practicing than stillness. Noise assails us on all sides—outside noise but, even more, inner noise: our anxieties, our stifled feelings, our repressed urges, our impulses, our longings, and, above all, our turbulent distress at losing contact with our imprisoned true nature. We are used to noise, expect it, and often cannot live without it—even using it to soothe our everyday worries. For comfort we look to multiplicity, which thunders in and around us, and miss the One, which we vitally need but which reveals itself only in stillness. The thought of coming face to face with ourselves terrifies us. And this is precisely what sitting in silence is intended to do: to make us face up to ourselves and our true nature and—on our way to that encounter—to everything that separates us from it.

There is also the stillness that speaks and is born of silence, but speaks only if we bear the silence patiently and focus our whole attention on the answer. In moments of black despair, we have all prayed to God for an answer—and God, instead of answering, has remained silent and, remaining silent, has thrust us deeper into the darkness. And then, if we hold out without complaining, the answer suddenly comes from this silence and floods us with light. And yet what is more alien to our normal way of hearing than absolute silence? Divine truth, however, does not speak to us in our normal language. And it is precisely the silence that confronts us when all our expectations are focused on a spoken answer that can suddenly rouse us to consciousness. This is something that Zen masters know.

There are countless Zen stories in which a student, filled with a passionate longing, comes to his master for an answer to the one question that sums up and expresses all his seeking, all his anguish. The master receives him. The great, all-deciding moment has come. The master knows himself that everything is at stake. What will he say? The student puts his question, waits breathlessly for the answer, and the unexpected happens: the master looks at him—steadily, piercingly—and says nothing! His silence has the weight, the solidity of bronze.

And realization hits the student like a thunderbolt. The entire edifice on which his question was based collapses. And something that questions cannot reach rushes into him. Burning, reeling, weeping, laughing, he wakes to the truth. One well-known example is the story of Master Juchi, which Hermann Hesse put into verse for Wilhelm Gundert when the latter's great book, *Bi-Yan-Lu*, [10] was published:

> *Master Juchi had, so people say,*
> *A peaceful, kindly, unassuming way,*
> *Was never heard to speak and never taught,*
> *For words are but illusions, and he sought*
> *To keep illusions faithfully at bay.*
> *And so, while others chose to air their learning,*
> *While novices and monks spoke out concerning*
> *The meaning of the world, its why and wherefore,*
> *And boldly found for each "because" a "therefore,"*
> *He listened and said nothing, always turning*
> *A warning finger upward, and the same*
> *Was his response whenever people came—*
> *Questioners who, careless or perplexed,*
> *Inquired as to the meaning of some text,*
> *The dawning of the truth or Buddha's name.*
> *Silent but eloquent, this pointing finger*
> *Grew ever more insistent, more commanding;*
> *Instructing, guiding, praising, reprimanding,*
> *Of the world's meaning and of truth it spoke*
> *So well that many a pupil, understanding*
> *Its gentle message, suddenly awoke.*

Silence can wake us only when it shatters everything that prevents us from experiencing Being. The chain that binds us snaps only when it is stretched to the breaking point—and beyond. That is why silence can produce this effect

10. *Bi-Yan-Lu, Meister Yüan-wu's Niederschrift von der smaragdenen Felswand,* translated into German with a commentary by Wilhelm Gundert (Munich: C. Hanser Verlag, 1960). Using original texts, this book provides the genuine seeker with a unique introduction to the mystery of Zen. It is the fundamental work on Zen.

only when it destroys the ground on which the questioner stands, and when the question itself is the distillation of a lifetime's quest and the seeker's whole life depends on it. The stories of the masters' silence and its impact on students cannot be understood unless this is the situation—unless the anguish of a lifetime is concentrated in the question and everything hinges on the answer. And what is true of silence is also true of the other means a master uses to help his students.

The Discipline of Silence

One way of leading a student on the path of Zen is to destroy all the concepts and images he uses to "grasp" the truth. This prevents him from confusing the image with the thing—"the finger pointing at the moon with the moon itself"—and it also prevents him from resting complacently on fixed ideas. If, during an instruction period, the student repeats something the master has just said, the master makes fun of him and says the opposite. When a saying is repeated, it ceases to be true; this applies even to the wise sayings of antiquity. This is why masters are often so harsh, even savage, in their comments on other masters' utterances. Nothing that is said about the truth can or must be said once and for all—even something said by a master, which becomes lifeless and positively harmful when it is parroted by someone else. A verbal bomb thrown at our assumptions must not be recycled as a pillow for more of those assumptions. When a master sees that his student is close to the truth, or has even tasted it already, his severity only increases. An example: A student returns from a pilgrimage on which satori has come to him. He respectfully approaches his master, who receives him in silence, and kneels down before him. Just as he is raising his head and preparing to speak, the master lifts his stick and deals him thirty heavy blows in quick succession. "Why have you done this, master?" asks the student. "I said nothing." "Even a word," replies the master, "and it would have been too late!" By stopping him from putting his experience into words, the master saves him from losing the treasure contained in that experience.

Another example: The student enters the master's room, and the master sees at once that he has experienced satori. He puts him to one last test. The student kneels without speaking and the master says to him amiably, "And so, now you have it!" "Yes, master, I have it," the hapless student replies. "You have nothing!" roars the master. "Get out of my sight!"

The old wisdom of the mystics—to see as if we did not see, to have as if we did not have, to do as if we did not do! But how hard this is, and how much harder for us than for the Oriental, who is less obsessed with the need to define and make everything definite. We have all had the heartrending experience of seeing feelings simply melt away because someone has tried to "understand" them and put them into words—or because we have done so ourselves. Perhaps we are lost in contemplation of a landscape, a sunrise, a flower, totally at one with what we are seeing and feeling and deeply aware of the fullness of Being in a way that only happens when all the barriers are down. Suddenly someone pops up beside us and says, "How beautiful!" And life seems to split down the middle. We are back within ourselves, and "beauty" is somewhere else—outside! Whatever it was that linked us with beauty in its true nature and ours has gone, and cannot be called back.

If this is true of everyday feelings, it is still truer of those fragile experiences in which Being touches us because we are suddenly open to its constant presence. I remember a dream I once had. I had gone into a church. People were milling around on all sides, and a tourist guide was showing them a small bronze figure of Christ. Suddenly one of its outstretched arms turned in my direction. I seized its hand, and was instantly filled with a feeling I cannot begin to describe. Being, in all its fullness, seemed to be flooding through me. Everything seemed totally meaningful and clear, and I was conscious of being completely sheltered, utterly at peace.

Then I suddenly started to wonder. I withdrew slightly and the question "What is this?" began to shape itself faintly in my mind. At once, the little statue crumbled into dust—simply disappeared! I had lost everything. Fear surged up in me and I woke to a sense of utter desolation and guilt. This is the way things are; there is a reality that disappears as soon as we define it, as soon as we ask what it is. Indeed, barely voicing the question is enough to dispel something that was there just a moment before.

This realization underlies all of Zen's vital utterances and greatly increases its significance for us; for if we are looking for something that can be "defined" beyond all doubt, we desperately need someone to tell us that this kind of seeking is actually concealing the truth of Life from us.

Paradox

Naturally we tend to see the world in terms of the objective knowledge that questions such as "What is this?" set out to provide. How hard it is to let Being in without at once losing it again by allowing objective consciousness to focus on it—but this is precisely where the inner way can help us.

If the foundations we stand on in natural consciousness actually prevent us from experiencing Being, then the master who wants to lead us to that experience must first do everything he can to knock them away. This is why his actions often startle like bolts from the blue, why he speaks in riddles, why shock tactics are his tenderness and nonsense his logic.

The student asks, "What does the 'coming of Bodhidharma' mean?" The master answers, "The oak tree in the courtyard." Another student asks, "What is Buddha?" The master replies, "There never was one!" Some more examples:

> The pupil asks, "What is everyday living?"
> The master raises his fly whisk.
> "Is that it?" inquires the monk.

"What is that?" says the master.
The monk makes no answer.
"What is the present moment?"
"No one ever asked me that before."
"I am asking now, master."
"You fool!"

There are countless answers like this—answers apparently senseless and exasperating. What are they supposed to mean? Is it easy or hard to work that meaning out? As long as we keep asking "What is this?" we remain the prisoners of our worldly consciousness, which, precisely because it is worldly, holds the supra-worldly at bay. The same applies to "When?" or "Where?" Life lies beyond the "five W's"—*who, what, when, where, why;* it "cannot be questioned," says Meister Eckhart. The answers to all these questions define something, project it onto objective, static consciousness, and reduce life to facts. Without facts, people feel lost. But what is to become of them if their reliance on facts is really total, and they see their own lives only in terms that turn every living thing into a "fact"? Being and their true nature are barred to them. If reality is to get through to us, we must learn to turn our backs on everything that cuts us off from it. When it claims to be absolute, objective consciousness becomes a wall, and we can tear it down only by daring to trust the truth of the intangible, numinous something that breathes in our deepest experience, avoiding any attempt to pin that experience down. This is why the hole punched in the tidy fabric of "objective" reality by the master's paradoxical answer can also become the aperture through which the great light sheds a first unexpected ray on the seeker.

Practicing Zen

The Meaning of Exercise

The East speaks to us in its wise books, but it speaks to us even more clearly today in the exercises it teaches us to follow, telling us that working on ourselves in this way will turn us into something more. But what does "more" mean? Different people offer different answers.

In fact, most people who follow these exercises today use them to restore or improve their performance or health, to become more efficient and give themselves a better grip on life. This is certainly useful, but has nothing to do with what Zen means by practice.

Hatha yoga, for instance, is taken up in this practical spirit and taught as a kind of calisthenics. This is undoubtedly good for people's health, improves their concentration, and makes them feel better in an everyday sense, but it no longer has anything to do with yoga's real meaning. Yoga is not meant to make a person more efficient or to help him develop "higher faculties," but to "yoke" him to divine reality.

People who want worldly power are often attracted, however, by the miracles of so-called yogis who have actually stopped being yogis and become fakirs instead. Even in the East, the aberration of wanting to work wonders is not uncommon. I once asked a Zen teacher what he thought of the wonders worked by Indian "yogis," and he said: "When a person spends years or decades developing certain physical or spiritual powers, he can always do things that strike others as wonderful at the end of it. But what has that got to do with the inner way? It's the other way round: If a person is practicing on the *way* and toward the *way,* he finds himself able to do seemingly miraculous things as time goes on, first in his own field of exercise, and later beyond it. But this is not what the exercise is about. The exercise is about his progress on the inner way, and that is what it points to."

Thus, a fundamental distinction is needed between exercises that serve the world-ego, i.e., pragmatic exercises, and exercises that serve the self-realization of our true nature. We can call these initiation exercises, which open the door to Mystery—the Mystery being in fact "true nature," the unfathomable center of all things. Coming to inner awareness of this center, dissolving in it, and making it the basis of everything we do is what all Zen exercises aim at.

Some exercises, however, seem to be helping us toward the center when they are actually leading us even more dangerously astray—breathing, relaxation, posture, and meditation exercises that temporarily dissipate tension and frustration, soothing us and making us feel, wrongly, as if we have made some progress on the inner way.[11] As long as the world-ego retains its grip, all that such exercises do is treacherously to encourage a state of mind and being that reinforces that ego.

Even Zen exercises can easily be misread as aiming at worldly efficiency or even miraculous feats. Stories like those of the master swordsman who freezes his opponent's suspended weapon in the air with a look, the master archer who scores a perfect bull's-eye in the dark and splits his first arrow with a second,[12] the master who wakes a dead man to life and brings a bird tumbling dead to the ground with one shout: true though they are, they can easily mislead us, if we are ruled by the ambitious world-ego, into taking up Zen exercises in the hope of achieving similar feats ourselves. But if we approach them like this, we are misunderstanding them and missing what they have to offer us.

11. Cf. Karlfried Graf Dürckheim, *Hara: The Vital Centre of Man,* trans. Sylvia-Monica von Kospoth and Estelle Healey (London: Unwin Paperbacks, 1977).
12. Eugen Herrigel, *Zen in the Art of Archery* (New York: Random House, 1971).

And it is equally easy, if it is only the world you care about, to misunderstand the Zen practice of seated meditation—zazen—and assume that its purpose is to help you to continue to lead your old life, but in a more relaxed, detached, and "serene" way.

This way the meaning and spirit of Zen practice are missed, and so is the answer it can bring to the vital aspiration of people in the West—the longing to feel true nature break through, to manifest it freely in everything they do and so become full human beings for the first time.

Zen exercise never tries merely to increase a person's knowledge or skills while leaving him otherwise unchanged, but sets out to make him over, waking him to his true nature and transforming him from it. And so all Zen exercises center upon the turning point of human transformation, upon satori, the Great Experience, in which the old ego disappears, true nature emerges, and the individual, transformed to himself, returns into the world in which he now bears witness to Being—knowing, creating, and loving in a new way.

To practice Zen is to work in a disciplined way toward a state of mind and being in which the Absolute is fully present and takes on form within us, while its all-embracing unity is experienced directly and becomes creatively active. How is this state of mind and being reached? By integrating the here-and-now ego with true nature and Being beyond the here-and-now. Its purpose? To bear witness to Being in here-and-now existence. The state of oneness we achieve when we are "integrated with Being" in Zen is not, therefore, just a matter of renouncing the world and disappearing in the Absolute. It is also a matter of returning to the world—now permanently at one with true nature and truly ourselves through contact with Being—and preserving that contact by acting in a manner consonant with Being. What, then, does "Zen work" consist of?

Dismantling the Ego

"Zen work" aims at achieving ever deeper contact and union with our true nature and—once the breakthrough comes and the new consciousness awakens (satori)—at taking form from and bearing witness to this true nature in our daily life and work. The turning point is satori. The precondition is the *dismantling of the ego.*

Dismantling the ego! People hearing this today react in very different ways, and with very mixed feelings. Many reject the whole notion out of hand. Psychologists are quick to suggest that too little—not too much—ego is far more of a problem than we think. And many people see in the fundamental call to "drop the ego" the typically Oriental danger of losing individuality, abandoning a cornerstone of European thought, vanishing into nothingness, and dissolving in the All-One. Anthroposophists are afraid of losing their "Christ impulse from the ego." None of this is the case. Zen is not in the business of destroying the ego, but of transforming the merely world-centered ego and changing the person determined solely by that ego into a person determined by his true nature. Nor does Zen reject the world, but merely attachment to the world.

When it speaks of "dismantling the ego," Zen is speaking—in full agreement with the Western spiritual tradition—of the basic condition we must fulfill to become truly ourselves and shape our lives in a manner consonant with Being. Dismantling the ego in this sense means chiefly dismantling the puny, power-hungry, self-assertive, and possessive ego, which is always anxiously focused on its own survival, status, and success. Even in the "objective" sphere, we all know that we cannot do anything worth doing or even emerge as "personalities"—integrated members of the community, sharing its values, attitudes, and aspirations—as long as this ego exists.

But dismantling the ego in Zen is not simply something we must do to live and think as members of the community. It is something we must do to release our spirituality—and this may be even harder if we are anchored in objective, logical, aesthetic, and ethical values than if we are anchored in the self-seeking ego. The more selfish a person is, the likelier he is to run headlong to disaster and, having touched bottom, to hear and heed the call to another way of life. The more rational and ethical he is, the greater the danger that his justified existence (justified because it accords with accepted norms and values) will retain its stultifying hold and so cut him off from real life—for even virtue, once it becomes a rigid system, is inimical to life.

Zen, like all Buddhism, sees attachment as the real root of evil, and people as evil to the extent that attachment makes them so. Attachment prevents us from thinking or living in better ways, and so cuts us off from the creative, redeeming power of life. This means that enlightenment, too, is possible only when attachment has been overcome. The three basic human failings that Buddhism repeatedly emphasizes—ignorance, desire, and hatred—are themselves mere offshoots of attachment.

Attachment always aims at possession. It is rooted in the hunger for permanence, the search for something fixed; it makes people hang on to anything they have once possessed, known, or been able to do. To "love" in this sense means to cling so tightly that one cannot let go. Once our notions and images of life set firm, we are "fixed" by them and cannot escape them. Images, of course, have gained in respect what barren logic has lost—rightly so, since it is in images and from them that life ripens into form. But images, once they harden and set, make it even harder for life to develop and mature; indeed, images and notions are often more effective than concepts in keeping the breath of life out. There is, however, a third and possibly even greater danger: ways of thinking, moving, and speaking that have become habitual and cannot be changed. It is as if people feared that their egos (and they themselves) would be catastrophically threatened by the giving up of ingrained gestures or harmful mannerisms—for instance, the permanently hunched shoulders in which a distrustful, fearful, or overweening ego takes refuge.

The fixed element is the worldview and life-style locked into concepts, images, and attitudes that have congealed and solidified. The fixing element is the defining ego, the "builder and guardian of the dwelling." This is why Zen practice always starts by dismantling the objective, defining ego, the ego concerned with possession and self-assertion, the ego that avoids pain, seeks pleasure, and distrusts everything, the ego that is constantly repeating the things it has once learned to do.

In the defining, attached ego, the indwelling fullness of what we *are* in our true nature is transformed into the objective multiplicity of what we *have*. Zen gives us back to our true nature.

Zen teaches us that there are two ways of neutralizing the ego: wearing out its energy by pushing objective thought or action to extremes, or totally withdrawing it from objective activity through meditation. Everything turns on experiencing and enduring nothingness, the void—for only in the void can the fullness, form, energy, and unity of Being be revealed.

The basic Zen exercise is zazen.[13] In Rinzai Zen there is also, chiefly, the koan, a problem the student is given to think out, but cannot solve by thinking. It is only when a person is at his wits' end that he is sufficiently shaken to see that he is on the wrong track. It is only when he reaches the breaking point that the inner eye opens and the consciousness that reveals him to himself as Being is released.

When this new consciousness is born, he continues to see the world objectively, but the objective vision is suddenly charged with deeper meaning, and he senses that his whole life is anchored in Being which *is*—beyond life and death, self and world, any and every "this and that." This process of transformation is also served by exercises in which a particular

13. Hugo Makibi Enomiya-Lassalle, *Zen: Way to Enlightenment* (New York: Taplinger Publishing Co., 1968).

skill is practiced to a point of completion that is not the product of ability, but the fruit of maturity that the adept attains by disciplining, dying to, and coming to himself again.

This is where the old Japanese exercises come in—archery, fencing, spear fighting, all the martial arts. So, too, do the tea ceremony and flower arranging. In all of these, correct breathing, correct balance, and correct stillness help to remake the individual. The basic aim is always the same: by tirelessly practicing a given skill, the student finally sheds the ego with its fears, worldly ambitions, and reliance on objective scrutiny—sheds it so completely that he becomes the instrument of a deeper power, from which mastery falls instinctively, without further effort on his part, like a ripe fruit. Whenever a person succeeds in ridding himself of the ego and becoming a pure instrument, he frees Being, which is striving all the time to manifest itself in him, allowing it to sing its everlasting song through his particular skill. And the more he identifies with what he experiences and expresses in that skill, the more fruitful and real it becomes throughout his everyday life.

The Purpose of Technique

The point of every exercise in which a specific skill is practiced is not improved performance as such, but what happens to the performer. Improved performance remains, of course, the immediate goal—but the point is the person achieving it, who purifies and transforms himself by seeking to perfect the exercise in the right way. What practice means in this case is not at all what it means when performance per se is the issue. Practiced in the right spirit, as a means to the *way,* exercise changes a person completely; his transformation then becomes not just necessary, but sufficient to perfect his performance. Skill always shows that a person has practiced, but the special kind of skill that goes with Zen's sublime teaching shows that Being has made over a person and itself expresses the change. This is why the East speaks of a Tao of technique, in which Tao and technique become one within the individual, so that technique expresses Tao.

The most striking account of the change wrought in a person by prolonged practice of a skill is given by Eugen Herrigel in his book on Zen archery. He shows that archery, "to the extent that it is a contest of the archer with himself," is a life-and-death matter. Why? Because it is an exercise in which "fundamentally the marksman aims at himself and may even succeed in hitting himself."

Endless repetition is common to all the exercises. Total concentration is needed at first, but as the actions slowly become automatic, the ego/object tension, which is rooted in purposive effort, gradually relaxes until ego and object (the implement, the instrument, but also the skill itself as process) become one, and the objective, defining, purposive consciousness is separated out and totally neutralized. Only when purposive tension is no longer necessary can its vehicle—the ego—be neutralized. And only when the ego disappears can the spirit (in the sense of supra-personal energy) come into play and mastery burst unchecked and as if of its own accord from the adept's true nature. At this point, mastery is no longer the product of conscious effort, but the revelation of true nature in a particular exercise.

The stages in the process, as described by Herrigel, are as follows: relaxing completely and shedding all tension, concentrating utterly, penetrating the mystery of breathing, mastering the "form" (external technique) completely through endless repetition, allowing the "spirit" to open so that the arrow can be loosed without effort, "devaluing" all interest (not merely in hitting the target, but also in inner progress)—all of this shielded, sustained, and carried forward solely by constant, tireless exercise, endlessly repeated and ever more unquestioning. Persistent exercise is the barrier that brings many people to grief. Not all the exercises are hard in themselves, but doing them properly is hard.

Practice, as Zen means it and Herrigel describes it, opens up a way that we in the West would be well advised to follow. No longer merely the means to a skill, it becomes a means of helping ourselves and others to break through to our true nature and give it form in the world. Seen in this way, exercise becomes a vehicle for the one really helpful form of guidance, and any exercise centered on personal transformation—on a person's being reborn to himself and his own creative potential, on manifesting his true nature in everything he does—comes close to Zen.

The turning point in exercise comes when our attention shifts from objective notions and goals to the mood, attitude, and movement that come from within and can only be inwardly sensed. This gives a new meaning to certain therapeutic practices that have been used so far mainly to restore health and productive energy. Drawing and painting, often used as therapy, provide one example. Practiced in the Zen spirit, they do not merely serve a diagnostic or generally liberating function, but become part of a calculated process leading a person to himself. Maria Hippius has described that process like this: "Anyone who practices drawing as a means of self-improvement can become aware of certain basic creative energies within himself and develop toward something that comes to him as a fundamental inner experience. In this way, he can gain a new 'understanding' of himself and of the world through essential and substantial experiences that he procures and brings to consciousness through the senses rather than the mind. Practiced in the right way, drawing can help him to see that his errors are errors along the way to becoming a full human being, and that he cannot become fully himself until he has made contact with his true nature and found his way back to the force that really sustains him.

"Like any therapeutic exercise, therapeutic drawing sets out to wake a person who has ground to an unproductive halt, gradually bring into play a new vital impetus, and call forth basic impulses, thereby mobilizing something deeper and stronger in his consciousness and conduct than the 'realities' by which he has previously attempted to live. His scarred and twisted persona, his failures and his apprehensions—all the things that cut him off from reality and truth—are allowed to fall away as the primal forces of Being gradually submerge them. Powers deep within his own nature may be mobilized, progressively shaping his own inner core and revealing his innermost potential as an individual. Stultifying complexes and inertia are replaced by a mysterious 'impetus from Being,' an impetus that is certainly weak to start with, but gradually gathers momentum—an impulse that comes from true nature and is caused (but now in the fullest sense) by the very same person who seemed to have reached a dead end.

"To achieve this result, the exercise of drawing, writing (graphotherapy), painting, or modeling must have a meditative, ritual character. No healing activity can succeed unless transcendence, i.e., the patient's true nature, is kept firmly in view. In the same way, no activity can successfully harness a person's inner powers and bring his full potential to light unless it has a 'sacred' character. It can precipitate the decisive change only if it comes from deep down, where the person is his undivided self, and only if every brushstroke is completely meant. This is the only way in which rediscovered sense qualities can revitalize him and restore the very special interplay of forces on which he depends. The adept suddenly senses, tastes, hears, and sees what is coming into being in and from himself, and discovers an entirely new inner mode of moving and perceiving in his minute, seemingly trivial activity, which he now learns to exploit for what it contains of Being and of quality."[14]

What is true of creative activity is also true of every physical exercise, for example, the practice of correct breathing, posture, and movement. It is only when mistakes in posture and breathing caused by defects in a person's life-style and by interference from the ego have been overcome, and the objective-purposive consciousness has receded, that true nature becomes an indwelling presence and is free to open and

14. Maria Hippius, "Das geführte Zeichen," in M. Hippius, ed., *Transzendenz als Erfahrung* (Munich: O. W. Barth-Verlag, 1966).

develop. We must learn to see all our movements from within as significant gestures. We must find out if and how far we ourselves are really present in our actions, or are merely the prisoners of convention and guided by certain fixed ideas in everything we say and do. We must be able to sense what it means to be fully present, from our true nature, in every movement, brushstroke, and gesture. This means that any activity—not just activities requiring special skills, but repetitive activities in office, kitchen, workshop, or factory—can be turned into an exercise. "Daily exercise" acquires a very special meaning when everything becomes a field for exercise in Zen, from the right way of breathing, walking (to be what we really are, we must walk "from" the right center), standing, sitting, speaking, and writing, to any working activity that uses technique. The only things that count are the basic approach and attitude.

Westerners usually regard the opening up of true nature and the self-fulfillment that results as a wholly "inner" process, and may well be surprised that the body is expected to play such an important part. Of course, the body in question is not the body we *have,* but the body we *are.* From the standpoint of the true self, there is both a right and a wrong way of being present in this body, the physical medium through which we express and manifest ourselves—in which we are "embodied." Our way of being present, of "being there," expresses what we are in a total sense, transcending the body/soul antithesis.[15] Working on a person's way of "being there" always means working on what he is in a total sense, in both soul and body. For this reason, too, all therapies that aim at self-realization but focus solely on the "psychological" element (i.e., psychoanalysis) will soon be completely outmoded.

Anything that contains the primal substance undiminished can provide a useful starting point and field for exercise when we set out to rediscover and release our true nature.

15. Dürckheim, *Hara: The Vital Centre of Man.*

This is particularly true of primal sense experience: color, sound, smell, touch, taste, and—above all—bodily awareness. But it is not just a matter of rediscovering primal, pre-personal experience. On the contrary, the original sense-qualities, when they are experienced in meditation, develop a new supra-sensual depth. Experienced and understood in this way, they form one of the roots of the supra-sensual spirit that unlocks the fullness of life. Instead of being taken for granted as an automatic part of all experience and disregarded, they must be raised to consciousness, seen for what they are, and recognized as playing a vital part in the discovery and development of the real self. This is perhaps even truer of bodily awareness and movement sensed from within. Every entrenched neurosis expresses itself in the body and strikes even deeper roots in its physical symptoms. A neurotic is a person who cannot find himself in his own body. And this is why coming to terms with one's own body—first becoming aware of bad habits and then freeing oneself from them—is an important factor in healing, indeed a vital one.

A person "is there" in the right way, is personally present in the true sense, when he mediates effectively between the Absolute and the relative, between Being and existence. Existence rooted in Being is what counts, and this is what Zen teaches. But the fundamental exercise is zazen.

Zazen

Any account of Zen, however brief, must give zazen—the central Zen exercise—its due.

Notwithstanding the many Zen, particularly Rinzai Zen, exercises that bring action into meditation, sitting is still the basic exercise: sitting in the right position, sitting quietly, sitting and meditating—zazen.

The student of Zen begins and ends the day with zazen. And during the day, whenever he has time—and the further he goes, the more time he finds—he practices zazen. Even at night, if he wakes without falling asleep again at once, he sits up and does zazen. Zazen is not meditating on a sacred saying or image, but just sitting and trying to shed all images and thoughts, actively trying to enter the void.

Westerners may at first be surprised that something that looks so much like doing nothing should play such an important—indeed a vital—part in bringing our real humanity to fruition in *the true self.* But it does, and is important not only to those who believe that the purpose and goal of all spiritual exercise is union with the Absolute—but equally to those who believe that this union vitalizes our way of living, loving, and creating *in the world,* and gives it deeper meaning. For the world is always our ultimate touchstone in the West, and even people who have attained final maturity, and have been transformed and liberated into Being beyond space and time, must bear witness to Being in the here-and-now.

We can no more say what zazen *is* than we can say what a sound, color, smell, taste, or hardness or softness is; we must hear, see, smell, taste, and touch it for ourselves. And so we must sit zazen for ourselves, and not just once but again and again—for weeks, months, and years—to know what it is or, more accurately, what it can be or, more accurately still, what we ourselves can gradually become with zazen's help and *be* even when we are not doing zazen. For zazen means and gives us something that is not there only while we are exercising, but always: an attitude that incorporates, expresses, and *is* Being, and which renews us and helps us to see new things in a new way and use every moment to the full, with Being constantly reflected in what we are (i.e., our way of "being there"), how we experience what we experience, and in the positive value of our actions—or, indeed, our omissions.

Practicing Zazen

One does zazen for the reason one does any genuinely spiritual exercise: to achieve union with something the Christian would call God, the Hindu Brahma, and the Buddhist . . .

Of the three, the Buddhist takes the most care not to say what cannot be said. When he speaks of Buddha-nature, he is merely referring indirectly to the intangible heart of all things—Being, which is everything that is. Being drops out of consciousness as soon as we become conscious of something, but the sacred tranquility that lies beyond all feelings can make it a permanent, indwelling presence, bringing us home to the truth of what we are. To become aware of our true nature in this way is at once our own good fortune, our way of helping others, our business in life, and the purpose of exercising, i.e., of doing zazen.

The path to this awareness leads through emptiness, through total detachment from everything that fills the contingent consciousness that is governed by the concepts, systems, and images of contingent reality and prevents us from making the breakthrough. In zazen we are meant to shed all worldly objects and emotions, all images, notions, and concepts. But our normal "waking" state is governed by the ego, and the ego is *never* free of objects—and so our next problem is to free ourselves through exercise from the ego, which is synonymous with the presence of images, ideas, and thoughts, as well as desires, anxieties, feelings, hopes, and fears. The natural consciousness is always "preoccupied" (i.e., full to start with), and this is the greatest obstacle to direct contact with true nature, with Being. To be liberated from objective consciousness is not, however, to be "unconscious." On the contrary, it is to be present and awake in a new subjective consciousness, which is no longer concerned with what we have (in an objective sense), but with what we really *are*—our true nature as the mode in which Being, the true nature of all things, is individually present in every one of us. When true nature comes fully to consciousness, we can also see it in all the "objects" around us. This is our personal opportunity, our very own way of being in a present beyond space and time—the everlasting now—in the midst of contingent reality.

The Technique of Sitting

Technique may seem a strange word to use in connection with a spiritual exercise designed to put us in touch with Being, which lies beyond the reach of objective consciousness and purposive activity, both of which are essential to the learning and mastering of any technique. The contradiction in fact disappears once we realize that technique is used to create the conditions for the Absolute to manifest itself and that the activity, when it is mastered and becomes automatic, is performed perfectly without reference to the will (guided by objective consciousness). At this point, Life can flow unchecked from the adept's true nature; that is, it can live itself out and become apparent in the activity itself.

In its fullness, order, and unity, Life is the animating, regulating, and unifying force behind everything—and when Being takes on form in a person, it can manifest itself freely in that form. Endlessly redeeming and creating, Life can melt fixed forms down and reabsorb them, and at the same time bring formlessness to form in an everlasting process of becoming. It is precisely this creative and saving Life that we obstruct by taking on fixed contours and clinging to them. These are the obstacles that zazen sets out to remove.

The student of zazen can no more *make* the exercise succeed than a gardener can *make* his plants grow. But a gardener can and must create the conditions for growth, by removing everything that stops his plants from growing, and encouraging everything that helps them to develop. In the same way, the student of zazen must get rid of anything that prevents him from becoming a medium for Being, and foster anything that helps him.

The following three factors prevent indwelling transcendence from showing through:

1. "Static" consciousness, that is, consciousness that deals in, clings to, and is filled with fixed entities (definite images, thoughts, notions, concepts, attitudes, positions).

2. An attitude—a way of "being there," spiritually *and*

physically, that obstructs the all-transforming movement of Life. The impulses, urges, desires, and anxieties embodied in this kind of wrong attitude are either rigid and thus prevent a person from becoming a clear medium, or formless and free-floating and thus prevent Life from revealing itself as living form.

3. Wrong breathing. Correct breathing, the everlasting movement of change, is the fullest expression of life itself. Wrong breathing constricts this natural movement, but as it grows "righter," its rightness fills the consciousness, automatically bringing the individual into inner harmony with life's ever-changing rhythm.

Correct Posture

What Master Dogen, the founder of Soto Zen, had to say on correct zazen posture is still valid today:

"You prepare for exercise by laying a thick mat in the selected spot and placing a cushion on it to sit on. You may sit in either the *kekka-fuza* (full lotus) or *banka-fuza* (half-lotus) position. In the first, you place your right foot on your left thigh and let it rest there, and you then place your left foot on your right thigh and let it rest there. In the second, you merely place your left foot on your right thigh. You should wear your clothing and belt loosely, but neatly. You next rest your right hand on your left leg, and your left hand on the palm of the right. You place your two thumbs together, tip to tip. You keep your body upright and carefully maintain a correct sitting posture by leaning neither to left nor right, neither forward nor back. You must also be careful to keep your ears directly above your shoulders, and your nose directly over your navel. Your tongue is held in contact with the roof of your mouth. Both your lips and teeth are closed. Your eyes should always be kept open. You breathe lightly in and out through your nose. In this way, you bring your body into the best position. You now take a deep breath and sway to left and right until you come to rest, firm as a rock, in an upright position. And now think about the unthinkable. How do you do that? By not thinking! And this is the deep and natural art of zazen."

The Zen master Hakuun Yasutani,[16] who died a short time ago, provided the following commentary:

" 'You sway to left and right until you come to rest, firm as a rock, in an upright position.' You move your body like a pendulum, first oscillating broadly and then gradually reducing the swing until the body eventually comes to rest in a central position of its own accord. You then sit firmly and enter the state of being motionless as a mountain. It is only at this point that your mind is collected (concentrated).

" 'Think about the unthinkable. How do you do that? By not thinking!' Beginners (and the meaning of the term 'beginner' depends on the yardstick applied) always have trouble with distracting thoughts during zazen. More advanced students, who are used to sitting, whose legs no longer hurt and who feel increasingly at ease, can become drowsy—and even those who normally get plenty of sleep readily fall into a kind of absent or abstracted state. These are the two diseases of consciousness. We call the first (persistent distracting thoughts) 'agitation,' or *sanran,* and the second (drowsiness or abstraction) 'somnolence,' or *kontin.* In zazen, consciousness is not supposed to vanish, but to enter a state of disciplined composure in which neither of these conditions can occur. Normally, consciousness moves so independently along its accustomed track that it is hard to keep an eye on it. That is why we must learn to avoid both agitation and somnolence. Both disappear if we approach the exercise in a really serious manner. Think of yourself as fighting a duel to the death, in which either you or your opponent will be killed. You stand facing each other with drawn swords. You cross blades. What is the point of complaining now that you are not completely on the spot, that insomnia has left you sleepy and confused?

16. Hakuun Yasutani was also the teacher of Philip Kapleau, author of *The Three Pillars of Zen* (New York: Anchor/Doubleday, 1980).

Even if you have never practiced zazen, this is one situation where no distracting thoughts will bother you—if your attention wanders for a moment, you will be cut down instantly. In the same way, anyone who seriously wants to attain the right state of consciousness for zazen can do it. If he fails, it is only because he is not really serious. It is distressing that we ordinary mortals should find it so hard to summon up the seriousness we need for zazen. To do it, we must bring our minds into the right state—and this is known as 'not-thinking' (the state that lies beyond the to-and-fro of conflicting opinions). It is, in fact, the central element in performing the exercise.''

A fuller description by Master Yasutani:

"First you must choose a quiet room to sit in. Take a mat which is about thirty-five inches square and not too soft, and place on it a small, round cushion, measuring approximately twelve inches across. Sit on the cushion and let your legs rest on the mat. You should not wear trousers, which make it hard for you to cross your legs. For many reasons, it is best to adopt the standard Buddhist posture (the full lotus). You do this by laying your right foot over your left thigh, and then your left foot over your right thigh. The main purpose of sitting like this is to achieve absolute stability, and you do this by establishing a broad, solid base and crossing your legs on this base, with both knees touching the mat. When the body is completely still, there is no movement to stimulate thought, and the mind also becomes still, as if of its own accord. If you find this position too difficult, you should adopt the half-lotus, simply laying your left foot over your right thigh. Westerners who are wholly unfamiliar with zazen may find even this too difficult; the knees will not stay down, and repeatedly have to be pressed down so that both touch the mat. If you find both the full and the half-lotus impossible, you should cross your legs in the normal way or simply use a chair.

"The next step is to place your right hand, palm upward, in your lap and to place your left hand, palm upward, in your right. Form a circle with your thumbs by bringing them together at the tip. You should remember that the right side of the body is the active side, and the left the passive. By laying the left foot on the right, you are suppressing the active side, and this makes for maximum tranquility. If you look at an image of Buddha, however, you will see that his posture is exactly the reverse—the right foot is on top. This is to show that a Buddha, unlike ourselves, is always active and saving others.

"When you have crossed your legs, lean forward, push your buttocks back, and slowly come back to an upright position. Your head should be straight, so that your ears are directly above your shoulders, and the tip of your nose directly over your navel. From the waist up, your body should be weightless and free of pressure and exertion. Keep your eyes slightly open and your mouth closed. With closed eyes, one easily falls into a dull and dreamy state. Your gaze should, however, be lowered and not fixed on any particular object. Experience has shown that the mind is quietest and freest of strain or fatigue when the eyes are lowered in this way.

"Your spine should always be straight. This is particularly important. If the body slumps, not only are the internal organs subjected to excessive pressure and prevented from functioning freely, but the vertebrae may also be placed under strain and press on the nerves. Since mind and body are one, anything that harms the body inevitably harms the mind too, endangering the clarity and 'single-pointedness' that are vital to effective concentration. From the standpoint of growing and maturing, a 'ramrod' posture is quite as undesirable as a slovenly one, for the first expresses pride and the second an abject lack of self-discipline. Both are grounded in the puny ego, and are therefore equally obstructive on the path to enlightenment. Always remember to hold your head up; if it is bent forward or to one side and remains in that position for some time, you will be left with a stiff neck."

Maintaining the right posture is essentially a matter of working all the time to keep the correct verticals upright and anchored in the firm horizontals of the stomach-pelvis-diaphragm complex, or *hara*. [17] The most helpful image here is that of the "rooted stick"; with every breath, its roots go deeper into the earth, while its trunk and crown grow upward. But again and again we find that we have slumped a little, letting the abdomen go slack or drawing it in, and depriving the spinal column of the natural supporting power it can have only when it is completely vertical—and that the head has slipped forward or back as a result. And so, again and again we must straighten up—never minding about the hollow back! A position that at first seems unnaturally erect and stiff (the "ramrod") instantly feels right when we follow orders and "push the buttocks back" (as Zen cheerfully puts it, "Let your anus see the sun!"), while pressing the abdomen slightly into the groin. Suddenly we feel the body straightening itself effortlessly, of its own accord—and feel ourselves growing and expanding upward, downward, and in all directions.

Working on Consciousness

The transformation of consciousness sought in Zen practice includes both the content and form of consciousness—in other words, we start by emptying consciousness, and then we transform consciousness itself.

Emptying consciousness. When we are trying to rid ourselves of the persistent images, notions, and thoughts that prevent us from "plumbing the depths," the first rule is to let them pass like clouds on the wind.

In its normal waking state, the ego always has objects of consciousness. One way of getting rid of them is to let the ego focus on an object that eventually swallows it! Breathing, or rather the closely followed rhythm of breathing, is the favorite "object" for this purpose. As this natural "out-out-in" pattern gradually infiltrates our consciousness, we approach the point where true meditation takes over from "concentration," object-centered tension is dissipated, and we are left in

17. Cf. Dürckheim, *Hara: The Vital Centre of Man.*

a rhythmically "tuned" state that entirely fills our consciousness. This tuned state is what matters: the music of Being rings out all the time, and we must become tuned instruments so that it can be heard through us.

Counting breaths is one traditional way of keeping images and thoughts at bay. We are told to count to ten and start again—this is meant to stop us from taking pride in our "score" or becoming drowsy from counting on indefinitely.

If we do not stare at the spot we look at in meditation, but simply let our gaze rest upon it, it too can effect the switch from objective to subjective consciousness. Suddenly it is no longer "outside," but "inside" too, and we and it are one. When this happens, both ego and object cease to exist.

We can also empty consciousness by concentrating on the point where our two thumbs touch, simply registering the sensation at the point where they meet. To eliminate "pressure" on the thumbs at that point, it is best not to place the entire left hand in the palm of the right, but simply to lay the fingers of the left hand on the fingers of the right. When this is done, the thumbs automatically touch very lightly.

Transforming consciousness. To transform consciousness is, first and foremost, to substitute sense consciousness for objective consciousness, and we can do this best by focusing on our own immediate sense impressions. The question here is, what do we really, subjectively sense when we objectively know, for example, that our thumbs are touching each other, our foot is resting, or our buttocks are touching the floor at a certain point? Normally, what we "sense" is immediately turned into what we "know"—but now we are trying to restore the original contact, to feel the quality of what we sense and the quality of our own sensations. We should focus on breathing in this way, not as something happening in a particular place, something we have or do, but as change and movement *which we are.* When we exercise, we must feel ourselves responding to the rhythmic quality of our own movements and must bring out their meaning as something we both experience and are. Any action that becomes automatic can be performed in this way. Indeed, daily life is full of these automatic actions, and the student of Zen learns to use them to make contact with his inner self again and again throughout the day.[18] This is also the secret of the mantra's power to transform. Recited over and over again, either aloud or only to ourselves, it breaks the spell of objective consciousness, opens the door, and allows us to become one with our own inner nature. It is sheer repetition, rather than content, that allows this. Obviously, it only works in the right way if the mind is entirely focused on union with the Absolute.

We can ease the transition from objective to sense consciousness in zazen if we stop thinking of consciousness as being located in the head (forehead) and think of it as being in the back of the neck or the upper part of the spinal column instead, that is, if we sense ourselves at that point and "see" from it. The spot on which our eyes rest in meditation can also be "seen" like this—and what we see then is totally different from what we see with defining, cerebral consciousness. The new consciousness might be said to be neither mental consciousness, which has developed in the cerebrum, nor pre-mental consciousness, which is located in the cerebellum and has a more primal quality, but post-mental consciousness diffused throughout the body—just as total change when we merge with Buddha-nature is also experienced as something affecting the whole body.

The state of consciousness we try to attain on the path to our true nature is not merely supra-objective, but supra-dualistic as well. We can bring it closer by "enduring" feelings, sensations, and even pain (e.g., in the legs), which have intensified to a point where they can scarcely be borne. When unendurable pain is nonetheless endured with complete serenity, a state of being beyond pain and non-pain *may* develop.

18. Cf. Karlfried Graf Dürckheim, *The Way of Transformation: Daily Life as a Spiritual Exercise,* trans. Ruth Lewinnek and P. L. Travers (London: Unwin Paperbacks, 1980).

Breathing

No one can practice zazen meaningfully and helpfully without knowing how to breathe correctly. The zazen approach to breathing shows particularly clearly how far Zen is from the merely artificial and how its way to the truth always leads through the deeply natural or immediate needs of a given situation. "This and this only" is the one rule, and everything that Zen demands of correct posture is summed up in the two words *this only*. This is why Zen breathing is a long way, for example, from hatha yoga breathing. The only change Zen tries to make is to eliminate the distortion of natural breathing that occurs chiefly when the ego predominates and the correct center of gravity is shifted upward, with the result that auxiliary muscles are called in to do the job that should normally be done by the diaphragm.

Bringing into awareness the real meaning of breathing as change and movement, as well as the meaning carried by each of the phases of natural breathing, has been found a useful way of dismantling ingrained bad habits in zazen. Put in the simplest terms, in seeking to achieve union with the Absolute, or whatever name one gives it, one must stop identifying with the objectively defining ego, which clings to its fixed positions.

When functioning properly, natural breathing goes a long way toward doing this job for us. It is a question of opening our eyes to the process and experiencing it consciously, i.e., participating in it consciously while exercising. We can do this very simply by learning to think of breathing not merely as a way of taking in air and expelling it, but as a movement in which we open and close *ourselves,* give *ourselves,* and, thus renewed, receive *ourselves* back again. When he breathes out, the student of zazen must feel that he is freeing himself of everything that has become fixed and static, and making room for the movement of renewal that he can experience when he breathes in. When breathing follows its natural, primal, and healthy rhythm, breathing in normally takes a quarter of the time required for the whole operation. Breathing out and the pause between out and in account for the remaining three-quarters and prepare for the natural expansion of breathing in. In this second phase, we (1) relax, (2) settle, and (3) merge; or, more accurately, (1) relax the upper body (shoulders, chest), which has been drawn up, (2) settle in the pelvic region, or *hara,* and (3) merge with the pelvic base. When we do this properly, breathing in becomes automatic and is experienced as revitalization and renewal of the whole system. One formula, which says it more profoundly and can be used to accompany breathing, runs: give oneself, give oneself over, give oneself up, and (breathing in) receive oneself back again, renewed.

Breathing out is thus the only phase in which we actually "do" anything; breathing in is automatic. Obviously, we only breathe like this—consciously fulfilling the purpose of breathing—during the concentration phase before every exercise. Once breathing becomes automatic, the meditation phase proper begins.

Only someone who has practiced zazen correctly and with the greatest regularity for at least a few months can judge what it has to offer. The traditional minimum exercise period is thirty to forty minutes.

The Three Stages of Consciousness and the Five Steps on the Way

We have seen that our true nature is the mode in which divine Being seeks to manifest itself in us, and that it cannot do this while the objective ego and its values hold sway. To become conscious (i.e., to "enter" awareness) of Being, we need a new consciousness, subjective consciousness, in which Being and consciousness become a single indwelling presence. The purpose of Zen is to liberate subjective consciousness.

We are so totally absorbed by the things we know, can

do, and are used to, that we rarely notice the reflected glow of a new, unknown, and greater life just over the rim of our ordinary consciousness. This ordinary consciousness is like an island and we are like islanders; we can imagine nothing outside our island, and although the sea is all around us, we have no idea what it is or how far it reaches. An inexplicable mystery is woven through our whole existence, but its only links with our ordinary consciousness are subliminal. Like stars in daylight, it is hidden from us by the light of our own objective consciousness, even though our purpose and destiny in life is to let it become manifest in and through ourselves. Every initiation process, every "way" of practice, sets out to make this happen—including Zen.

The way we human beings follow is the way of developing consciousness, and this consists of three stages.[19] We start at the *pre-mental* stage, where we are still "beyond" antitheses, where undivided consciousness expresses undivided life. Our ultimate goal is the higher, *post-mental* stage, which also lies "beyond" antitheses; this is the stage aimed at in Zen. The *mental* stage lies between the two and is governed by the defining ego.

Thus, the word *beyond* has a double meaning that applies to two stages: pre-mental and post-mental. The "beyond" itself is an active principle, sustaining and stimulating us on the deepest level of our consciousness, though we gradually lose touch with it as our intellect develops. And it is something we can find our way back to by outgrowing the consciousness that alienates us from our roots. Zen wisdom focuses on that spiritual level at which our ordinary consciousness is left behind, and Life is experienced post-mentally and not pre-mentally. Obviously, this experience comes more easily if Life is still subliminally active deep within us. If, on the other hand, we can no longer sense its presence, take it seriously, or accept its manifestations as anything but childish or primitive, we will find it hard to make contact with Zen.

19. Jean Gebser, *The Ever-Present Origin* (Athens, Ohio: Ohio University Press, 1985).

We cannot survive unscathed even during the stage when developing objective consciousness has alienated us from our primal, pre-objective consciousness, unless we are still secretly in contact with Being. If objective consciousness and its logic, aesthetics, and ethics sever this contact completely, we eventually reach a point where the only alternative to total stagnation is breaking through to the third, post-mental stage.

The three stages of consciousness can be subdivided into five steps. The transition from pre-mental to mental is the first. The second, third, and fourth are all taken at the mental stage of consciousness, which serves as a springboard to the post-mental stage.

The second step is emergence and development of the objective, dualistic consciousness, which lands us simultaneously in the antitheses of ego/world and ego/true nature. To start with, however, the ego/world tension is the only one we feel. Suppressing true nature and our roots in Being, we concentrate entirely on the world, on succeeding in it, surviving in it, and doing what it asks of us, and the gap separating us from Being widens.

The third step comes when the ego/world tension crushes our true nature, and the resultant anguish drives us in on ourselves. We now try to evade the world's demands, but these demands are unceasing, and we are torn between living for the world and living for our own inner selves. True nature calls from the inner life, and by trying to live that life only, we accentuate the tension between our inner needs and the world's demands. This tension is the central feature of the third step. When the strain increases to breaking point, we are ready to take the fourth.

We take the fourth step only when a first experience of our own true nature—and of the Absolute in our own true nature—has liberated us, filled us with joy, and sent us looking for stability somewhere outside the inner-life/worldly-life antithesis. This means turning our backs on the world and trying repeatedly to sense our true nature in "private" meditation, to dwell in Being beyond the antithesis. Since contact with Being releases us from anguish, we naturally try to prolong it. Of course, this pursuit of unworldly tranquility may be simple escapism, an attempt to live in the past or to reclaim the sheltered world of childhood. But it can also start something new, generate a new sense of purpose, and lead to genuine fulfillment.

All this time, the ego and our links with the world are still inescapably there, and so a day inevitably comes when we realize that the peace we seem to have found outside life's contradictions is actually the peace of indolence. Repressing our true nature was one way of failing to become a complete human being—and we fail again now if we try to pretend that we have no ego, that we are not in the world, and that the contradiction between absolute true nature and contingent reality has simply disappeared. Just when we think we have outrun all of life's contradictions, we run slap into the one contradiction that cannot be removed, that will not go away. And so we are forced again and again to face up to the ego and our human destiny. We must return to the world and accept the pain caused by the tension between relative and absolute. If at this point we forget what the fourth step has taught us and simply regress to the old ego, all may be lost. But if we can genuinely outgrow antitheses by accepting them, we can at last make the breakthrough to post-mental consciousness, which was already close when the fourth step was taken. This is the fifth step, the decisive step into the true self, where ego and true nature become one.

When we take the fifth step, we experience satori and the opening of the inner eye, which sees Being and existence as one. It is only at this point that we can stop seeing dualistic existence and non-dualistic Being as opposites, and start perceiving Being *in* existence. When we take the fourth step, we try to lose the ego in true nature. When we take the fifth step, we must accept the ego all over again. It is only by learning to see antitheses as the form in which the not-two presents itself to us when it passes through the prism of the defining consciousness that we can accept the pain caused us by the conflict of light and darkness, good and evil, Being and non-Being—and make something positive of it. The fact that we are now anchored in true nature, somewhere beyond suffering and non-suffering, does not mean that we stop suffering, but simply that we can now suffer *usefully.* From now on, our pain is no longer the pain that has no purpose, embitters, means nothing, and cannot be escaped; it is the pain that benefits us and makes us over. Now that we have experienced something beyond cause and effect, and have seen through that relationship, we can meet life's reverses in a new way and use our new freedom to turn them around and make them positive. We have reached the ground of all things, and can now accept our destiny—however hard—shape it, and make the most of it in a way that often seems superhuman to the ordinary consciousness. In fact, all of this only shows what human beings *really* are, deep down, when wholeness is achieved. The ways in which we experience the world and respond to it have been transformed. The Absolute lives on "subjectively" within us, and the pain of relativity also acquires a new meaning; for, whatever happens, we are now aware of creative, redemptive Being as an omnipresent force, constantly, lovingly drawing us home to the ground in which all things are one, and also constantly remaking us and releasing us back into the world.

The five-step formula runs through the whole of human life, as long as life keeps on the move and advances dialectically toward fulfillment in the not-two. Our conscious life is tensioned between poles, with first one and then the other "winning," and it ceases to be real in a nonpolar universe where these poles are suspended. We reject the relative when we turn our backs on the world, but it is only by accepting it again and finding the Absolute, which we have now experienced, in the very heart of relativity that we can approach fulfillment.

Zen thinks, lives, and practices the five-step dialectic of life. The dialectic we go through in practice (and going through it is more than merely thinking it) has symbolic force for human life as well, when it is lived, suffered, and shaped "to the end that is fulfillment."

I have my Zen teacher, Takeharu Teramoto, to thank for a text of inexhaustible profundity—"The Tale of the Wonderful Art of a Cat"—which gives a uniquely vivid picture of the five-step dialectic.

Takeharu Teramoto was a former admiral and a professor at the Naval Academy in Tokyo. His practice *(gyo)* was fencing, and the story of the five cats was passed on to him by his fencing master—the last in a school where it had been handed down from master to master since the early seventeenth century as a secret guide to practice.

The Tale of the
Wonderful Art of a Cat

There was once a master swordsman named Shoken. His household was plagued by an enormous rat, which ran boldly back and forth even in broad daylight. One day, Shoken put his cat into the room and closed the door behind it, so it could catch the rat; but the rat sprang at the cat and bit it in the face so savagely that it ran off howling—and so this attempt came to nothing. Next, Shoken brought in a number of neighboring cats with good reputations and put them into the room. The rat crouched in a corner and leaped at any cat that came near, biting it and putting it to flight. It looked so ferocious that none of the cats was eager to risk taking it on again. At this stage, Shoken lost his temper and set out to chase and kill the rat himself. But in spite of all his skill, it slipped past his every blow and he could not catch it, although he put his sword through doors, shojis, and karakamis in trying. The rat darted like lightning through the air, dodged his every slash and thrust, sprang at him, and bit him in the face. Finally, sweating and exhausted, he shouted to his servant, "Six or seven leagues from here, there's a cat that's supposed to be the cleverest in the world—go and get it!"

The servant fetched the cat. She looked much the same as the others—neither particularly clever nor particularly fierce—and so Shoken expected nothing special of her. All the same, he opened the door cautiously and let her in. The cat advanced very calmly and slowly into the room, as if she too were expecting nothing out of the ordinary. The rat, however, gave a start and did not stir. The cat simply walked unhurriedly up to it, picked it up in her mouth, and carried it out.

That evening, the defeated cats met in Shoken's house, respectfully offered the old cat the place of honor, bowed down before her, and said humbly, "We are all considered hardworking. We have all practiced our skills and sharpened our claws so that we can win against rats of all kinds, and even weasels and otters. We would never have thought that such a strong rat could exist. How did you manage to beat it so easily? Please do not keep your secret to yourself, but tell us how you did it!"

The old cat laughed and said, "True enough, all you young cats are hardworking, but you do not know the right way, and so you fail when something unexpected comes along. But first tell me how you have practiced."

A black cat stepped forward and said, "I come from a family famous for its rat-catching, and decided to follow the same path myself. I can jump over a screen two meters high. I can force myself through a hole so small that only a rat can get through it. Since I was a kitten, I have practiced all the acrobatic tricks. Even when I'm waking up, still half-asleep and struggling to rouse myself, one glimpse of a rat flitting along a beam—I've got it at once. But that rat today was stronger than I, and I suffered the most terrible defeat of my career. I am deeply ashamed."

"What you have practiced," said the old cat, "is technique and nothing else [*shosa,* or purely physical skill], but you are constantly asking yourself, 'How can I win?' and so you are always clinging to a goal! When the great masters of the past taught 'technique,' they did it to show their students *one form of the way* [*michisuji*]. Their technique was simple—and yet it contained the loftiest truth. But technique itself is the only thing people care about today. Of course they've come up with plenty of new tricks on the 'such-and-such results from doing so-and-so' principle. But what is the real result? Some new sleight of hand and nothing else. And so the old way has been forgotten and people have worn their brains out trying to outdo one another with better techniques. Now every single possibility has been exhausted and there aren't any stones left to turn. This is what always happens when technique is the only thing that matters and people rely entirely on their cleverness. It's true, of course, that cleverness is a spiritual function, but if it isn't based on the way and aims only at skill, it puts you on the wrong track, and everything you do turns out badly. So look for the truth in yourself and practice properly from now on."

Next a large tabby cat stepped forward and said, "I believe that mind is the only thing that counts in the martial arts; that is why I have always tried to develop my mental power [*ki wo nero*]. As a result, I feel that my mind is as hard as steel, free, and charged with the 'spirit of *ki*' that fills heaven and earth [Mencius]. The moment I see the foe, this omnipotent spirit casts its spell on him, and I've won before I've even started. Only then do I make my move—very simply, doing only what the situation requires. I can hear my opponent think, I can use my power to steer him left or right as I choose, and I always know what he's going to do before he does it. I never give technique a thought—technique looks after itself. When a rat runs out along a beam, I just give him a piercing look. At once he comes tumbling down and I've got him! But that rat is a mystery; it comes without form and goes without a trace. What's it all about? I don't know."

"It is true," the old cat said, "that what you have sought is the effect that comes from the mighty power that fills heaven and earth. But what you have attained is merely psychic power and is not good in the true sense of the term. The very fact that you are conscious of the power on which you count for victory works against your winning, since your ego is in play. What happens when your opponent's ego is stronger than your own? You hope to crush him with your superior power—and he turns his power on you! Do you really think that you alone are strong and everyone else weak? What are you going to do when you meet something that your own strength, great as it is, is not sufficient to defeat? That is the question! The inner power that you feel and that seems 'free,' 'as hard as steel,' and 'to fill heaven and earth' is not the mighty power [*ki no sho*], but only its reflection in yourself. It is your own mind, and hence only the shadow of the great spirit. Of course, it looks very like this great, all-embracing power, but it's really something totally different. The spirit of which Mencius speaks is strong because it is permanently illuminated by a great clarity—but your mind is strong only under certain conditions. Your mind and the spirit of which Mencius speaks come from different sources, and so have different effects. The difference between them is the difference between an eternally flowing river, like the Yangtse, and an overnight flood. What kind of power do you need when you find yourself face to face with something that contingent spiritual power [*kisei*] can never conquer? Remember the old proverb: 'A cornered rat will even bite the cat.' When your foe is cornered and facing death, nothing can touch him anymore. He forgets life, pain, himself—and no longer gives a straw for victory or defeat. He no longer has any intention of protecting his own safety. That is why his will is as hard as steel. How can you hope to defeat him with spiritual powers for which you take credit yourself?"

An older, gray cat now came slowly forward and said:

"Everything you say is true. Psychic power, however great, always has an inner form [*katachi*], and anything, however small, that has form is tangible. And so for many years I have sought to develop my soul [*kokoro*, the power of the heart]. I do not employ the power that overcomes others from the mind [the *sei* used by the second cat]. Nor do I use claws and teeth [like the first cat]. I make peace with my opponent, allow myself to go along with him, and do absolutely nothing to resist him. If he is stronger, I simply give in and make him feel that I'm doing what he wants. You might say that my art is the art of catching flying stones in a loose curtain. Any rat, however strong, that tries to attack me finds nothing to jump at, nothing to catch hold of. But that rat today simply wouldn't play my game. It came and went as mysteriously as God himself. I've never seen anything like it."

"What you call making peace," said the old cat, "is not rooted in true nature, in the great nature of all things. It is a manufactured, artificial way of making peace—a trick—and you are consciously using it to escape your enemy's aggression. But because you think this—if only for an instant—he sees what you are up to. If you try to seem conciliatory in this frame of mind, you merely confuse and obscure your own aggressive instinct and take the edge off your own perceptions and actions. Anything you do with a conscious intention inhibits the primal, secret impetus of nature and checks its spontaneous flow. How can you expect to work miracles like that? It is only when you think nothing, want nothing, do nothing, and surrender yourself and your own rhythm to the rhythm of true nature [*shizen no ka*] that you shed tangible form—and counter-form becomes impossible. When that happens, there can be no more enemies to resist.

"I do not believe for a moment that all the things you have practiced are useless. Everything—absolutely everything—can be a form of the way. Technique and the way can also be one and the same thing, and the all-governing spirit is then contained in technique and speaks through the body's actions as well. The power of the great spirit [*ki*] serves the

118

human person [*ishi*]. If your *ki* has been liberated, you are endlessly free to respond to everything in the right way. If your spirit is genuinely at peace, neither gold nor stone can harm it, and you need no special skills in battle. Only one thing counts: there must not be a breath of ego-consciousness anywhere, or everything is lost. If you think about it even for a moment, all of this becomes artificial and no longer flows from true nature, from the primal motion of the body of the way [*do-tai*]. When this happens, your enemy, too, will resist instead of doing what you want. And so, what method or art do you need? It is only when you are entirely free of consciousness [*mushin*], when you act without acting, with no intentions or tricks, in harmony with the nature of all things, that you are on the right way. So have no intentions, practice having no intentions—and simply let things happen from true nature. This way is endless and inexhaustible."

And then the old cat went on to say something astonishing: "You must not imagine that what I have told you here is the last word. Not long ago, there was a tomcat living in the village next to mine. He slept all day, and there wasn't a trace of anything that looked like spiritual power about him; he just lay there like a block of wood. No one had ever seen him catch a rat, but there were no rats when he was around—and wherever he showed up or settled down, there wasn't a rat to be seen! One day I went over to see him and asked him to explain the whole thing. He said nothing—and still said nothing when I repeated my question, and repeated it twice after that. But it wasn't really that he didn't want to answer; he obviously didn't know what to say. And so I saw that those who know do not speak, and those who speak do not know. That cat had forgotten himself and everything around him as well. He had become 'nothing,' he had achieved the highest form of nonvolition. You might even say that he'd found the divine way of knighthood—conquering without killing. I'm still a long way short of that myself."

As if in a dream, Shoken overheard all of this. Coming up, he greeted the old cat and said, "I have practiced the sword for many years now, but have still not reached the goal. Now I have listened to your wise words and feel that I understand the true meaning and purpose of my way—but I implore you to tell me more about your secret."

"How can I do that?" the old cat said. "I am only an animal, and rats are my food. How can I know about human concerns? All I know is that swordplay is not merely a matter of defeating an opponent, but an art that can ultimately lead a person into the great brightness of the radiant ground of death and life [*seishi wo akiraki ni suru*]. Even while he is performing his technical exercises, a true master should constantly perform the spiritual exercise that leads him to this clarity—and to do this he must study the doctrine of the basis of life and death in Being and of the meaning of death [*shi no ri*]. You can attain ultimate clarity only by freeing yourself of everything that leads you astray from this way [*hen kyoku*, the middle distance], and particularly of defining thought. If true nature and contact with true nature [*shin ki*] are interfered with neither by the ego nor by anything else, they are perfectly free to manifest themselves whenever this is necessary. But if your heart clings—even fleetingly—to anything, true nature is imprisoned and turned into something fixed and static. When this happens, there is also a fixed and static ego, and something fixed and static outside that resists it. And so there are now two things standing facing each other and battling for survival— and the wonderful workings of true nature, whose essence is constant change, are impeded. This is the grip of death, and the clarity of true nature has been lost. If you are in this state, how can you meet your enemy in the right frame of mind and look calmly on victory and defeat? Even victory, if it came, would be a blind victory and would have nothing to do with the meaning and purpose of true swordsmanship.

"Being free of all things does not mean a vacuum. True nature as such has no inherent nature of its own, but lies beyond all forms. It takes in nothing from outside, but its vital force sticks to anything, however trivial, to which we cling, however briefly—and the primal balance of energies is lost. If checked even slightly, true nature is no longer free to pour itself out abundantly. When its balance is disturbed, it floods the points it still reaches, and the points it does not reach are starved. In the first case there is too much energy and no way of stopping it. In the second there is too little, and the spirit of action is weakened and fails. In both cases it becomes impossible to do what the actual situation requires. And so, when I speak of being free of all things, all I mean is this: If one hoards nothing, depends on nothing, and defines nothing, there is neither subject nor object, neither ego nor anti-ego. When something comes, one meets it as if unconsciously and it leaves no trace. The *I Ching* says: 'No thought, no action, no movement, total stillness: only thus can one manifest the true nature and law of things from within and unconsciously, and at last become one with heaven and earth.' Anyone who practices and understands swordsmanship in this manner is close to the truth of the way."

When he heard this, Shoken asked, "What do you mean when you say there is neither an ego nor an anti-ego, neither a subject nor an object?"

The cat replied: "When there is an ego—and because there is an ego—there is also an enemy. If we do not set ourselves up as egos, there is no one and nothing to oppose us. When we speak of an opponent or enemy, we really mean an opposing principle. Whenever a thing has form, it also has an anti-form—and it has form as soon as it becomes definite. If my true nature has no form, then no anti-form exists. Without an antithesis, there is no opposing principle, and this means that there is neither an ego nor an anti-ego. If we let ourselves go completely and become entirely, fundamentally detached, we are in harmony with the world, at one with all things in the great All-One. Even when our enemy's form is extinguished, we are completely unconscious of this, in the sense that we do not dwell on it. Our mind moves freely on without defining anything, and our actions flow straight from our true nature.

"When our spirit is entirely free and unoccupied, then

we and the world are entirely one. This means that we now accept it beyond good and evil, beyond liking and disliking. Nothing holds us back and we no longer cling to anything. All the antitheses we encounter—profit and loss, good and evil, joy and suffering—come from ourselves. That is why there is nothing in heaven or on earth more worth the knowing than our own true nature. An ancient poet says: 'A speck of dust in your eye and three worlds are too narrow; care for nothing and the straitest bed is broad enough.' In other words, if a speck of dust penetrates the eye, the eye cannot open, for it can see only when there is nothing in it. This can serve as a metaphor for Being—the light that shines and illuminates, in which there is nothing that is 'something,' but which loses its virtue the moment 'something' enters it. Another poet says: 'If I am surrounded on all sides by enemies, one hundred thousand in number, my form is crushed into nothingness. But my true nature is eternally mine, however strong the foe may be. No enemy can ever penetrate it.' Confucius says: 'Even a simple man's true nature cannot be stolen from him.' If our spirit becomes confused, our own true nature turns against us.

"That is all I can tell you. Simply look for the truth within yourself. All a master can do is tell his student the basics and try to explain them. But only you yourself can find out the truth and make it your own. This is called self-appropriation [jitoku]. The message is transmitted from heart to heart [i shin den shin] in a special way that lies beyond formal instruction and scholarship [kyogai betsuden]. This does not mean that what the masters taught was wrong, but simply that even a master cannot pass on the truth. This is not true of Zen only. In the spiritual exercises of the ancients, in cultivation of the soul and in the fine arts, self-appropriation has always been the vital element—and this is transmitted only from heart to heart, beyond all tradition and instruction. The purpose of 'instruction' is always merely to point the way to something all of us already have without knowing it. And so there is no 'mystery' that a master can 'pass on' to his student. To instruct is easy. To listen is easy. But it is hard to become aware of what one

122

has within oneself, to track it down and take possession of it properly. This is what we call looking into our own true nature [*ken-sei, ken-sho*]. When we do this, we experience satori, the great awakening from the dream of error and illusion. To wake, to look into one's nature, to perceive the truth of oneself—all of these are the same thing.''

Zen for the West — Western Zen

In its essence, there can be no doubt that Zen, as taught in the East, is not merely Oriental, but holds the answer to one of the vital needs of people in the West as well. Only people who cannot see what Zen is really about are put off by its specifically Eastern trappings.

We must remember, however, that Easterners and Westerners do see the purpose of human life differently—and we must face up to the differences if Zen's basic insights, teachings, and exercises are to help us. The fundamental difference is between the ways in which East and West see the coming of Life to *form*.

Human beings are ruled by two conflicting instincts, the urge to escape the world and the urge to shape it. There is a permanent difference between East and West regarding the relationship between the two, and each runs the danger of seeing one side only. The danger in the East is that of simply letting go and dissolving in the Absolute, while the danger in the West is that of letting fixed forms choke the vital impulse, of seeing life only as a series of fragmented details. Both East and West can learn important lessons from the dangers that threaten them.

In both East and West, to be genuinely enlightened is to see both sides—and to see that they are indivisibly connected—whether or not one's own tradition stresses one side at the other's expense. Even when it counts as the more important of the two, "seeing the whole" makes sense only as a prelude to "seeing the parts," and seeing the parts makes sense only when it comes of repeatedly seeing the whole. Contraction and expansion *together* make up the natural rhythm of breathing and growth. And yet there is a difference of emphasis between East and West: the East emphasizes union with the Absolute and ultimate extinction of the ego (and even the individual soul) in Being, while the West emphasizes the coming of the Absolute to form in the here-and-now. For us Westerners, this question of form is central, and our nature and traditions are such that giving the Absolute a form is our special responsibility.

The purpose of trying to do anything well in Zen is to achieve union with the Absolute. Even when the immediate aim in performing an exercise is to perfect a skill, that exercise is really concerned with what is going on inside as a person sees where his ways of acting and thinking are wrong, discards his bad habits, and moves from tentative contact to a genuine, deepening awareness of Being in his true nature. The only value of what he does or produces "along the way" lies in the degree to which it reflects his contact with Being. In the West, however, we are the heirs of the Platonic tradition; we think that form has inherent meaning and value, and try to perfect it for its own sake. We feel a duty not only to human development, but to formal perfection as well. Life's meaning, as promised by our share in Being, is not simply redemption; it is also the "work" that bears witness to Being.

This is true of everything people make, and even truer of people themselves. We see human perfection in the human *person,* expressing Life in a valid form (in Christian terms, the Word becoming flesh).

124

This belief that all creatures—and human beings too—fulfill themselves in a physical, specific, and perfected form lies at the heart of the Western intellectual tradition. An essential part of that tradition is the conviction that Being must take on form in persons—an assumption that the East, with another outlook and tradition, does not share. Indeed, it is significant that the Japanese had no words for *personality* or *work* (in the sense of a specific thing made by a specific person) until very recently.

The three essential facets of Being—fullness, order, and unity—are revealed as clearly to people in the East as they are to us. In Eastern deities, as in our own, they are reflected in the attributes of power, wisdom, and love. In Buddhism itself, they appear as the threefold treasure: Buddha, the doctrine, and the community of disciples.

Of course, in both East and West, the threefold unity of Being is also reflected in the view that people naturally take of one another. Like the Westerner, the Easterner is drawn to, loves, and respects the person who expresses the fullness and unity of Being in his energy and capacity for loving, but who also has firm outlines that neither energy nor love can blur. Eastern art, like that of the West, has an unmistakable feeling for form, perfect form to which nothing can be added, and from which nothing can be taken away. But form has a different significance in the East.

When we in the West take aesthetic pleasure in an artifact—a picture or statue, for instance—our pleasure comes from what we see. But the Easterner looks beyond what he sees to the underlying reality, from which all forms come and to which they return, but which is itself beyond both form and formlessness. For him, a flower in full bloom is only one of the countless ways in which the Absolute manifests itself—a specific reflection of it. For us, the form in which Being reveals itself is itself the point, and formal perfection completes and consummates a process. This is the process of becoming, and we see its ultimate goal not as release from a multiplicity of forms into the One, but as revelation of the One in form (absolute in contingent form). At the second stage of consciousness, the impulse from Being that makes us seek perfection becomes trapped and distorted in fixed forms, and the primal experience is rationalized, rigidified, cut off from Being, and ultimately stifled—but this is only an aberrant form of what is really meant. The East calls this condition "the Western sickness of form," and we are now becoming aware of it ourselves, and starting to rebel against the merely formal and fixed. Zen and Zen exercise can help us to make this rebellion fruitful. This is why artists and psychologists are turning to Zen, and why people who have lost their beliefs are increasingly using zazen-type meditation to empty themselves and prepare for the primal experience of Being. This experience underlies all live religious feeling, but once-for-all interpretation of it leads to pseudo-belief and lip service, and turns practice into dead formalism.

Once, only intellectuals and artists saw the truth about form. Now a whole generation is dimly starting to realize that forms—the forms we make and the forms we are—are alive only when Being shines through them. The East can teach us a lot about making this happen. Zen meditation sets out to remake us, turning us into mediums for Being, and its insistence on correct posture means that the message is, as it were, written into our bodies as well. This emphasis on "person" as "form" and "form" as "person" introduces a new element, making it necessary to take Zen practice further and bring it closer to Western and traditional Christian conceptions of both person and form. What is needed here is a Western Zen.

The threefold unity of Being is active in every living creature, and every living creature bears the mark of its fullness, essential form, and unity, sustaining us, shaping us, and bringing us to wholeness within the Whole. But its essential form (logos, the word) is clearer to us in the West, and this is why giving it external form—in what we do, make, or are—is our special task. For us, an artifact is perfect when the "idea" behind it is fully expressed in its form—and for us the "person" is the idea behind the human form.

The underlying law, "idea," or life principle of our true nature comes to us as an image in our consciousness, and hovers before us as a form that it is our task to realize. Basically, however, Being within us is not so much an innate image as an innate way—the inner way along which the Absolute takes form as we follow it step by step. When we set out consciously upon this way, we experience satori, and our eyes are opened to the signatures and signs that the Absolute uses to reveal its laws, order, and essence, and to manifest itself in individual human beings.

One of the signs that tells a master that his student has awakened and is an entirely new person comes when that student is no longer afraid to be himself. Because he has tasted Being and is now free to become uniquely and utterly himself, he can behave naturally even in front of the master. But here the emphases differ between East and West: the Oriental master sees individuation only as a sign that contact with Being has freed his student of the ego, while we feel that the change that has made him entirely himself was what the experience was really about. For us, the purpose of awakening is to bring out a human being's individuality and to make him fully a person for the first time; we believe he is not a person simply because Being is in him, but because it manifests itself in his particular shape. For us, as for the Oriental, a human being is perfect when Being shines through him and is radiantly reflected in whatever he experiences, is, and does, but we take this perfection above all as meaning that Being has come to valid form in him, is personified in him, and is perfecting others through him.

Even Eastern Zen knows that Being can be experienced only in the form it assumes in the individual's true nature, and that to experience individuality properly is to experience Being as well. If we assume that Zen rejects form, we are on the wrong track, for Zen sees Being not as transcending forms, but as transcending antitheses, i.e., as transcending form and non-form and therefore present in every form as well.

And so there is also room in Zen for form—and for the human person seen as form. This is why a Western Christian will get a gently knowing smile if he tells a Zen master that God is a person and not the impersonal All-One. Of course, the more he insists on the personal element, the more he lays himself open to the suspicion of clinging to that "God" of whom Meister Eckhart said, "When the ego passes out of being, God also passes out of being." Zen denies only one conception of God—the conception that corresponds to the defining ego. I once asked the abbot of the Zen monastery at Sendai, Master Miura, who had read my book on Meister Eckhart, what he thought of the links between Eckhart and Zen. At first he looked at me and said nothing. Then he shot his right hand out like a sword and looked for a moment at the tiny gap between thumb and index before saying: "It's like that. There's barely the thickness of a leaf between them. Better not to touch it!" What did he mean by "the thickness of a leaf"—and why did he say not to touch it? What he was really saying was this: "How can we be sure that Eckhart's Godhead does not include the great Unity, lying beyond person and non-person, of which we speak? And how can you really be sure that the Absolute does not reveal itself to us, too, in a personal form—while we avoid giving it a name for fear that this will merely tie it down in a concept of God rooted in the ego's fears and hopes?" And yet—there is a difference! Even when he has experienced Being as something that cannot be grasped or defined, perhaps the Christian—and not only the Western Christian—*must* still venerate the mystery as "supreme form" and give it the holy name without hesitating. The East, however, shies away from doing this, and surrounds the Absolute with silence.

The West has an instinctive respect for form itself, and thus for the energy contained in form as well, But we, too, are expected to transform ourselves and liberate within ourselves the energies that create form as we advance on our way—and the teachings and practice of Zen can play an important part here. In fact, Zen wisdom—and Zen practice—can be of the greatest help in releasing human creative energies. There is surely nothing more inimical to creativity than the defining ego and the images and concepts in which it moves or fails to move, and which Zen sets out to eradicate. And surely nothing releases a person's creativity more effectively than breaking away from the concepts that imprison him, plunging into the void, and letting the Absolute take over.

People often ask: What is the use of telling us about ways and methods that seem to depend on masters—since we have no masters? The point to remember here is that some of the things a master in the East has to do to prepare his students for satori are already done when a Westerner starts on the quest. Acceptance of the ego, self-assertion, self-reliance, and the disasters repeatedly brought on him by his own conceptual, technical, and organizational skills—these are the things that prepare the average Westerner for something else and eventually bring him to the crossing point without his being aware of it. When we really come to that point and hear—even once, but unmistakably—the voice from "beyond," then we can also hear the master in ourselves, the voice that speaks to us in all of life's crises, telling us to change course and set out upon the way. Today we can already sense the endless vistas that open up within us when the structures in which we have immured ourselves collapse. And this is a sure sign that we are almost ready to start looking for the way to freedom. The moment we become aware of ourselves as the prisoners of fixed concepts and systems, we are ready for this way, where we see our own suffering for what it is, treat our innermost experience as insight, accept the discipline of everyday life as our practice, and at last become willing to take help where we can find it. Help and helpers are nearer today than we imagine—if we will only let them help us.

The vital thing is to realize that Being—as fullness, logos, and all-embracing unity—is entering the inner heart of humanity, and that humanity itself has matured and is ready to receive it. There are millions, not merely thousands, of people who have looked death and ultimate terror in the face, and experienced in this last extremity something that death cannot touch. There are millions of people who have been brought close to madness by despair at their own inability to understand, and who have suddenly sensed something that mere understanding cannot grasp. There are millions who know what it is to be totally alone, and who have found comfort and shelter in the all-embracing One. This is how Being comes to our rescue in life's darkest moments. Everything depends on taking it seriously and seeing it for what it is: inner strength that the everyday world cannot touch, fundamental meaning beyond all understanding, and love whose power is limitless.

To experience Being's saving power is one thing, but there are millions who have also sensed within themselves the ability and duty to shape their lives in a manner consonant with it—feeling for the first time the impetus and promise that drive people to follow Life's law, which is written into the world and which the world must obey. Rounded personality, formal perfection, system and order—these are always the aims of people who cannot see further than the natural ego. But as ultimate aims, they belong to the era that is drawing to a close. They are being replaced by other aims in which the essential core of what the world-ego is and does fulfills its real purpose by becoming a window for Being.

Each of us has focused thus far on being a "personality"—self-reliant, productive, and consciously dedicating our energies and virtues to objective ideals and objective social values. But the time has come to move on and concentrate on becoming a real person, permanently open and faithful to the way, taking on form and accepting it in others only when it allows Being to show through, when it leaves room for further change.

A new generation is growing up today, a generation that has experienced Being for itself, has maintained contact with it, obeys its laws, is wary of its own weaknesses, rejects hypocrisy, and is dedicated to the service of a new world. As the old supremacies lose their power and the old taboos their magic, the old illusory ideals are being rejected and the sober truth of Being is coming into view.

The darker the clouds on our horizon, the readier we are to welcome the light that scatters them utterly. Do we look to the clouds or the light? That is the everlasting, all-dividing question, the fateful question that faces us today. We shall determine who wins out: the old generation that has lost touch with Being, cannot change its ways, and is hurtling to destruction; or the new generation that has developed and matured to become a vessel and medium for Being, and is advancing steadily toward new life—and taking the world with it.

Men Made Easy

Avambre Press

Published by Avambre Press
 PMB 144
9663 Santa Monica Blvd.
Beverly Hills, CA 90210

Publisher's Cataloging-in-Publication Data
Oh, Kara
  Men made easy : how to get what you
  want from your man
  / Kara Oh – Beverly Hills, CA :
  Avambre Press, 1999.

        p.   cm.
  ISBN 0-9667875-9-5
     1. Man-woman relationships. 2. Interpersonal
  relations. 3. Intimacy (Psychology).
     4. Women—Psychology I. Title.

HQ801 .044 1999   98-96649
158/ .2—dc21   CIP

With love and admiration,
I dedicate this book to my mother,
Eve Deacon

Help Kara Write Her Next Book

Tell us how the Twelve Simple Secrets are working in your life. Your stories will become a new book titled:

TWELVE SIMPLE SECRETS ABOUT MEN
Women Share How Men Made Easy *Has Changed Their Lives*

Talk to us. Tell us how men are being different with you, what new things they're doing to make you happy, and how you're becoming a happier and more fulfilled woman. You don't have to be a writer, just give us the details and we'll edit it for the book. We want women to be inspired and learn how they can successfully improve their lives. (Include your address so we can get approval to use your story.)

Send your stories to:

MEN MADE EASY
PMB 150
3600 S. Harbor Blvd.
Mandalay Beach, CA 93035
or Email: KaraOh@KaraOh.com

Visit our web site (address below) and talk to other women, find out where Kara will be appearing, read articles about love, sex, and romance, enjoy our joke pages, add your name to our mailing list, and download four free communication games.

www.MenMadeEasy.com

Watch for Kara Oh's next book,
MAXIMIZE YOUR MAN
Turn a Frog Into a Prince and He'll Love You Forever

Contents

Welcome—Page 1

Chapter One—Page 7
How you can make your dreams come true.

Chapter Two—Page 17
Why *you* have the power in your relationship.

Chapter Three—Page 35
Why a defensive man cannot love.

Chapter Four—Page 47
Why men crave intimacy more than women do.

Chapter Five—Page 63
How most men express intimacy.

Chapter Six—Page 77
Why monogamy is so difficult for men.

Chapter Seven—Page 93
Why men need to feel successful.

Chapter Eight—Page 109
Why men are driven to make women happy.

Chapter Nine—Page 125
Why men are willing to face rejection.

Chapter Ten—Page 135
Why men are so cautious about commitment.

Chapter Eleven—Page 147
Why men need concise communication.

Chapter Twelve—Page 159
Feminine Grace and Intuition:
Without them the Twelve Simple Secrets won't work.

How to Make Her Happy—Page 173
A Quick Guide For Guys

Acknowledgments

The birthing of this book has been filled with love and encouragement from many people. My mother and great friend, Eve Deacon, seems the most appropriate to mention first. Her support is boundless. I will be forever grateful.

I thank my friend, Warren Farrell, Ph.D., for writing his wonderful book, *The Myth of Male Power*. It opened my eyes.

I thank Duane Unkefer, my editor and friend for his encouragement and enthusiasm for what I have so desperately wanted to share with the world. He is a major reason why I continued.

I thank Henry Baggish, my first cultural anthropology teacher, who transformed my passion for travel to wild and exotic places into a need to discover where we came from and why we are the way we are.

I thank Cork Millner for telling me on my first day of his writing class, "You are now a writer."

I thank Dale Laudermilk, my dear, sweet, understanding friend. His belief in me was often greater than my own. My gratitude cannot be measured.

I thank Martha Whitt for her final edits and words of enthusiastic support.

To all those at the Jenkins Group who moved the book along, thank you. Susan Howard, Theresa Nelson, Eric Norton, and of course, Jerrold Jenkins. I thank Barbara Hodge for the cover design. She—with her creativity and intuition—was a welcome gift that arrived late in the process. I am grateful.

I thank John Lindberg, who believed in my project enough to want to be my distributor.

I thank my special friends who believed in me...some even when I didn't: Evelyn Jaffe, Linda Adams, Caroline Fergusen, Carol Fell, Sally Hamilton, Jane Haberman, Gerd Jordano, Jill Manning, Helena Wooden, Kathleen Fors, Marie Ann Strait, Kira Slade, Louise Gerber, Kathleen Carrigan, Kathleen Schienfeld, Marti Glenn, and Wendy McClure.

I thank all the people who have taken my seminars over the years. With each participant I learned a little more and loved a little deeper.

I thank all the men who so openly shared what was in their hearts and souls. They often said they were telling me things they'd never told anyone before. For that, I am honored. Without them, this book would not be possible.

I thank my daughter Amber, my son Brent, and my ex-husband Harvey Bottelsen for their continued love and support.

Finally, I thank my soulmate, my partner, and husband, Carl-Wilhelm Illemann, whom I met just as I was finishing this book. I never knew true love until he entered my life. He is beyond all my girlhood and womanhood dreams come true. The Secrets in this book do work, because when I asked him what I needed to do to keep him loving me so deeply, he said, "Just keep doing what you've been doing."

Men Made Easy

How to
Get
What
You Want
From
Your
*M*an

KARA OH

Avambre
Press

Welcome
Fairy tales do come true.

Within the pages of this book are Twelve Simple Secrets that I developed after interviewing hundreds of men. These Secrets will allow you to peek into the heretofore well-guarded private recesses of a man's heart and soul.

As if by magic, the Secrets will cause your man to treat you more and more like a queen. He won't be able to help himself. He'll respond as if in a trance. He'll begin to change in ways you had hoped he would in the beginning of your relationship, ways in which you probably gave up on long ago.

Twelve Simple Secrets
that will change your life.

Do you still believe in romantic love? Do you long to have it be a part of your relationship? Are you willing to admit that you want the little-girl dreams of a handsome prince carrying you off to his castle to live happily ever after? You're not alone. Most women do.

Some people say the fairy tales created the dreams. I believe the fairy tales were written because the dreams were a natural outcome of many women's deep heart longings to be cherished and adored; to be protected and cared for; to be thought of as beautiful in the eyes of a man who would do anything, even slay dragons, for her love. But somewhere along the way, the minutia of daily life filled the void and you almost forgot about the dream...almost. Instead, you settled: settled for comfortable, settled for occasional, settled for "It could be worse." Once you know all Twelve Secrets, you'll no longer be settling because you'll watch your relationship change, right before your eyes...effortlessly...and discover that your fantasies are beginning to come true.

Expectations only disappoint us.

The expectations that many women carry to the altar are pretty high. Most men fall short—often quite short—of those expectations. But the Secrets revealed in the pages of this book can make most any man become more like that mythical Prince Charming. He'll become more attentive, more romantic, more loving, more caring, and a lot of everything else you dared not hope for.

A man doesn't usually pay much attention to his relationship. Either it works or it doesn't. A woman is more attuned to the subtle nuances that give her what she craves within her relationship. As you read this book, you'll feel yourself shifting from within, and you'll find yourself interacting with your husband or boyfriend in brand-new ways. As you shift, he will. Like the Pied Piper, you lead and he follows. As you learn the Secrets, and take them to heart, you'll see how truly simple it is to completely transform your relationship.

• • •

For several years, I facilitated women's self-discovery workshops. I heard the heartache and disappointment that surrounded their relationships. I saw the destruction that divorce and crushed dreams could cause. I watched women cry, held them in my arms, and wiped their tears.

I could empathize because I grew up wanting the same dreams. I had a good marriage for almost thirty years, but there wasn't any passion or romance. I used to cry myself to sleep, silently huddled on my side of the bed. He was a good man, I told myself, but a lot was missing for me. After eighteen years of marriage, both my husband and I began a path of self-discovery; then, ten years later, we realized we had become different people, wanting different things. After a difficult year-and-a-half struggle, we divorced.

We're both happier now and still good friends. I've since discovered what it's like to be with a romantic, passionate man who makes me feel beautiful and womanly, a generous man who cherishes and adores me, who wants to take care of me and make me happy, while respecting my strength and independence, and I will never again settle for less. That's what fulfills my deepest heart's desire. That's what makes me feel most fully and completely a woman.

• • •

People ask me how I came to know these Secrets about men. Very simply, I made men a focus of study. I'm very intuitive and, because of the self-discovery workshops I facilitated over several years, I developed the skill of understanding people. It served me when it came time to understand men.

Throughout this book I make some pretty bold and broad generalizations about men, and sometimes about women. Obviously, there will be exceptions to each and every claim I make. After all, we are all individuals. But almost without exception, men have agreed wholeheartedly with each of the Secrets, and they're grateful that I'm sharing this information with women. Believe it or not, just about every man I spoke to agreed with the following comment made by a window salesman from Houston, "There's nothing that comes anywhere near what it feels like to love and be loved by a woman. My wife makes everything else worthwhile."

We can learn from ancient cultures.

Because cultural anthropology is my educational background, when I ponder why we do the things we do, I come from a larger perspective. I use logic and intuition in concert with what I have learned about psychology, culture, biology, evolution, as well as anthropology. Could my conclusions be wrong? Of course. Are they useful? Absolutely! If you believe as I do that love and trust grow out of greater understanding, then you'll agree that every shred of wisdom adds depth to your relationship and your ability to create everlasting love. The Secrets revealed in this book will open your eyes so much that you'll feel as if you've been blind.

I've been blessed to be able to travel all over the world. I've been particularly interested in visiting tribal cultures in places like Papua New Guinea, Indonesia, and Africa. I've seen most of the tribal behavior that I discuss in this book, much of which is driven by, and evolved because of, survival. Comparing what I've observed

firsthand to the ancient cultures I learned about in my studies of cultural anthropology, it's obvious that not much has changed. I used what I know of cultures today and made conclusions about how life for ancient men and women might have been, then compared it to our modern ways of interacting and behaving.

Understanding creates more harmony.

You'll have amazing leverage once you can look beneath your man's outer shell, the one that has all the answers, never gets emotional, and doesn't quite understand why you want romance. Not only does this book give you some reasons for his sometimes frustrating behavior, it also points out why you and he are so very different. Once you understand that much of what he does and how he reacts is a variety of automatic responses—such as needing to succeed, to solve problems, and how easily he's aroused—you'll be better equipped to get what you want from him and your relationship.

Culture—that which we learn and pass on—is as powerful in determining our behavior as physical evolution, and in many ways, even more so. Personal pride, integrity, competition, and of course the all-powerful social shame can do wonders to keep us in line. Culture is strong, but it can be overridden...when you know what to do.

We want more from our relationships.

Today, thankfully for most of us, survival is not in the forefront of our concerns. Quality of life is what we care about. We want more from our experiences and from our relationships with others. The Twelve Simple Secrets will

give you more of what you want because the seemingly Grand Canyon–sized chasm that separates men from women can actually be bridged.

On the next page you will begin a playful adventure that will carry you to new places of the heart. A glorious new life filled with the magic of ever-deepening love awaits you. Come, follow me to a cottage by an enchanted forest, filled with dreams-coming-true and happily-ever-afters.

Chapter One
How you can make your dreams come true.

Once upon a time there lived three fair maidens who had all seen a wee bit of life, which probably means we shouldn't be calling them maidens, but hey, this is a fairy tale. These particular women lived in a picture-perfect village on the edge of an enchanted forest as, of course, all forests are.

Many years ago, no one quite knows how it started, a strange malady befell the women of this village. It caused them to let go of their dreams, to be less than they thought they would be, and to make excuses for why their relationships were not as they'd hoped. Everyone accepted it as inevitable. The villagers called it The Settling and it wouldn't go away.

These three women had been friends since childhood. Carol, with long auburn tresses, was the oldest and most experienced at the wise age of forty-one. With big brown eyes, high cheekbones, and a smile that never stopped, she was instantly likable. The others looked up to her because she had been married twelve years and had two small

children. Carol had owned a successful dress shop but was now enjoying being a full-time mom. Her marriage had fallen short of her girlhood expectations, but she figured it could easily be worse. Although her marriage had begun with lots of love, over the years her husband had become distant and unexpressive. She missed the way it was. Carol was aching inside but didn't know how to change things. She numbed herself by staying busy with her children and her friends.

Jenny, at thirty-nine, was the next oldest. She had fiery red hair and freckles to match. She was a strong, outspoken woman and worked as the assistant manager at the only bank in the village. She'd been divorced six years ago and only recently gotten married to the man she had been living with. She had wanted to start a family, so she convinced her boyfriend to get married. Now she was worried because they seemed to argue all the time. She wanted him to be more attentive and romantic, but whenever she mentioned the subject, he just walked away. Their resentments were growing.

Finally, there was Beth, who, at the tender age of thirty-five, was the baby of the group. She was the perky type, with a peaches-and-cream complexion and long golden curls. She had always struggled with her weight, and after her most recent breakup, she'd gained even more. She managed the village bookstore. Her third serious relationship had recently broken up and she was beginning to wonder if she was ever going to find the right man. She worried that maybe she was being too fussy.

Carol, Jenny, and Beth made a point to get together every Thursday for lunch. They'd seen each other through the ups and downs of life: marriage, childbirth, boyfriends, breakups, and divorce. You name it, at least one of them had gone through it. Probably not so different than the life you share with *your* girlfriends.

One day, during one of their weekly get-togethers, they began to complain—again—about their husbands and men in general. They dissected every nuance of their relationships, their disappointments about love and romance, the bits and pieces they felt they understood about men, and what had gone wrong along the way. Their conclusion? Men were lame, insensitive, and boorish, and whatever was going on in their thick heads was beyond anything *they* could figure out. As with everything else that wasn't quite right, they blamed it on The Settling. But no one ever had a solution.

Carol, even though long married, spoke with frustration. "I feel like I'm always groping around in the dark. Thomas seems so close-mouthed and if I try to talk to him about it, he clams up even more. It's just not worth the headache to care."

Jenny agreed. "Yeah, I try to get Brad to be more romantic, to talk to me more, but it's like I'm talking to a brick wall. It's easier to just let it go."

Beth frowned. "What I don't understand is how, after only a few months with a new man, he quits doing all the wonderful things he did in the beginning of the relationship. When I find Mister Right, I want him to adore me forever." Her eyes got misty.

Their waitress, Ginger, an irritatingly gleeful type, had been picking up bits and pieces of their conversation and, having waited on them several times in the past, was familiar with the women and knew this was usual conversation during their lunches. Ginger decided to be bold and say something.

"I'm sorry to butt in, but I can't help notice that you

talk about men a lot, and it doesn't seem you're that happy with them. Do you mind if I make a suggestion?"

The women, although instantly defensive, agreed to listen to her.

"Obviously you like men or at least want them in your lives, but from what I can tell, you're stuck and don't know what to do to make things better."

As you can imagine, our friends stared at this snippy little waitress with a look of *What could you possibly know?* But, curiosity being the powerful force that it is, Jenny spoke up. "What on earth are you talking about?"

"I've been visiting a woman who lives in that cottage on the edge of the forest; you know the one. She's teaching me how to transform my relationships with men into golden opportunities of happiness," Ginger gushed.

"This woman is teaching me how to turn what I thought were mediocre men into absolute princes. I'm having the time of my life, and so are the men. The Settling is gone from my life and I'm more optimistic than I've ever been."

Beth, with a youthful streak of optimism, spoke next. "Ginger, if what you're saying is true, I want to know about this woman. I still have my dreams and I don't want The Settling to take over my life."

Ginger, recognizing a sister rebel, continued. "This woman will teach you her Twelve Simple Secrets about men. The Secrets could have helped me avoid a lot of heartache and helped me turn at least two of my past relationships into 'happily ever after.' It breaks my heart to think about it. But things are already looking up and I'm excited about my future.

"Diedra, that's her name, welcomes anyone who's sincerely interested in turning ordinary relationships into

exceptional, lifelong love affairs. After hearing what she has to say, you'll know things about men that even men don't know, and certainly more than almost every other woman on the planet. Then you'll be able to cast a magic spell over just about any man. It's powerful stuff and works almost instantly. It's fun to fool around with because men are simply thrilled with what you're doing even though they don't have a clue that it's going on. They just know that all of a sudden you've become irresistible, they can't keep their minds off of you, and they're dying to make you happy.

"Once you know her Twelve Simple Secrets, she guarantees your relationships will become truly magical. You'll experience lots more love, romance, and even steamy passion, if you want it. And Beth, since you're single like me, there will be a terrific man in your life in no time. All this because of the Secrets and because you're going to learn what it *really means to be a woman*. I know because that's what's been happening to me."

Ginger, like a conspiratorial missionary, looked into the hopeful eyes of the women. "You've got to trust me and at least meet her."

Carol was the most wary. "This just sounds impossible."

"Don't you want your relationships to be better?" Ginger pleaded. "Don't you want to know what life could be like without The Settling?"

"Men have always been the same," Carol argued. "I can't believe things could change just like that. As for The Settling, we've lived with it all our lives."

"That's just it." Ginger was excited. "It hasn't been all your lives. Think back. Remember when you were young girls? You dreamed you would some day meet a

wonderful man who would want to make you happy and cherish you forever. You dreamed you would be the fair maiden, blissful in your life with your prince."

Ginger could see a deep stirring within the women. "Can you remember how it was? The Settling hadn't taken hold yet because you still had your dreams. And don't you remember the hopes and dreams you had when you got married? You don't have to accept The Settling, and men really can become princes."

"I still have those dreams," Beth said, "but with each year and every man that passes by, I become more disheartened. I'm beginning to think that all men are inconsiderate, selfish, and insensitive." Beth twisted her napkin.

Jenny's voice was a whisper. "I had those dreams when I moved in with Brad. But day-to-day life took their place. I'm beginning to not care anymore. Even the fighting has become routine. But my dreams of romance, enduring love," she looked up hopefully, "of having a soulmate, have just drifted away. It crept up so gradually that I never noticed. What happened? We were so in love in the beginning."

Carol had to reach farther back, but she agreed. "My life with my husband and children is so busy with work and family that all those dreams are just a flicker of memory. I think about them once in a while and I feel silly. You know, just schoolgirl stuff. That's not real life. Thomas is a good man, but he's so distant. Sometimes it doesn't even feel like I'm married."

Ginger smiled. "I like you ladies. I've heard your conversations about men and I thought the same thing…until now. It doesn't have to be like that. One of the women in my group had the same kind of husband. As she learned the Secrets, she came alive as a woman, and her

husband began to notice a happy, attractive woman around the house. As she began to love herself, she felt more sensuous, sexy even. When he began to show some interest, she happily encouraged him. She says they're like newlyweds."

"Almost every man can be a prince." Ginger's voice rose with enthusiasm. "If you still love your husbands, even if it's a tiny bit, Diedra will teach you how to turn them into the princes of your dreams." Ginger leaned close. "And they'll love all that you're doing. Honest. The beauty of the Secrets is that they make men fall madly in love with you, even if you've been married for years. And if you're single, you'd better know what you want in a man because you'll have more than one to choose from."

Jenny's curiosity was growing. "What kind of things does Diedra teach?"

Ginger thought for a moment. "Well, have you ever wondered why men quit being romantic, why commitment is so difficult for men, why men don't listen when you talk, why sex is all men seem to think about, why men seem so insensitive? Or have you wondered why men won't talk about what they're feeling, why passion goes away, why good men are so hard to find, or why it's so darned difficult to understand men?" They waited, hanging on her words. "Well, the Twelve Secrets will answer those questions. You'll understand men so well it'll seem like you're looking directly into their hearts and souls. You'll actually understand them better than they understand themselves. When you understand men that well, you'll know exactly how to turn your relationships into your fantasies come true. They'll begin to change in ways you've always wanted and start treating you like a queen."

"I don't know," Jenny said. "It sounds like we're supposed to become docile, mindless, adoring wives."

Ginger laughed. "Hardly. It's the complete opposite. It's about you becoming totally awesome. For the Secrets to be most effective, you have to admit to being, and want to become, the terrific women that you were meant to be. The more empowered, self-confident, and happy you are, the better the Secrets will work. Come on, there's nothing to be afraid of."

The three friends looked at each other with a *What do you think?* twinkle in their eyes. Could men really change that much? They *were* curious, and very tired of The Settling.

They asked a few more questions; then Ginger made a comment that convinced them. She said, "It can't hurt to try it, and if you don't do something different, why on earth would you expect anything to change? If all you do is complain and accept The Settling as inevitable, your lives will continue to be the same."

Beth pleaded with her friends. "The 'same' is what we've been getting for a long time, and, admit it, we're all tired of it. Doesn't magic and dreams coming true sound a whole lot better?"

Then Carol said, "Okay Ginger, we'll do it. Sign us up." Jenny and Beth smiled with the excitement of a new adventure.

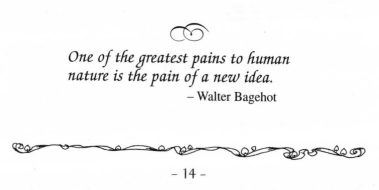

One of the greatest pains to human nature is the pain of a new idea.
– Walter Bagehot

When asked what she hoped to gain from one of my MEN MADE EASY seminars, one playful attendant said, "I'd love to have a fairy godmother who would wave her magic wand and make my life perfect." Maybe you've wished you could get exactly what you wanted by wiggling your nose like Samantha in the old *Bewitched* TV series. Magic *can* happen, but it's up to you to create it. For years, we women have wished our relationships with men would be different, but we never knew what to do. As you've learned, wishing isn't enough. With the Twelve Simple Secrets, you'll finally know what to do. Your relationship will begin to take on a new life, sparkling with the love that you enjoyed when you first met.

**The secret to change is
to do something different.**

With this book, you hold in your hands the opportunity to completely transform your relationship. You will become your own fairy godmother and finally make your schoolgirl dreams come true. If you want to be happy from within, and have your relationship become more loving, romantic, and even passion-filled, the Twelve Simple Secrets are what you've been waiting for.

• • •

3 things you can do:
  At the end of each chapter you'll find suggestions for things you can do to transform your relationship and take charge of your level of happiness. The more you do, the more you'll learn about yourself, and the more effective the Twelve Simple Secrets will be.

✓ To begin the process, get a three-ring binder and some lined paper to keep your notes in.

✓ Then write down five things you want from your relationship that you don't have now or don't have to the degree that you would like.

✓ Now, write down just three things you'd like to improve with your husband or boyfriend during the time you read this book. If you're not involved with anyone, do this with men in general. You can do it in the form of journaling or lists, whichever is most comfortable for you. Just play with this and be curious. You may learn something new and interesting about yourself.

Chapter Two
Why you have the power in your relationship.

Secret #1
The key to what you want is Feminine Grace.

The time for their first appointment had arrived and Carol, Jenny, and Beth found themselves standing in front of a storybook cottage that sat nestled just inside the enchanted forest. With excitement built over a week of anticipation, they looked at each other, then stepped onto the path that led through a flower-strewn garden. Carol, the self-appointed leader of the group, knocked on the door of the cottage. They were guided by a crookedy old woman to a comfy room at the back of the house. With a mischievous smile, the old woman turned and left them alone. Watching her depart, our fair maidens wondered if they'd made the right decision.

Huddled on the sofa, they waited. Then, as if from nowhere, a woman was standing by the fireplace in front of them. She seemed to glow with joy and her eyes sparkled. She walked toward them, both arms outstretched.

"Welcome to my home. I'm Diedra O'Connor." Her

voice was warm and soothing.

After introductions were made, Diedra sat in the big overstuffed chair in front of them and began to speak. "I'm glad you're here. You're going to learn things about men that will answer just about every question you've ever had. You'll discover The Settling cannot hold a joyful woman down and learn how a happily empowered woman can turn almost any man into a prince.

"Throughout our weeks together, be on the lookout for magic. You may feel it within you, you may see it in someone else, or you may find it happening after you leave this place. One of the ways you'll know you've experienced magic is when hearts open effortlessly and love, harmony, and friendship flow. You'll begin to see it everywhere because you'll be the cause of it. You'll have many magical moments over the next weeks and months and serendipity will appear in the most wonderful ways. As you pay attention and your awareness grows, you'll find magic swirling all around you."

Diedra's loving tone relaxed the women and they eased into the embrace of the down cushions.

"My Twelve Simple Secrets about men will help you have charmed relationships, filled with love and romance; relationships that will endure through time. I realize two of you are married, but, Beth, the Secrets will allow you to attract a wonderful man into your life. It'll be fun to hear what happens to you as we travel through the lessons.

"Everything I'm going to share with you is simple and nonthreatening. Any man will be thrilled with what you're learning so you can feel safe to repeat anything I say.

"So tell me, which of you would like to have magical relationships?"

The women hesitated, as if it might be a trick question,

but, eventually, each one raised a hand.

"Good. Part of getting something is daring to want it. The Settling has blinded you to any other way. Each of you can have dream-come-true relationships with the men you love. I'm here to teach you the Secrets that will make that happen. By the end of our time together, your men will be so in love with you that you'll be dizzy with the thrill of it. Some women know these Secrets naturally, but, somehow, over time, the women of this village have forgotten what they need to know to have exciting relationships that continue to grow in love.

"I learned these Secrets from the Wise Woman of the North Forest many years ago. She made me promise to pass them on after I found my Perfect Partner. The Twelve Simple Secrets were gleaned from men, but it took the Wise Woman to realize what she was hearing. Men don't understand themselves that well because they don't usually think about what's going on inside of them. We women are more interested in the mysteries of why people are the way they are. Once you've received all Twelve Secrets, you'll know men better than they know themselves. Can you imagine the leverage you'll have with them?" They all smiled enthusiastically.

"We're here to talk about men but, first, we've got to talk about you. Do you like being women?"

It seemed a silly question to them, but they agreed that they did.

"What do you like about being women?" Diedra pulled an easel with a chalkboard next to her chair.

"Speak up and I'll write it on this board." The women hesitated. "Come on, what do you absolutely love about being women?"

They began to comment as Diedra wrote their responses

on the board.

"Expressing emotions."

"Wearing beautiful clothes."

"Being creative."

"Being loved by a man."

"How it feels to have a man's arms around me."

"Being pregnant...and being a mother."

"Ball gowns."

"Multiple orgasms."

"Makeup."

"Women friends."

"Shoes."

The list grew as the women gained enthusiasm.

Diedra smiled and wrote all their responses on the board. "These are great answers and I'd like to add one more: choices. I think one of the most wonderful things about being women is how many *choices* we have. We can be soft and feminine; we can be strong and assertive; we can be mothers, workers, artists; we can feel deeply and weep without anyone questioning us. We can even be giggly and silly."

Beth said, "I love it when I can let loose and cry. It's so cleansing."

Diedra nodded. "But Beth, what would you do if a *man* began to cry in front of you?"

Beth stammered, "I don't know. I've never had it happen."

"If you were at a gathering of people and you saw a woman crying with a couple of people holding her, you'd feel some heart tugs and curiosity, but probably not much more. If a *man* was crying and someone was holding him, you'd think something horrible had happened. Men don't have permission to be emotional. It's got to be a crisis of some kind. And generally, we're uncomfortable when a man cries, for any reason.

"Aren't we lucky that we can feel all of our emotions most any time we need to?

"Also, women can hug and touch and hold hands. Most men swat each other on the behind, sock each other in the arm, or, if they do hug, it's a quick, stiff embrace with a slap on the back, signaling it's over.

"We have a narrow idea of what's acceptable behavior for men. If they don't work, produce, and provide, they're looked down on. If they're creative, they're often thought to be unmasculine or gay. They can't show their emotions or they're thought to be weak. Isn't 'sissy' or 'coward' the worst things a little boy can be called? Men rarely go to therapy. They're supposed to know all the answers. They can't work in a field that's traditionally women's work without their masculinity being questioned. Women can work in much broader categories than men can. Men simply have fewer choices.

"On top of all our career and life choices, look at your list: We get to wear beautiful clothes, makeup, change our hairstyles, dress up in gowns, high heels, and jewels; we get to wear pretty, sexy lingerie, or slip comfortably into a pair of blue jeans and a T-shirt. We get to be moms and wives. We get to feel our emotions. It's pretty great, don't you think?"

The women nodded agreement. "Now, tell me what you *don't* like about being a woman."

"Oh, that's easy, PMS."

"Being considered the weaker sex."

"Fear of being attacked."

"Job discrimination."

"Having to wait for men to make the first move."

"Getting old."

"Being judged by my appearance."

"Feeling insecure about my body."

The list grew. "Those are all legitimate complaints, but...even with all that, who's glad to be a woman?"

They all quickly raised their hands. "Yes, it's a spectacular gift to be women. We have more choices and options than at any other time in history. But let me ask you this: Who's *ecstatic* to be a woman?" After some hesitation, the women raised limp hands. "As I expected, not much enthusiasm. It's a new idea, but, if you're going to put my Secrets about men into full gear and create beautiful relationships, get rid of The Settling, *and* become magnificent, happy, empowered women, you must learn to be out-of-this-world in love with being women."

With a self-conscious smile, Carol asked, "Can you tell us exactly what you mean? I like being a woman, but, beyond that, I've never really thought about it."

Diedra leaned forward. "When you love being a woman: First, you're totally and completely comfortable with yourself, which makes men—and everyone else—feel comfortable.

"Second, you're in touch with your creativity and love of beauty and enjoy expressing it.

"Third, you're comfortable with your sexuality and allow it to flow through you. But you don't flaunt it; you do it with grace and style. You love that part of yourself because it's an expression of your femininity. When you're comfortable with your sexuality men can tell. They have a built-in radar that picks it up from across the room.

"Fourth, you're beautiful, no matter what God gave you, because you glow from within. That kind of beauty has nothing to do with what's in fashion magazines, it comes from being happy."

Diedra's enthusiasm was growing and she spoke with a power that riveted the women to her every word.

"Finally, if you love being a woman, *you can't help but like men*." Diedra was beaming.

"You've all met this kind of woman. She's often not an outstanding beauty, but…she's comfortable with who she is, she has style, and it's obvious she likes herself. She's the woman men are hovering around at a party. And women like her too. This way of being is what I call Feminine Grace." Diedra's face glowed brighter and her voice grew stronger.

"Any time you're expressing your femininity and feeling good to be a woman, you're in a state of Feminine Grace. That's when you're the most magnetic, the most beautiful, the most joyful and loving, and the most self-confident. It's when you feel great about being you. And you relish your individuality. You can choose to be unhappy about being a woman or you can be ecstatic. Either choice will color every aspect of your life. But a woman with Feminine Grace is the most powerful kind of woman there is. Which would you prefer?"

Diedra's question hung in the air like cathedral bells just rung…then she put a card on the easel, which read:

Secret #1
The key to getting what you want
is Feminine Grace.

Then she asked, "How do you express your Feminine Grace? Each of you give us an example."

"Well, this is a simple thing, really, but when I wear a skirt I feel feminine." Jenny smiled. "I like how it feels on my legs. I hadn't thought of it before, but when I wear a skirt, even if it's to the market, I'll find myself paying more attention to my hair and makeup."

"One way I feel it is when my husband dances with me. I feel his masculinity most strongly then." Carol looked down. "It's been a long time."

"How about you, Beth?" Diedra wanted each of them to get a feeling of Feminine Grace.

"Well…my favorite is when I'm in love. I'm totally aware of being a woman, and I feel beautiful. I take better care of myself and I want to look nice, even when I'm home alone. I feel like I'm glowing. It's very yummy."

The others laughed.

"When I've asked men what they like about women they say things like: how creative we are, how we can express our emotions, how wonderful we are to look at, our curves and soft skin, how we can do so many things at once, how loving and nurturing we are, how we create beauty. When they're talking I can hear awe in their voices. They absolutely love our femininity. We express ourselves with our femininity by the way we walk, the way we talk, the way we look at them when we're impressed with something they've done or said. They're especially awed, to the point of being pretty helpless, when we do the extraordinary things, like wearing high heels and stockings, makeup, and nail polish, especially on our toenails. That doesn't mean not to wear jeans and T-shirts, but, when you do, do it with style and a sense of being a beautiful woman.

"These may seem like little things, but they're big, I mean *really big,* to men. Men are mostly visual and they notice when a woman looks nice, especially if it's for them. You have no idea how much power you have over men. You each use it to some degree, but you don't fully

appreciate how helpless men are in the presence of a woman they're attracted to. You hold the key to their physical needs for sex; their need for intimacy; their need for belonging through the creation of family; and their need for order, beauty, and comfort—all of which we'll talk about in our future meetings.

"Most modern women are self-sufficient and capable of accomplishing almost everything for themselves. Consequently, men are at a loss as to how to interact with and how to treat women today. Women have had to adapt and change with their circumstances. Men have mostly been the provider and their ability to change and adapt is not as well defined. They respect the modern woman but they're uncomfortable with a woman who doesn't need them. *Feminine Grace allows you to be the kind of woman men want to love and, at the same time, be self-sufficient, self-confident, and capable of almost anything you put your minds to.*"

Diedra turned serious. "Give me some examples of when you're the opposite, the antithesis of Feminine Grace."

"When I complain." Beth covered her face in mock embarrassment.

Carol offered, "When I'm bossy, or disrespectful of others."

Then Jenny added, "When I'm feeling insecure or self-conscious. I feel helpless when I'm that way."

"Those are good examples. My grandmother used to call it being 'ugly.' It's a great term when your behavior is unattractive. It's a strong word that gets the point across. So, if you catch yourself being 'ugly,' look for ways to be more beautiful, poised, and graceful. You'll find it a revealing process. And who wouldn't rather be beautiful than ugly?"

There was obvious agreement.

"If you want more love, affection, passion, romance, appreciation, and companionship from a man, you've got to do your part. The most effective way you can do that—which, coincidentally, will give you even more than you've been asking for—is to love being a woman and express yourself with the beauty of Feminine Grace."

One is not born, but rather becomes, a woman.
– Simone de Beauvoir

Women are powerful beings—*really* powerful. We give birth. We create home life, comfort, and beauty. We can do almost anything we put our minds to. Men will give up their fantasies of having sex with lots of beautiful women to marry us. All they want in return is for us to be women and love them as men.

Generally, it's women who press for marriage. But ironically, it's men who are happier and healthier when married. Something is amiss here. I believe women are less secure in marriage because, more often than not, they're dependent on a man for financial support. If they have children and work, they're exhausted. Women have huge expectations regarding marriage and, almost always, marriage, and the husband, fall short of those expectations. Feminine Grace includes a strong sense of personal power, without which women don't know how to get what they want from the men they love. Ironically, most men say they get a lot of pleasure out of making their partners happy. It gives them the satisfaction of a job well done. Those same men say they can't win with a woman who complains, belittles, and manipulates. That kind of behavior—which stems from insecurity or insensitivity—disappears as a woman develops self-love. Truly beautiful women love themselves and are comfortable with who they are.

We enjoy fairy tales but the flip side of them is that we've been taught since girlhood that we're not complete without a man. Men need women for love and intimacy and because they have a biological drive to procreate, provide, and protect. But being in a relationship doesn't distinguish a man's identity, not like it does a woman's. A woman who never marries has traditionally been called an "old maid." That's changing, but there's still the stigma. There's no equivalent for men. Because men generally do the choosing, women who don't get chosen can feel inadequate and less attractive, which often leads to anger and resentment. Through that anger and resentment women proclaim they don't need a man. But the anger says they do. Actually, the same thing can happen to women who get chosen, because they've frequently settled for less than they thought they were going to get.

Joseph, a successful architect told me, "I sometimes wish it was different, but I can't help that I'm attracted to the physical appearance of a woman." He, like most men, can't help it. It's in their biology so they shouldn't be blamed. It makes sense that those prehistoric men who were attracted to (and could quickly get aroused by) the physical appearance of a woman had more opportunities for sex. Consequently, they impregnated more women, sired more children, and more of their offspring survived to pass on those "quick start" genes. Those are the men we interact with today.

Women complain that men are superficial and should

be able to look beyond the physical. Well, men, being the sexual beings that they are, are rarely interested if the sexual attraction isn't there. "Why can't men see past the appearance of a woman?" one angry, overweight woman complained in a Warren Farrell seminar on men/women issues. When I hear a woman who doesn't like her own body—which clearly this woman didn't—making that complaint, what I want to ask her is, "How can you expect a man to look beyond your physical appearance, when even *you* don't like the way you look?"

Feminine Grace is feeling good about yourself, inside and out, which includes how you look. It's caring about yourself and your appearance because you like yourself and it gives you pleasure. Vanity is excessive concern for your appearance. Lack of confidence feeds vanity. Men say, over and over, that a self-confident, happy woman is much more appealing than an insecure "10" any day.

What's missing for women is the sense of personal power that comes from Feminine Grace.

With Feminine Grace:
1. You don't need a man to feel complete, but you're happy to admit if you want one.
2. You're empowered by being a woman, never using it as an excuse.
3. You're comfortable being you and like who you are.
4. You enjoy expressing your uniqueness in how you look, not following trends.
5. You're eager to learn, grow, and improve yourself.
6. You express yourself with knowledgeable confidence.
7. You know who you are and you're proud of it.

8. You like your body and how you look, and you take care of yourself.
9. You take responsibility for your life, not blaming others for your circumstances.
10. You're happy from within, not needing others to make you happy.
11. You like people and people like you.
12. You genuinely like and appreciate men.

Feminine Grace is not just being "feminine." There's a consciousness about it. It's coming into rapport with being a woman and loving it. For example, a corporate woman can attempt to compete with men and try to be equal, which is impossible—an apple and an orange, while still fruit, will never be the same—or she can be fully a woman, confident in her own expertise and knowledge, interacting with others as a woman, not an approximation of a man. That kind of woman is respected by her peers—male and female—not resented or looked down on. She dresses as a woman, not as a man, but, understanding and respecting men, she's careful not to be sexual in her attire. (Men say they can't work with a woman who dresses sexy and not think sex.) It's a matter of decorum, taste, style, and self-respect, mixed with a desire to let her beauty show through.

Some well-known modern icons of Feminine Grace are Sophia Loren, Maya Angelou, Katharine Hepburn, and Susan Sarandon. Some who continue to leave their mark even in their death are Audrey Hepburn, Princess Diana (who was just getting there), and, of course, Grace Kelly. And how about the late Florence Griffith Joyner? Even as a world-class athlete, she certainly enjoyed being a woman. Women who embody Feminine Grace are obviously comfortable with themselves; they enjoy their individuality, they like men, their sexuality flows effortlessly, what they do they do with confidence and grace, men and women like and respect them, and their beauty glows from within. Yes, these women are beautiful, but not because they're fashion queens. They're beautiful because they know who they are and they like themselves.

Who do you know who exemplifies (and who do you think is the antithesis of) Feminine Grace?

Feminine Grace is joy, accomplishment, and love that comes from within. It's time to begin to acknowledge your feminine power, a power that comes from loving being a woman. You'll then accomplish your dreams because you believe in yourself, and do so with creativity, sensuality, love, and happiness in your heart.

Women are the relationship experts.

Women evolved to be nurturers and caretakers of relationships. Obviously, prehistoric women who were best at nurturing their children had more children survive to pass on those same nurturing genes. Women who created strong ties between members of their tribe were more likely to be cared for if their mates were killed or died. The early woman had to attract and keep a mate to hunt for her and her children. Today, fortunately, survival is not in the forefront of our thoughts. We have the luxury to want more personal and emotional fulfillment.

Women expect too much from men.

In Papua New Guinea, one of the last bastions of tribal living, I observed that the men spent most of their time with other men. They talked and laughed while they carved,

worked, made tools, and, a favorite activity was to sit around while they smoked. Past and upcoming sporting events were a hot topic of conversation when they weren't practicing.

The women had much more going on. They did laundry at the river, worked in the gardens, cooked, sewed and wove, and tended to a variety of household chores—always surrounded by children, other women, and elders. I watched how they talked all day long. Everywhere I went, it was a beehive of activity.

How different women are from men. These tribal people are basically the same as the prehistoric people from whom we all evolved. It wasn't that long ago that all people lived communally. The "modern" era is a new experiment in social interaction, and, in many ways, it's not working very well.

A woman today doesn't have that constant female companionship. Now she makes lunch dates for an hour. Then she goes home or back to work still craving more talking time, more together time, more interaction, and someone to do "chores" with. At work she has to focus on the job at hand, with only an occasional stolen moment to chat. And who's at home? Her husband or boyfriend. But he isn't interested, and her disappointment in him grows, never realizing why. She complains, he gets defensive, resentment takes over, and love dies.

A man and a woman living alone in one house is a new idea. It isn't possible for one person to fulfill all of another's needs, so it's not surprising that people settle for less than they expected or leave each other in a hurtful divorce.

Men look to women as the relationship experts. Sustaining relationships, loving, nurturing—women do these things naturally; it's second nature. The relationship

is not a focus for men like it is for women. Men unconsciously assume that once they do the work of winning a woman, she'll take care of the relationship. A problem develops when women expect men to participate in the nurturing of the relationship. They don't think to and generally don't know how. They trust women to know what to do and instinctively follow their lead. Men do try, but they're certainly not natural at it.

If a woman tries to get a man involved in the relationship by complaining, badgering, manipulating, and making him feel bad and wrong, he'll be repelled. If a woman leads with Feminine Grace, enjoying being a woman and appreciating the masculine qualities of the man she loves, communicating her needs in a loving way, he can't help but become more attentive, caring, helpful, loving, and romantic. It's simple: Men are attracted to women who are beautiful in appearance and in action, and who appreciate them as men. And *when a man is attracted to a woman, he wants to make her happy.*

"You know, most of my adult life I've focused on what's bad about being a woman. Right now I feel energized, like I could do anything I put my mind to." Jenny was effervescent.

"Whoa, look out for Superwoman." Beth teased. "I wish I felt like that. I haven't felt beautiful in quite a while, but I'm inspired to get back in shape. I don't like feeling unattractive."

Carol's eyes danced. "I feel beautiful and womanly. I wonder if Thomas will notice. But how do we stay this way?"

Not waiting for Diedra, Jenny jumped in. "I have an idea. Let's each pick a woman we think represents Feminine Grace and who we most want to emulate. That way, we have a more concrete image in our minds. We can even get pictures and put them up where we'll see them every day."

"That sounds fun." Carol looked at Diedra for agreement. Diedra gestured for them to continue. "And we can remind each other of the benefits of being women."

Beth added, "And remind each other that we want to do things in ways that are beautiful and not ugly. That really did it for me. I can totally relate to when I'm being ugly, and I'm always upset with myself afterwards. Always...I just realized something. All those stereotypes about women that are so demeaning are all about ugly behavior. That inspires me even more."

Carol looked at the others. "Good point, Jenny. Let's do this as a team effort. How does that sound to you, Diedra?"

Diedra laughed. "Looks like you're on a roll. I say, 'Go for it and have fun.' I'll look forward to hearing how it goes. Next week I'll show you how to *instantly* get any man to think you're wonderful." They stood up, excited to begin their adventure.

The women waved good-bye to Diedra as they chatted together down the road back to the village and to their lives that would never be the same.

4 things you can do:
✓ As the women chose to do, find a picture of someone whom you think embodies Feminine Grace, someone you

can model. Put it where you'll see it regularly. Choose more than one woman if you like.

✓ Write down five qualities of Feminine Grace that you feel you already have.

✓ Write down three qualities of Feminine Grace that you would like to develop. Make a plan for what you must do to develop each one.

✓ Now, list three ways you express ugly behavior, and be honest. After each item, describe how that quality is impacting your relationships and your life. How does each one make you feel when you do it? When you find yourself being "ugly," stop yourself and ask how you can shift into Feminine Grace. This will take time to develop. If you forget, it's okay. With each opportunity, you'll catch yourself sooner, and eventually your ugly behavior will be replaced with Feminine Grace. As that happens, you'll notice you're getting more of what you want: from others, from yourself, and from your life.

Chapter Three
Why a defensive man cannot love.

Secret #2
Men need to feel understood
and accepted for who they are.

After their hellos, Diedra guided her new students to the sofa. "Now, let's get into the heart of this thing and talk about men. What don't you like about them? We'll make a list on the board. Come on, let loose."

"They're smelly."

"They're hairy."

"They're in charge."

"They're rude."

"They rape and molest."

"They make war."

"They think with their penises."

"They're always horny."

"They don't respect women."

"They leave."

"They cheat."

"They won't talk."

"They live for sports."

"They don't call."

"They don't help around the house."

"They can't find things."

"They don't feel their emotions."

The women continued with laughter, frustration, and anger until the board was filled.

"Okay, that's a nice long list. Now tell us what you *love* about men." Poised with her chalk ready, Diedra waited.

"How they make us feel protected."

"How hard they work."

"How great it is to make love with them."

"Their muscles."

"Their bodies."

"Kissing them."

"How they enjoy our cooking."

"How sweet they look when they're holding a child."

"How easy it is to turn them on."

"How they like to solve our problems."

"How they look at us when they're in love."

The women, with lots of *ooh* and *aahs* and *oh yeses,* enjoyed creating the new list. Then Diedra asked, "How does it feel as you focus on *this* list compared to the previous list?"

Carol smiled. "I feel softer."

"More feminine." Jenny sighed.

Beth, with tears forming, said, "Sad, because it makes me wish I had a man in my life. But I feel more open to men, more hopeful. Something I haven't felt in a while."

Carol held Beth's hand and added, "You know, when Beth mentioned feeling open, I realized I'm not open to my husband when I'm thinking he's a jerk, or worse."

"Thank you, Carol; you just made my point. If you're thinking men aren't okay the way they are, you're not available to love them, not really. The men react by building defensive walls around themselves, and guess what?—They're not available to love you *either.*

"Now, for our second Secret." Diedra put the card on the easel for them to read.

Secret #2
Men need to feel understood
and accepted for who they are.

"If a man doesn't feel understood, he gets frustrated. If he doesn't feel like a woman is even interested in learning to understand him, and continues to judge him, he gets defensive. And rightfully so. Men complain that women don't really want to hear what they have to say. That's interesting, isn't it?—Since most women complain that men don't talk to them enough.

"Of course, we want our partners to understand us too, but that will come as you use the Secrets.

"A man wants a woman who accepts him and likes him. When a woman constantly reminds a man he's not okay as he is, he becomes so guarded that he's not open to love. He shuts down. If he's married, his heart hardens and the love he felt in the beginning of his marriage dries up. The wife wonders what happened, often blaming him for being less attentive and emotionally unavailable, compounding the problem. If a man is single and a woman disapproves of him, he discontinues the relationship and runs the other way as fast as he can. Then the woman blames him for being afraid of commitment.

"Have any of you ever wanted to or tried to change a man?"

With laughter and sheepish grins, they all raised their hands. "How would it feel if your husbands tried to change *you*?" The laughter disappeared.

"Men are simple. They're either attracted to you or they're not. A woman can *become* attracted to a man by how he is with her, but it rarely happens that way with men. They're attracted to how you are and how you look. If they're not, they're not interested in starting a relationship. Carol, when Thomas decided he wanted to marry you, the woman he fell in love with was the woman he wanted beside him for the rest of his life. He didn't fall in love with your *potential*, he fell in love with *you*.

"How many of you have fallen in love with a man's potential? Or how often have you heard other women say, 'I love everything about him except—fill in the blank—but when we get married I'll get him to change'?"

All three heads nodded yes.

"Men know women want to change them…and they hate it. They absolutely hate it because it means we don't think they're okay the way they are. One reason we do this is because we enjoy beautifying and improving things—including men and children—and making them better. Ancient women did not *need* to weave patterns into baskets for the baskets to function.

"Instinctively we raise children from helpless beings into the best they can be. But it doesn't work with men. All it does is alienate them. How are they going to love you if they're protecting their hearts from your attacks? Yes, Jenny, you have something to add?"

"This is so revealing. As you were speaking, I realized I've been trying to change Brad practically since I first met him. And I did the same thing to my ex-husband. But I see areas where Brad can do better or be happier and I

want so desperately to help him be the best he can be. It's probably kept us from loving each other more. But how do I change how I see him?"

"Because it's natural for women to see a man's potential and his imperfections—and we have such high expectations—it's hard not to say something. *But if you want him to be the best he can be, following the Secrets is what you need to do.*

"Jenny, you can learn to better accept your husband by making a mental—or better yet, a written—list of the qualities you love about him. Go back to when you first fell in love and revisit those strongest feelings. Carol, you create a list for your husband, and Beth, do this about men in general. It'll work the same.

"As you consider each item on your list, focus on how each one makes you *feel.* Then, when you think of your man or look at him, you'll begin to attach those nice feelings to your experience of him. It's a simple process that takes just a little bit of effort. Throughout the day, focus on those feelings. This is an amazingly simple way to create more love. It's one of those magic tricks.

"By the way, if your partner is being disrespectful, you cannot let that go by. It will counter everything we're trying to accomplish in these meetings. A woman isn't able to love a man who's disrespectful.

"Okay now, let's do something that should help you understand and accept men more fully. Everyone close your eyes. Take a couple of deep breaths; then, as you exhale, relax your body, especially your face and shoulders. Now, picture your husband, or some man you feel good about, standing before you. Think about the qualities you like about this man. How do those qualities make you feel? Take another deep breath and let the feelings fill you up. Okay, look into his heart. See how vulnerable it is. How he protects it behind a shield of tough stoicism. Think about what his family and his culture have taught him: Be strong, be brave, don't complain, chin up, don't cry, don't feel, provide for the family, be responsible, go to war and possibly die for others. Imagine his pain, his insecurities, his longings, his need to love and be loved, all of which cannot be expressed, all of which he is most likely unaware. Breathe that in....Now, for the next few moments, feel that great big, soft, vulnerable heart of his."

Diedra let the women sit for a few moments, their eyes closed, their bodies relaxed. She could see an occasional tear roll down a cheek.

"Okay, you can open your eyes now. How do you feel? What was that like for you?"

"I feel softer and more loving toward my husband." Carol sighed. "I want to go home and just be there for him."

Jenny whispered, "I could see how lonely and isolated Brad must be."

Beth wiped her tears. "I never realized I had such a narrow view of men. It's like I only saw them as strong and in charge, or rude and insensitive, never as someone with real feelings."

Diedra glowed with love. "Yes, if you remember to focus on what's inside their hearts, their potential for softness, for feelings that have nowhere to be expressed, and their need for love, you'll find you're different with them. It's very sweet.

"This process is especially necessary if you can't find anything to appreciate. Beneath even the most hard and hurtful heart is a soft, wounded child. That doesn't mean you should let a bad man in your life, ever. But hurts can build up and continue to damage you. If you focus on that

wounded child who only knows how to strike out, you can begin the process of healing. If a man has done bad things to you, it only harms you to blame all men. If you continue to hold hatred and anger in your heart, those harmful men get to continue to damage you. Love yourself and let go."

"Diedra, I don't think I could do this process with my ex-husband. He constantly berated me and called me names." It was obvious that Jenny still carried some hurt.

"You know, most men have the potential to become a prince...but some just don't. You've got to use your feminine intuition—which we'll talk more about—and stand tall in your womanly powers of Feminine Grace. That's when you make smart decisions for yourself, as you apparently did by divorcing him. As you develop your Feminine Grace, you'll be able to stand up to men who are disrespectful and say yes to those who are considerate and caring. Your feminine intuition will help you know the difference and Feminine Grace will give you the strength.

"In our next lesson I'm going to explain why men actually crave intimacy even more than women do." Our three maidens looked puzzled but Diedra only smiled.

One of the best things about love—the
feeling of being wrapped, like a gift,
in understanding.

– Anatole Broyard

In my research and on radio interviews I've asked men what it's like when a woman makes them feel understood and accepted for who they are. One radio host laughed and said, "I expect it'd be pretty darned nice, but I've never had the pleasure." After asking how they would respond to a woman who made them feel that way, several men said, without hesitation, "I'd marry her." Somehow it didn't seem like they were kidding.

Men only know how to be men.

"Don't women know how awful it feels when they try to change us and constantly disapprove of how we are?" Ben, a carpenter from North Carolina, said with pain in his voice.

Men know that women complain about them and they say it feels awful. Because most of the complaints are about men being men, it causes them a lot of confusion and frustration. One man I interviewed on the golf course explained, "I only know how to be a man. I try to do what she wants, but it's never enough, never right." Men like to solve problems but this is a problem they can't seem to get their arms around. Men only know how to be men.

When I ask men what they don't like about women, the majority say complaining, criticizing, and the way women try to change them. Married men tell me they don't feel much love toward their wives when they're "in trouble" all the time—especially if it's because they're simply being men. A group of single men agreed when one man said, "I've almost given up on dating. So many women are mad at men. What did I ever do to them?" And another man added, "And they blame us for every bad thing another man did to them. Men can be pretty bad, but I don't deserve that." The bottom line of that conversation was that angry women turned the men off completely, no matter how attractive the women were. The men joked that it was a whole lot easier to find another guy to grab dinner with.

It hurts men when they know women want to change them.

Men don't try to change women all that much. A man who decides to marry a woman is in love with the woman just as she is at that moment. He doesn't want anything about the woman to change, but he knows it usually does, which explains some of the caution about commitment.

Women would hate it if they knew a man wanted to change or, even worse, improve them. Yet, women do it to men almost without exception. To get involved with a man because he has potential is unfair and disrespectful. And we know in our hearts that men don't really change, so we go into a relationship or marriage deluding ourselves. No wonder the divorce rate is so high.

If you want men to respond to you in ways that are caring, admiring, and loving, you must first begin to see them differently. It's true that men are responsible for most of the violence, sexual crimes, and wars, but most men are decent and don't deserve to be treated as if they have some horrible disease. They need to be seen as individuals, which in turn will make you *treat* them differently. As you see into men's hearts and understand them more deeply, you'll begin to accept them and appreciate their masculine qualities. When that happens, you'll automatically quit blaming them for being men. Without blaming the defenses can come down.

Understanding and acceptance: It's as simple as that. A man will fall all over himself to make you happy because you are, most likely, the first woman to give that to him. You, armed with Feminine Grace, are the key to these kinds of changes, the changes you've wanted all along.

• • •

4 things you can do:

✓ Make a list of five masculine qualities you love about your husband or boyfriend. Then appreciate him for those qualities. And give him sincere compliments. Men get very little appreciation and few compliments. If you like how he looks, let him know. If you like something particular about his body—his muscles, chest, or broad shoulders—let him know. If you like how he makes love to you, especially if you want him to keep doing it that way, let him know—and don't be afraid to be specific. If he does something nice for you, tell him how it makes you feel. It's so easy. Anything he's good at that you admire and appreciate, tell him. Let him know when you're proud of him. You'll make him feel good because he'll know he's making you happy. You'll find him wanting to please you. It makes him happy to make you happy.

The masculine virtues that men value the most are strength, sexual power, courage, being successful, making money, being a protector, and being a good father. If you focus on these qualities, and understand your depth of appreciation for the ones you value the most, and let him know how you feel, you'll be doing him a loving service for which he will be grateful.

✓ List three things you'd like your man to do more of, such as how he treats you, what he says to you, how he helps you around the house. Get him to do more of those kinds of things by appreciating him and letting him know how good it makes you feel when he does them. You have to be very specific for it to sink in. Men don't do that well with subtlety. "I love it when you compliment me," is good, but it would be better to say, "It makes me feel

wonderful when you tell me I'm beautiful. When you compliment me, it makes me feel open to you." Then give him a big sexy kiss. *That* he understands.

✓ Do this next exercise at least two times this week. To get him to help around the house more, first, you've got to stop complaining—you know that doesn't work anyway. Instead, catch him doing something that's helpful; then praise him for helping out, and tell him how good it makes you feel. When he brings a glass in from the TV room say, "Oh thanks, that's nice of you to help. Did I ever tell you what a good husband you are?" Then give him one of those big kisses. For some men, especially if you've been doing it the other way for a long time, it may take a few repeat efforts, but, if you're patient, and loving, responding with grace and poise, he'll pay attention and begin to shift in how he interacts with you. The goal is to get him to *want* to help out.

✓ Three times this week, appreciate and compliment the men you work with or interact with in businesses. You'll find the effect is like magic. Waiters, mechanics, your co-workers: compliment them on their attire, or appearance, how good they are at some skill. You'll find them tripping over themselves to do nice things for you. The next time they see you they'll most likely have big smiles on their faces.

Men have had very little appreciation in their lives, so you'll be an important source of support for them. They'll feel understood and accepted, possibly for the first time in their lives. This is when you'll begin to see the true power of Feminine Grace and how simple and effective it is. You'll see how easily magic can happen.

Your Notes

_____

_____

_____

_____

_____

_____

_____

_____

_____

_____

_____

_____

_____

Chapter Four
Why men crave intimacy more than women do.

Secret #3
Your are his only source of intimacy.

Diedra could see the enthusiasm on the faces of her new students. "What was it like to acknowledge men this week?"

"I've been dying to tell you what's been happening!" Carol was bubbling with excitement. "Over the years, I've gotten into the habit of complaining a lot, which I now realize made me feel ugly." She made an appropriate face. "So I decided I'd practice Feminine Grace. It felt a bit fake but I reminded myself that this was about getting what *I* want while giving him what *he* wants.

"When Thomas came home from work the evening of our last meeting, I had on a pretty dress and I'd taken extra care with my hair and makeup. I told him to go sit in his favorite chair after he changed his clothes. Then I took him his favorite drink, sat on the arm of his chair, and told him how much I appreciated how hard he worked and how thankful I was that I could be home with the kids. Then I leaned down and gave him a slightly longer kiss than would be expected. When I got up, I looked him in the eyes, kissed him again, and went to the kitchen. All week I stayed focused on the things I most admire about him. It felt different because I'd gotten in the habit of focusing on what made me unhappy. I felt good appreciating and complimenting him all week, without going overboard. It's strange, but it made me feel womanly and kind of in charge. Each day he's warmed up a little bit more. I'd never noticed it before, but he's been pretty guarded for a long time."

Diedra smiled. "Appreciation instead of complaining. Now that's a trade most men would accept.

"What about you, Jenny? How did it go this week?"

Jenny was subdued. "You know, I made that list, about what I most like about Brad, and it was actually kind of sad. As I did it, I began to feel the same nice, loving feelings as when I first met him. I realized I've wasted the last year seeing his faults and trying to fix them, instead of enjoying all the loving feelings I could have had. What I've gotten instead is fighting. Focusing on what I like is causing me to like him better.

"All week long I let Brad know how much I love his body, how smart I think he is, what a great lover he is, and how pretty he makes me feel. And I meant it. The list did it for me. He's become the attractive man I met. I've noticed him staring at me. When I look over at him, he just smiles."

Beth was practically jumping out of her seat. "I had so much fun this week. Every chance I got I appreciated or complimented men. It was so cute how they tripped over themselves doing things for me. Men seemed totally different to me, as if I'd put on a pair of those 3-D glasses. I just assumed they were all princes and that's exactly how they behaved."

"That's terrific, girls. And this is just the beginning.

Carol and Jenny, you'll soon discover a total transformation of your husbands. They'll be happier and more in love with you than ever before and you'll be getting more and more of what you want.

"So with that, let's move on to the third Secret." Diedra placed a card on the easel that read:

Secret #3
You are his only source of intimacy.

Diedra slowly made eye contact with each of the women. "You are an extremely important person in your husband's life. Once you understand that, you'll be able to give him more of what he needs. Then, because he'll feel safe, understood, accepted, and appreciated—probably for the first time—he's going to cherish you like a rare treasure.

"Would someone please define intimacy for us?"

Jenny tentatively raised her hand. "I think intimacy is sharing yourself completely."

"Okay, so how would that look?"

"I guess by two people expressing their emotions with each other."

"Thank you, Jenny. That's a good description of intimacy. By that definition, do each of you have women friends you're intimate with?"

They nodded. "Okay, who knows men who have that kind of intimacy with their male friends?"

No response.

"Who has that kind of intimacy—where you're both expressing your emotions—with the man in your life?"

Carol offered, "I let him know most of what goes on with me, but he doesn't tell me what's going on with him."

Diedra continued. "It doesn't appear that there's much

intimacy going on between you and your husbands, or between them and their friends. Will one of you explain why you think that is?"

Jenny offered, "Well…from what you've been saying, I think it's because men just don't know how to express their emotions."

"Yes, that's part of it. The other part is that not only do most men not know how to express their emotions, they don't even have access to their emotions. Since they were little boys, they've been taught not to feel. 'Big boys don't cry, be a man, chin up, be strong, keep pushing, don't be a sissy.' " Diedra was silent for a moment.

"Let me tell you a little story about a man named David. He's been married for twelve years, has two kids, a nice house, two cars, takes his family on a vacation every year. He's created a comfortable, stable life for his family. But, his life has just been shattered because today he lost his job.

"On his way home, his concern for his wife grows. How is she going to react? he wonders. Arriving home, he's greeted by his wife, Betsy, while the kids play in the backyard. He puts his arms around her, wanting to protect her from the world. After explaining what has happened, he pulls her toward him. She cried in his gentle embrace.

"A sweet scene, I'm sure you'll all agree. But where does David go for comfort? Who will hold *him* while *he* cries? Who can he talk to about *his* fears and concerns for the future welfare of his family? And how do you suppose it makes him feel as a man to have lost his job?"

Diedra was silent, tears filling her eyes. The women saw how passionately she felt about this subject she had chosen to teach.

She continued. "Men commit suicide more often than

women. They don't attempt it as often as women, but when a man wants to kill himself, he usually uses something that works, such as gun, a car, jumping off a bridge, hanging. Women are frequently reaching out for help. Often, maybe unconsciously, they choose their timing so they can be found, or they tell someone, and they use something like pills that will be slow and reversible. Men don't think anyone is there to help them, and since they don't usually have a support system, it doesn't occur to them to solve their problems with outside help. It's amazing how often the wife and close friends say, 'I had no idea,' when asked if they knew he was upset.

"For most men, the only person they can be intimate with, and express their emotions to, is their romantic partner. But two of their greatest concerns—sex and career or money—can't usually be completely shared with her because she's tied to his need to perform successfully for her, to be a man. He'll share some of his emotions, fears, anxieties, and longings, depending on how safe he feels, but not to the full depth that he might be feeling them. And the more concerned he is, the less likely he'll say anything at all."

Diedra's passion grew. "Are you beginning to understand the isolation that most men experience?"

Beth leaned forward. "I hear what you're saying, but why don't men just go to their male friends? *They* ought to understand what he's going through."

Diedra smiled. "That seems logical, but it doesn't work that way. Because men aren't comfortable with emotions and because they've grown up cheering each other on—to get back up after being knocked down, to be tough, to hold it together, to be a man—and so much a part of their relationships is competitive, that's mostly all they

know how to do. Generally, they're comfortable giving each other only a few minutes to share a personal problem; then it's back to a discussion of the latest sporting event, or the business deal they're working on. Besides, most men's friends are colleagues, so it's not *appropriate* to share personal issues. If either of your husbands has a close male friend with whom he can express his emotions, encourage him to nurture those relationships, because it's extremely rare."

Frowning, Jenny said, "My husband certainly doesn't have a friend like that. Which means I'm 'it' for him, right?"

"Yes, basically. But what if you've been complaining, trying to change him, and making him feel like you don't understand him and that you don't approve of him as he is? How open do you think he's been?"

Looking disheartened, Jenny said, "Not very."

"And how sad, since you're the only person with whom he might have been able to let down his defenses and be himself. You can see why it's pretty risky for most men to expose themselves by being that vulnerable. Think about the times when he did share some of his emotions or problems. Did you listen, really? Did you give him caring eye contact? Were you considerate of how fragile his emotions might be? Were you kind and understanding of his dilemma? Or did you immediately begin to comment on what he had shared, possibly cutting him off, maybe even correcting him, or telling him that he shouldn't be feeling that way? Maybe you tried to bolster him by telling him to pull it together. How do you feel when he does that to you?…Just like you, he needs understanding and respect."

Carol leaned forward. "It's strange; as this is sinking in, I actually feel stronger, which makes me feel more in balance with my husband. Last week I focused on Thomas's masculine qualities that I admire, and consequently he seems more manly to me, and more attractive. I appreciate his loneliness and isolation, and my heart goes out to him, but because I see him as more masculine than ever before, understanding his softer side makes me feel more womanly. Does that make sense?"

"It makes perfect sense because you're beginning to see that there's a lot more to your husband than you realized. Our perception of what men are has been too narrow. What I'm trying to show you is a fuller, richer picture of what it means to be a man. When that happens, your understanding expands, and you see him and all his many facets. Your love is expanding, and the more fully you love a man, the more you connect with your feminine self. You're creating magic, wouldn't you agree?"

Won't you come into my garden?
I would like my roses to see you.
— Richard Brinsley Sheridan

Women have mothers, sisters, girlfriends—and even some men friends to go to when they need to share their emotions. No one questions or judges them. But men really have no one. You are the only one with whom he can share some of his inner self. It's a position to be honored, cherished, and nurtured. Think about it. What a wonderful gift you can give to the man you love.

A group of men in one of my sexuality workshops shared what had happened on the occasions that they allowed themselves to get emotional. They said they felt they "weren't really listened to," they felt "misunderstood," and often were told "they were doing it wrong." Bill, a carpenter, said, "My girlfriend asked me to share my feelings with her but when I did, and even cried, she got scared and said she didn't know how to react. She eventually left me. I'm never going to do that again."

Women—and most men—have too narrow a view of how men are supposed to behave.

Deep within women is the ancient belief that men are the protectors, the strong ones, that men should support women—not be supported by women. At least not because he's being fragile. Women want to be able to count on men; it's a natural part of our makeup. If they see men lose control emotionally, how do women continue to respect them as men? To look up to them as the strong ones? Women say they want men to be more emotional, to cry, but only to a point. The real problem is that women—and most men—have too narrow a view of how men are supposed to behave.

Throughout society, even today, boys are being taught to be men. A professor from California shared this common story with me. "When I was a young boy, I was playing softball. When it was my turn to bat, I missed the ball badly and lost the game. On the way home I began to cry and my dad turned around and said, 'You stop that crying right now. Quit being a baby. Be a man.' And do you know what? I didn't cry again for twenty years, not even when he died."

"Be a man" means not to express their emotions, to be tough, to become the provider, to sign up for the possibility of a draft. Studies have shown that as babies, little boys are held less, handled more roughly, and allowed to cry longer than little girls.

In Warren Farrell's book *The Myth of Male Power*, he explains how early pressures of being "men" affect males. Until boys and girls are nine, their suicide rates are identical; from ten to fourteen, the boys' rate is twice as high as girls'; from fifteen to nineteen, four times as high; and from twenty to twenty-four, six times as high. That's a sickening trend.

There's a Catch-22 here. Women want to be with a man with whom they can feel womanly; meaning he's stronger, protective, willing to care for her and hold her when she hurts. Men want that too. But men need a safe environment in which to express a fuller range of emotions. In our culture today, we, their romantic partners, are the *only* outlet for that expression.

We must see a more complete picture of who men are.

To create enough safety for her partner to express his emotions more fully, a woman can do several things to keep the relationship strong and vibrant. Don't try to do serious therapy. That should be with outside help. Simply allow him to share his feelings without fear of judgment or negative consequences. And don't try to be his mother, telling him what to do or how to do it. Neither are healthy for a romantic relationship. Stay the woman he loves, who is supporting him to feel. See a more complete picture of who he is as a man. The fact that he has emotions should make him more appealing as a person, not less appealing as a man. Focus on those masculine qualities that you admire, the ones that make you feel most feminine. Is it his physical strength, his intelligence, his take-charge ways, his prowess as a lover, or how he makes you feel like a woman?

Realize that you are the woman he trusts and loves. As you fall in love with yourself and enjoy being a woman more, he'll soften and become more open and hopefully feel safe enough to begin to feel. Encouraging him to express all of who he is gives him the rare opportunity to be more human. That's something to celebrate.

Carol spoke next. "Diedra, I've been married for several years. A lot of habits have been set in place. How do I create more trust so Thomas will begin to open up to me? I'd like that very much if he would, and I think it will make us closer."

"You're right about being closer," Diedra agreed. "You know what happens with your women friends when you express your emotional selves: It becomes a special bonding experience.

"The first way to help your husband develop more trust is to stay focused on what you like and admire about him and to appreciate him regularly. Don't complain. Don't try to change him. If you have a problem you need to discuss with him, do so with Feminine Grace. Be respectful, clear, and concise. Don't blame, but explain what you're feeling and what you need. As you do this, he'll slowly become less defensive.

"As Thomas begins to relax around you, feeling better about you and himself, you can begin to open some dialogue that will encourage him to talk to you from deeper in his heart.

"What you can do is pick a time when he's relaxed, but not doing anything else like watching television or reading. Just sit with him for a while. Then, ask him a not-too-probing question. Maybe something like, "What have you been enjoying most about work lately?"

"When he answers, I want you to notice something that's common among men: I call it the Moment of Silence. He may not say anything for a few moments. Don't talk. He's gathering his thoughts. Then, when he begins to talk, don't interrupt or comment on what he says. In past conversations, not knowing about this, you probably jumped in with your editorial comments. Don't! Allow all silences to sit. He's still gathering his thoughts.

"When you stay silent, he'll feel more comfortabl and less guarded against your need to comment on what he says. We often speak whenever there's an opening and want to dissect what's been said. Women interrupt each other all the time. Remember, men say women don't listen to them. Instead of listening, we're often waiting to jump in with our comments. We'll talk more about developing your communication skills in future lessons. When you stay silent and wait, he'll most likely speak more personally. Let each silence sit. Unless he asks you a question, he's still gathering his thoughts. Each time, he'll drop a little deeper into his heart and eventually, if not this first time, in the next few conversations like this, you'll find him expressing from a much deeper, more personal place. This is one more way that magic simply happens.

"You'll know when he's done because he'll tell you, either by saying it directly or by asking you a question about something else. Even when he's done, don't comment on what he said in any editorial way. Simply acknowledge and appreciate him for expressing himself. Then go back to light conversation.

"During those silences, notice how well you listen, or

not; notice if you want to argue and make him wrong; and imagine how he's feeling, how he might shut down and discontinue the conversation if you say what you're probably dying to say. When you listen, focus on his soft heart and try to feel what's going on within him.

"Here's something very important that you must adhere to…always: A man feels betrayed when you tell someone something private about him—just as betrayed as you would feel if he had an affair. I mean this! It has to do with loyalty…and they don't ever want to be perceived as weak. Overall, men don't think women are very loyal, especially about keeping private matters private. A good rule of thumb is to never say anything that you couldn't say in front of him, and never, ever belittle him to anyone else. It's about respecting him. Respect and trust: without them, there cannot be love."

"But, Diedra," Jenny argued, "sometimes I need to tell someone when things aren't going well for Brad and me. I'd go crazy if I couldn't."

"Of course you need someone to talk to. Just as he does. Just don't tell someone else those very private things he's revealed about himself. Let him know with whom you share your personal life and keep it with that one—or in your case—two people. This can be difficult for women, but it's a matter of building, and in some cases, rebuilding trust. Of course, share with your friends. Share that you're frustrated, or angry, or whatever, but be considerate not to belittle or bad-mouth him or reveal his innermost secrets.

"Once Brad begins to trust you, he'll become more comfortable telling you his deeper feelings. This may take a while though, because you've been doing it the other way for a long time. Listening is the most endearing quality you can develop, especially when you haven't allowed your husband to speak freely in the past.

"Think about when women get together. They often talk across each other, interrupt, have several conversations going at one time, and somehow they still keep track. Men go crazy with this. Men take turns, they listen to each speaker, and follow only one conversation at a time.

"Prehistoric women spent all their time together. There were children of all ages to be watched and cared for. There were elders who needed attention. Pots to stir, baskets to weave, and all the while, the women talked. We are the descendants of those busy women.

"Men focused on hunting. Hunting was serious business because a successful hunt meant the tribe would continue to survive, and always, it was a test of manhood. Men planned, made weapons for, and told stories about hunting, and practiced games to prepare physically for the next hunt. Then, after the hunt, they told stories about how it went. Is it so different for the modern man? Sports and business are merely modern forms of hunting and preparation for hunting. Men need to focus and women are comfortable doing several things at once. It's simple when you look at it that way, isn't it?"

Carol smiled. "I admire Thomas's ability to focus on something so completely, but it can also drive me crazy. What you've been saying will help me be more patient."

"I'm sure it will. By understanding the differences in communication styles, you can give your husband something that he's longed for and would never have gotten: to be heard and to have the opportunity to trust enough to allow his emotions to be expressed. What a grand and wondrous gift you can give him."

"I appreciate what you're saying, about men not having anyone to express their emotions with, but I'd like Thomas

to listen to me better, too. How do I get that to happen?"

Diedra thought for a moment. "I'll be covering that in our discussion on how to communicate better, but for now, let me say a couple of things. First, as you let go of ugly ways of interacting with him, he'll do the same, which will lead you both into greater levels of respect and trust. Remember, if you lead with love and acceptance, he'll follow. As you focus on what you admire about him and he sees you becoming more beautiful and alluring, you'll become more interested in each other. So, some of it will take care of itself. Remember when you were first in love, how you talked for hours? Some of that will come back as your love grows anew. Also, remember that he's generally no more interested in the little details than you are the plays in the final quarter of last weekend's football game.

"For those times when you really need him to be there for you, rather than complaining—which you already know shuts him down—use Feminine Grace and tell him lovingly that you need to talk to him. By the way, the words "we need to talk" strike terror into the hearts of all men. They assume it means there's a problem, and it's their fault. So, ease his anxiety and let him know up front that he's not in trouble. Be respectful and check to be sure that the time is right with him. If it's not, find out when he'll be able to give you his undivided attention. After you've told him what you needed to say—in a non-blaming, non-judgmental way—let him know how good it made you feel that he listened so attentively. Trust me, this works unless you choose a bad time or begin to blame or accuse him. Include a sexy kiss if it's appropriate.

"The key to creating this kind of magic is to live every aspect of your life with Feminine Grace. It's simple: Be conscious and try to do everything you can with beauty, joy,

respect, and appreciation, even when you're not feeling it. Your alternative is to be unattractive or even ugly. It's a matter of self-respect and self-love. You choose. And acting 'as if' you're a joyful person will eventually help you develop the habit of being joyful. When you're feeling joyful, love flows into you and you don't feel the need for someone else to give that to you. Their love is just cherries on top of the natural love you feel from within. Your life will be completely transformed, filled with more love than you ever imagined possible."

"Diedra," Carol said, "this has been really interesting. I'm looking forward to trying your listening technique. I really would like Thomas and me to have more intimacy."

"I'll be curious how it goes. Not every man can open up." Diedra explained, "It's more the woman's way. You'll like the next lesson because we're going to talk about how men express intimacy most comfortably. You'll be surprised and, at the same time, you'll realize that you already knew it. I look forward to sharing it with you."

After seeing the women to the door, Diedra stood for some time, watching them walk toward town. They're in for some interesting times, she thought. Smiling, she turned and stepped back into her cottage.

2 things you can do:
✓ At least two times this week, interact with a man, any man, and be aware of his soft, protected heart. Notice how this makes you feel about him. Focus on his wonderful masculine qualities, but, at the same time, remember what society has done to shut him down. In your binder, write about your

experiences and anything new you notice about men.

✓ Engage your husband or boyfriend in a conversation in the way Diedra described. Practice your listening skills. Notice if you want to interrupt and what you feel compelled to say. Be aware of how different the conversation is because you stay silent. Be sure to use a lot of eye contact. Acknowledge him when he's done. If you don't have a partner, practice with any male friend. Write in your binder what the experience was like and how it was different from past conversations.

Chapter Five
How most men express intimacy.

Secret #4
Sex is the only way most men know how to be intimate.

Before Diedra began the class, she asked Beth how it was going.

"I've been focusing on feeling better about myself. My last breakup was pretty devastating. Then I gained a lot of weight. I've got about ten pounds more to go to feel good in my clothes again, but I'm doing it for me this time, not men. I'm staying open to men, but I notice myself thinking they're jerks for not noticing me. It's an old habit to be angry at men. My last boyfriend enjoyed insulting me. It was awful. I don't know how I got into that situation in the first place."

"I've been saying that most men can turn into princes, but some men simply aren't worth a woman's time and energy. When a woman lacks self-esteem, she's more likely to tolerate a disrespectful man because she needs a man in her life, and she's afraid to be alone. If she lacks

self-love, she's not going to care enough about herself or have the inner strength to stand up for herself. As a woman develops the qualities of Feminine Grace, her standards rise: to the point that she would much rather be alone than with the wrong man."

Jenny took her turn. "The most wonderful thing happened this week. I did exactly what you said to do, Diedra, and my husband opened up and told me things he said he'd never told anyone before. I waited until he was done watching the football game; then I sat on the sofa with him and offered to rub his shoulders. While I was doing that, I asked him, 'If you could do anything you wanted, and you knew you'd have plenty of money, what would you want to be doing?' Then I stayed silent. It seemed to take forever, but I just kept rubbing his shoulders.

"Finally, he started to talk about doing something that I would never have guessed. I kept silent, with an occasional 'I'm listening' kind of noise like hmmmm, or 'that's interesting.' When he was done, I told him how pleased I was that he told me. I was dying to say, 'Well, why don't you just do it?' but I didn't. For three hours, we laughed and cried together, him talking and me listening. Then we made love like we used to, in the beginning of our relationship. It was wonderful."

She stopped and took a deep breath. "And do you know the best part? Brad said he felt lighter and happier than he'd felt in a long time."

Diedra smiled. "As you can tell by Jenny's experience, intimacy of that kind is magical. Do you see how much power you have in your relationship? When you take the lead with Feminine Grace, he'll follow blindly because *you're* what he wants. At least when you're being beautiful. But I must caution you, not all men are able to

open up like Brad did. For most men, they've been shut down for so long they just can't seem to let go of all their defenses. Here's the next Secret."

Secret #4
Sex is the only way most men know how to be intimate.

"To which gender does society give permission to be emotional?" Diedra looked at each woman.

After a moment, Beth said, "Women, of course."

"That's right. And what does society say if men are emotional?"

Carol offered, "They're not masculine."

"Right, and who has permission to be sexual?"

"Men?" Jenny took a turn.

"Yes. What do we call him if he's too sexual?"

There was no reply. "Okay, answer this question. What do we call a woman if she's too sexual?"

Quickly, the three responded. "She's loose."

"She's a slut."

"She's cheap."

"Trashy."

"She's a tramp."

"A whore."

"Are you getting the picture? Of course, we have our names for men, but they don't come as quickly to mind and they're not as degrading. We might call them a jerk or a dog or a womanizer, but we don't make nearly as harsh a judgment of them. Why do you suppose that is?"

Beth raised her hand again. "It's like you said: Men have *permission* to be sexual."

"Yes, exactly. And at the same time, they're *not* given

permission to be emotional. But men are human. They need closeness and connection with others, just as you do. We saw how close Jenny and Brad felt after he opened up. But since most men don't have the opportunity—or are able—to be emotionally close, what's the other way they've been given permission to be close?"

Carol thought out loud. "Men get their intimacy needs met sexually because that's the only place that society has given them permission to get close to another person, to let loose and feel. It's so obvious."

Diedra nodded. "It is, but even men don't realize this. Although they agree when you talk to them about it.

"Women get to express the full range of their emotions in a variety of ways. But it's through sex that men get to feel most deeply. The sad thing is, even with sex, men can't completely let go. Women aren't judged by their emotional expertise. But men are judged for their expertise in sex. Just because they like it—a lot—and just because they usually want as much as they can get, doesn't mean it's always a great time for them.

"They have the responsibility of being 'The Man.' They've got to do most of the initiating, romancing, seducing, usually being the aggressive partner. They've got to keep an erection, they've got to please the woman, and somewhere in there they want to have a good time.

"And here's another piece of the puzzle. An awful part of all this is that sex—his vehicle for closeness, love, and emotion—is still, in our permissive culture, considered naughty, dirty, bad, even disgusting, and on and on. So, the one way he's allowed to be intimate is tainted. How's that for a sad state of affairs? It seems we give the men all the dirty jobs, doesn't it?"

"Where's my magic wand? I want to make it all better

for them." Carol tried to be light. "Actually, my heart aches for them. I'm glad I'm not a man.

"Here's a question for you, Diedra. Every time you unveil some new aspect about what it's like for men, it feels as if I already know it...yet, I'm certain I've never heard most of this before. Why do I feel this way?"

"Does anyone else relate to what Carol just said?" Diedra asked. Beth and Jenny nodded. "That's your feminine 'knowing,' your intuition. You *do* know all of this, but over the last twenty years or so, we've been focusing on being self-sufficient women, strong women, women who don't need men. Consequently, we've lost touch with much of the natural 'knowing' that women instinctively have about men and relationships. We've done a great job with our relationships with each other, but, at the same time, our relationships with men have suffered.

"We don't have magic wands, but the Secrets I'm teaching you can *become* your magic wands. Your feminine intuition and your natural rapport with, and interest in, love and romance are the reason you need to be the one to bring about these changes in the men you're involved with. I know you'd like the men to do things to nurture and deepen love, but most men don't think much about it. They do, however, want a happy and vibrant relationship, but they expect it to just happen. That's why, even though it doesn't feel as romantic, you've got to take the initiative. But trust me, your men *will* become more romantic.

"If you use your intuition in concert with the Secrets you're learning in our meetings, you'll create a synergistic effect. When you add your Feminine Grace, well, that's when you'll get real magic. Here's a way to remember it: Understand and accept him, trust your intuition to lead you into what feels like the unknown, combine with Feminine

Grace, and you'll have two people who are happier and more in love than they ever dreamed they could be."

Anybody who believes that the way to a man's heart is through his stomach flunked geography.

– Robert Byrne

Often, when we think of people being emotional, we think of them crying, or getting angry. But one of the most powerful emotions that can be expressed is love.

When a man expresses his love, his heart is exposed.

Men don't generally feel comfortable expressing their emotions with words, and, for a lot of men, *love* is one of the most difficult words to say, next to the words *marriage* and *commitment*. When a man acknowledges his love he puts himself in a position of vulnerability because his heart is exposed. And men know that women tend to assume marriage is on the horizon as soon as she hears those words. So, they shy away from expressing their love. But men feel very deeply.

Most men I've surveyed say they'd prefer sex with love, even single men in their twenties and early thirties, when it seems all *they* might care about is scoring—not that they turn down appealing opportunities. Men usually prefer love but without the strings attached. Since men use sex to express intimacy, it makes sense that they would rather have sex be as full an experience as possible. On the flip side of that, because women carry so many expectations with sex, men often avoid getting as emotionally close as they might otherwise, simply to keep things from getting too complicated. And sometimes men just want sex, with nothing personal involved. That's more rare for women, so they don't understand how a man can have sex and not feel that it means anything.

You are the conduit for his expression of love.

When a woman understands that sex is how most men express love and intimacy, she'll want to be more sexual if she wants to receive his love. When she does that, she becomes the conduit for him to more fully express his emotional self.

Unfortunately, women haven't been given the same permission to be sexual that men have. Consequently, many women are shut down sexually. Even when a woman wants to be more open and expressive, those old negative lessons from childhood are hard to reverse. Most women were taught to be "good," meaning don't have sex until marriage, and then they should become sex goddesses...but only in the bedroom. Of course, a lot of women haven't adhered to that directive, but the cultural expectations are a strong part of our thinking. All too often, sex is a "special" thing that's kept in a pretty little box, stored on the top shelf in the closet, and then, once in a while, brought down for special occasions.

Women have a lot of issues about their bodies, which keeps them from being as free and easy with sex as they could be. Men absolutely go crazy for a woman who is comfortable with her body. And—hear this—men don't

expect you to have a perfect body. They are much less concerned about, and usually don't even notice, all the little imperfections that you may be focusing on. They're grateful that you'll get naked with them at all.

Another factor is that many men don't know how to make love to a woman. Women are complicated and extremely individual in what they like, want, and need. Men enjoy the challenge of discovering each woman's little differences, but they also fumble around, trying to guess the right combination. Frequently, even after years of marriage, women aren't comfortable telling their partners what they like, and then blame their partner for not being able to figure out their mysteries. Most men love to please a woman sexually—it's the ultimate accomplishment for men—and at least once in each of my sex workshops a man would say, "We want to make women happy, but they've got to tell us how." If women realized how badly men want to know what their partners like—so they can please them and be great lovers, i.e., great men—women would be more willing to let their partner know what they like.

When two people love each other, hearts and souls intertwine.

No matter how it's discussed in philosophical and religious circles, we're all sexual beings. We're here to procreate, which requires the act of sex. But we're also here to learn how to love. When two people make love—notice the phrase, "make" love—to each other, hearts and souls can intertwine and mesh in a shared moment that lasts minutes and even hours. When a woman can release her inhibitions and flow with her sexual energy, magic happens.

I've asked many men what made their best sexual experiences great. One Kansas City man summed it up for many of the others when he said, "Sex is great for me when it's obvious my wife is experiencing pleasure. But the best is when I can feel her love for me." That, more than anything, shows how strong the emotional connection is for men. "She liked it," is the simple way one man put it.

As you cultivate your Feminine Grace, you'll like your body more, be more comfortable expressing yourself, and relax. As you do so, your ability to enjoy sex will expand, and you'll become a more enthusiastic, available partner. The more you do that, the more love and intimacy you will create with your partner. From there, romance will flow, because he won't be able to get you off his mind.

"Diedra, I'm feeling frustrated." Carol sounded lost. "I can see that the lack of love I've been feeling in my marriage is partly due to our lack of physical closeness but I never thought of it quite that way before. I've been blaming it on him and that he doesn't seem to care. I miss the connection we once shared but, after so many years, how do I create the kind of changes you're talking about?"

"Well, one thing for certain is that sex begets sex. The more you have it, the more you think about it and the more you want it. Physical closeness is something you share only with your partner and it should be cherished.

"To revive passion, it helps to focus on the physical aspect of your relationship...so make love twice a day."

Carol practically jumped out of her seat. "Diedra, I

have children. There's no way!"

Getting the reaction she expected, Diedra laughed. "I didn't necessarily mean what you thought. You just have to redefine what making love means. Making love doesn't have to mean intercourse. Let it be long, slow kisses; lots of touching; holding each other; and gazing into each other's eyes. Make hello and good-bye kisses last at least ten seconds. Besides, it's important for kids to see loving parents.

"Make a date once a week to make love. Take turns creating a romantic atmosphere. Light candles, wear a sexy outfit, feed each other mangos or chocolate or grapes, play sensual music. Your sexual energy will begin to flow and you'll find yourselves looking forward to 'date night.' Because sex begets sex, chances are pretty good that you'll begin to enjoy sexual pleasures more often than once a week.

"Another thing that helps is to sleep naked. 'But the children,' you may say. Why is it okay for *them* to be naked but not the parents? Just keep a robe next to the bed and be relaxed about it. It's good for children to get a healthy view of love and nudity. If you can't bring yourselves to sleep naked, sleep in something sexy. For him, silk boxers are soft and sensual. For you, anything that makes you feel beautiful."

"Brad says he doesn't mind my floppy T-shirt that I sleep in." Jenny sounded defensive.

"Men don't usually complain much. Men consider women to be the leader in the relationship, so they just get used to however it is, even though they may not like it. My question to you is, do you feel beautiful and sexy in it?"

"Well, no. But it's comfortable."

"You have to set your priorities. What's more important; your comfort or the possibility of invigorating your love life?" The others laughed. "I know, I know, comfort is

pretty appealing. But sleeping naked will become comfortable in no time. I'm talking about igniting the sparks that brought you together. Remember how much you enjoyed making love when you first fell in love, when it didn't matter where you did it or what you were wearing? You can bring that back if you want it, but you have to want it. It's easy to climb in bed at the end of a long day and fall asleep. But, if you make a commitment to have some love play before you fall asleep, often it will turn into lovemaking. A little kissing, a little naked hugging, and voila, you're making love, growing closer, and—you'll have to admit—sex is the best sleep aid around. And mornings will most likely become more fun too.

"Another thing to consider regarding sex is that it doesn't have to be about orgasms. That puts a lot of pressure on both of you and it's not a necessary part of lovemaking. Let go of orgasm as the ultimate goal and just meander as you touch, move, and kiss. Simply let it flow, and enjoy.

"Something else that really makes a difference is to wear sexy underwear. Lingerie reminds you that you're a sexual being and makes you feel more alluring. Your husband, seeing you looking sexy for him, will find his interest perking up. So to speak." Everyone laughed.

"Be sure to create some alone time. Go on a date once a week; go away for a weekend every other month; and a vacation once a year. Vow not to talk about work or kids except during specified times. If you're nursing, you may only be able to get away for a couple of hours, but focus on love and romance. If money is tight, swap baby-sitting with friends; go camping instead of staying at hotels. Be creative. The investment is worth it. A divorce and two households is a whole lot more expensive."

Diedra asked her students, "Are you feeling inspired?" They all nodded and told her to continue.

"Get some books on sex, love, and romance. Trying new things and having the books around will help you keep love and sex a priority. Read out loud to each other, and maybe get turned on a bit. Take turns trying new ideas—make it fun and adventuresome.

"All these suggestions will help you become more interested and enthusiastic. This is so important that, next week, we're going to devote more time to how to expand your interest—and his—and become much more enthusiastic.

"You've been doing a great job incorporating the Secrets into your lives, so this should be particularly fun. See how your husbands respond when you go to bed naked or with a sexy new nightgown. Go on a little shopping spree and buy some new lingerie and enjoy the sensual pleasures. Notice how different you feel. Beth, even though you don't have a partner, you should still wear sexy lingerie and either sleep naked or wear something sexy to sleep in. It will help you release your sexual energy. You'll be sexier because you'll feel sexier. Men have a built-in radar. Letting that energy flow and using your Feminine Grace to interact with men should get a few heads turning because you'll glow with a woman's inner beauty. And *that* is potent stuff!" Diedra winked. "When you meet someone interesting, remember to make him feel comfortable by staying comfortable with yourself. All you need to do is feel beautiful.

"Another way to help your sexual energy flow is to fantasize about making love. Try it and see what happens to your libido. Talk about magic! Make it fun, not a chore.

"Remember to do all of this with Feminine Grace and you'll find the passion between you and your husband

growing with each day. And Beth, you're going to notice the men paying more attention because of your inner glow.

"Making love creates a special bond like no other. In our monogamous culture, it's the only thing we promise to save for them. Because lovemaking is sacred, never, ever use it as a reward or punishment. It kills your husband a little each time you do it. It makes it less pure, less beautiful, less loving."

"I'm excited to go try some of these things, but I'm nervous too." Jenny offered.

"Just be playful," Diedra smiled, "all of you, and let the magic flow. When you come back you can let me know how it went and how the men in your lives responded. And Beth, just feel sexy and see what happens."

4 things you can do:
Remember that sex for him is his most comfortable outlet for intimacy. The more sexual you become, the more intimacy you both will share. Gauge yourself by what you know your partner likes. Some men are more conservative than others, so you'll have to determine what will be the most effective way to achieve renewed passion and intimacy.

✓ Think sexy. Pick at least one time per day to focus on feeling sexy. This may be foreign to you, but it works, even if you have to pretend. Pretend long enough and it becomes real. Keep it a focus and it will begin to happen naturally.

✓ Buy sexy lingerie this week, if only one piece. Push your comfort level and buy something that seems *too* sexy. Buy at least one pair of thong panties and give it a fair trial.

You'll find them to be comfortable and they're very sexy.

✓ Flirt with and tease your husband at least three times this week. Let him know you're feeling sexual. That's when he'll show more interest, especially if you've been turning him down for a long time. As your sex life wakes up, he'll be thinking about you more.

✓ Continue to focus on his masculine qualities. Admire and compliment him at least two times this week.

You may find you have some resistance to doing all these things. You may be harboring some resentments. That's natural after years of less-than-glorious love. But remember, someone has to make the first move and *it isn't going to be him*. Once you begin the process, he'll start to notice you more, think about you more, appreciate and compliment you more, and his love will grow. Relish feeling more like a woman and enjoy the man who's turning into a prince, right before your eyes.

Chapter Six
Why monogamy is so difficult for men.

Secret #5
Men have high hopes for monogamy.

Our three maidens, looking lovelier than ever, waited to be seated at one of Ginger's tables for lunch.

"Hi, ladies. Why the big smiles?" Ginger was sparkly as usual.

Carol was the spokesperson. "Ginger, we came to thank you. We love Diedra and what she's teaching. We're not even halfway through and our relationships are already noticeably better. We wanted to let you know."

"Hey, what'd I tell you? I knew you'd like her! Just be sure and tell your friends. Wouldn't it be great if every woman knew this stuff?" After chatting a bit more, they ordered lunch.

Jenny quizzed Carol first. "So, how's it going at home?"

"Well, the other night after I put the kids to bed I ran a bath, with bubbles, and lit some candles around the tub and in the bedroom. Then I asked Thomas if he could help me with something. He wasn't very interested, I could tell,

but I led him into the bathroom. The look he gave me was priceless. First it was confusion, then I saw a tiny light go on in his head; then there was a hint of this mischievous little-boy grin. Just a hint." They all laughed. "I put my arms around him and said, 'How about taking a bubble bath with your wife?' Then I started unbuttoning his shirt. We kissed, like we used to; then got in the tub and fooled around. After I dried off I went into the closet and slipped on his favorite nightgown that hadn't seen the light of day for a long time. Well, he responded immediately, if you know what I mean. We went to bed and made love for over an hour.

"We've been much more physical since then. I'm feeling younger and more beautiful—and he seems so much happier. It's like we've fallen in love again. Actually, it's better than that, because we're smarter now and we appreciate each other more. Thomas has been calling me during the day to say 'hi,' which he hasn't done in years. He's even doing little things around the house to help out. And he's taking more time to play with the kids. They're loving it."

"Carol, that's terrific."

Beth was on the edge of her seat. "Can I tell my news? I met a terrific man at a friend's party. I had on my new sweater and wool pants, so I was feeling especially pretty." She stood up and turned around. "And you can see I've lost more weight. When we were introduced I was immediately attracted to him, so I made nice eye contact and smiled: you know, trying to help him feel comfortable. Well, we hit it off right away. I listened, like Diedra suggested, and when I spoke he seemed to hang on my every word. I'd ask him a question; then, after answering, he'd want to know *my* answer. It was the most comfortable

I ever felt with a new man and I didn't feel like I was at his mercy, waiting for him to like me. I felt like I was in control, and I stayed feminine and focused on his masculinity. It was like I was guiding him. And he kept telling me what an interesting woman I was."

Carol was smiling. "What fun. You know, you probably took a lot of pressure off of him by being so comfortable with yourself. Have you talked to him since then? What's his name?"

"It's Steven, and, yes, he called the next day." Beth beamed. "We're going on our first date this weekend. We've talked on the phone twice. He's really nice."

When Beth finished, she and Carol stared at Jenny.

"What?" Jenny laughed. "You want me to share too?"

"Uh-huh," Carol and Beth teased in unison.

"Well, it's like Brad is seeing me for the first time. I've been telling him how sexy he is and why I think so. Which makes me see him as even sexier, which makes me feel sexier. You know, that magic thing. And we've been sleeping naked, which has done amazing things for our love life. I feel wonderful."

• • •

At Diedra's that afternoon Jenny asked to speak. "I've been focusing on the sexual part of my relationship, which brings up an old worry of mine. I'd like to know what you have to say about monogamy."

"You must have been reading my mind because that's today's topic. But first, let's see how everyone's week went. How many of you were inspired to buy new lingerie?"

All three raised their hands. "Good for you. Does anyone have anything to say about that? I'm fishing here."

Diedra smiled.

"Well, I bought a pair of thong panties." Beth blushed. "I thought they would be uncomfortable, but they're not and I have to admit that I do feel sexy in them."

"That's what I'd hoped you'd say. Seductive lingerie is like taking a magic potion, whether there's a man in your life or not. It changes you instantly.

"So, ladies…you want to talk about monogamy? Well, I don't think it's natural for people to be completely monogamous." There was dead silence. "But I think most men and women like the concept.

"Here's the Secret you need to know about monogamy." She put the card on the easel:

Secret #5
Men have high hopes for monogamy.

"Because we aren't focused on survival, we have the luxury of choosing our partners for love. There's no better way to deepen love than monogamy. That's its greatest value. When you have that kind of commitment to each other, you become more bonded than in any other way. Physical intimacy is a powerful force. When you promise each other that you'll share it with no one else, you have the opportunity to reach unbelievable heights of spirituality and loving. Unfortunately, I don't think most people know how to take full advantage of this God-given opportunity.

"But the instinct to mate with more than one partner is strong, especially for men. The desire to have sex has a lot to do with the primal drive to procreate, but I think it's mostly unconscious. Biologically, men can mate with and impregnate many women in, say, the nine-month period it takes for a baby to gestate.

"Within the men we love is a primal drive to mate with many women and pass on their seed. But most men admit that sex is better when there's love. That's our highly evolved spirit, rising above our primal selves. When people can focus on personal fulfillment they have the luxury of choosing their partners for love. And love is a pretty nice feeling, worth working for, and even sacrificing for.

"Most people want to be monogamous when they marry. But men are easily aroused through visual stimulation, and they like variety. It's amazing that men are willing to be monogamous at all, but they are."

Diedra continued. "Polygyny works in cultures where it's the accepted form of marriage. Men want sex pretty regularly, and if a woman is pregnant or nursing for up to two or three years—as in many cultures—she's not really available or even very interested. With another wife, the husband has an available partner. Also, men can procreate for many years more than a woman, so he can choose a younger, stronger woman to serve his needs for sex and procreation even though he's aging. As older wives age, they're often happy to let the younger woman take over the 'chore' of sex. I say chore because love is probably not the reason they marry. And with multiple wives, a woman won't get thrown out to fend for herself, as often happens today with the way we practice serial monogamy."

"I don't like what you're saying," Jenny said. "It's not at all romantic. I don't think Brad is that way."

With a gentle tone, Diedra explained, "Jenny, you can create romance with the Secrets. I realize that's what you want, and it's what your husband wants too. That's why he chose to marry you. He wants the deeper kind of loving as much as you do. What I'm trying to tell you is that monogamy is going against deep biological drives that

have been with us from the beginning of human existence. Our social systems and spiritual desires have evolved, and most of us are blessed with not having to focus on survival. Today, men and women both choose monogamy when they marry. But natural instincts are strong. I just want you to fully appreciate that. It's a significant part of understanding men. I'll get to what you need to do to better insure a monogamous relationship."

"Why does it bother us so much if cheating is so natural?" Carol asked.

"Well, I think it goes back to survival. If a man has sex with another woman, he might leave the first wife and her children. If the hunter leaves, she and her children might die. And if *she* cheats, he might have to care for another man's child. I'm always impressed with a man who is willing to take on another man's children. It's one thing to work to support his own, but, when they're not his, he's an exceptional man.

"Today, love and bonding are an important part of the exclusive pact of monogamy. Because of the promises you make to each other—plus all the fairy tale expectations that are part of our picture of marriage—it feels like your heart is being torn out when your partner cheats. The emotional aspect is very important. Even if a woman doesn't really know the man she's having sex with, she needs to at least pretend that he cares. Men instinctively know that women's hearts are connected to sex, so it hurts them deeply when their wives cheat. A man can, more easily, be in love with his wife and have sex with another woman without it meaning anything. He can plant his seed and move on. But women don't understand, because their experience is usually so deeply emotional.

"Let's not forget how important you are to your

husband. You are his confidant, his nurturer, and the person who holds his heart in your hands. That's a powerful position. He doesn't want to lose that to another man."

"So, where does that leave us?" Jenny sighed. "I was so elated when I arrived but now I'm feeling kind of sick."

Diedra apologized. "I didn't mean to take away from your fun, but this is a subject that had to come up sooner or later. It's too big a topic. Let's have some tea and come back to it in a bit, shall we?"

*I wasn't kissing her, I was
whispering in her mouth.*
– Chico Marx

Most men freely admit that they like being married and having family, hearth, and home, and the emotional security that those elements bring, plus, they hope, a steady supply of sex. That's why so many men choose marriage. Women hold the key to all of that. Men don't want to jeopardize their marriages, but they often do, because their need for sex, intimacy, and sometimes variety, is too great.

Men feel important, special, and manly with the women with whom they have their affairs. Their wives see every aspect of them and often let them know they're nothing special or, worse yet, a disappointment as a husband and a man.

The most frequent reason men give for breaking their promise of monogamy is, "My wife lost interest in sex," or "My wife won't do certain things for me, so I need to go elsewhere." I usually ask when the interest in sex went away and most often they report that it happened when the

children arrived. How sad since children are an important reason the marriage should be stable, happy, and loving.

Many men admit they have affairs simply because they like the variety, even though things are often fine at home. What they don't admit—partly because they're unaware of it—is that they need to feel important in a woman's eyes.

Many young men get used to having a variety of partners because women are so available. For many, "scoring" is the name of the game. It's often a difficult decision for a man to "settle down" with just one woman...for the rest of his life—an ominous thought for a lot of men. Fortunately, as men age, the desire to score diminishes and they begin to care more about quality, which includes love and a deeper connection with their partners.

> **Most people assume that at some point
> in their marriage, the passion will go
> away, and they'll have to simply settle.**

People tend to settle for what they have, assuming—because that's the way most everyone else's relationships end up—that ecstatic love, romance, and passion will probably go away. If they knew how to keep the fires of love burning, there would, no doubt, be less cheating and less divorce, if for no other reason than they would never want to risk losing such a good thing.

It's an interesting aside that women are having more affairs today than in the past. There are several possible reasons for this, such as they're out in the world more; they've had more partners in their life and enjoy variety; they have greater expectations of being satisfied sexually; the passion has gone out of their marriages; the 90's

me-first go-for-it attitude; and the emotional reprieve they get from the stress of being a working woman trying to raise a family. But that's not the issue at hand; creating a dynamic relationship is.

Most men say they roam because their wives lost enthusiasm for sex.

There are many things you can do to better insure that your partner doesn't roam. A Wisconsin baker explained what many men have said, "I love my wife but it doesn't feel very good when she isn't interested in me. I wouldn't have affairs if she showed some *enthusiasm* for sex." The operative word here is enthusiasm. When a man decides to marry, he hopes his wife will fulfill all his sexual needs as well as give him the home life, emotional security, and intimacy he craves.

But what does enthusiasm mean? It means being open, willing, and eager to be spontaneous and try new things. One man, sad about his divorce, explained, "My wife had sex with me out of obligation. It was horrible. I'd pretend to have an orgasm so she'd relax. It was awful." If a woman is rigid about what's acceptable, is simply enduring sex, her husband will eventually lose interest. It's too hard on his ego. Some women know the pain of having a husband who isn't interested and know how humiliating it can be.

Men generally have a broader range of what's acceptable than women do, plus more curiosity. They have fantasies they wish their wives would, or assume their wives will not, be willing to attempt or participate in. If a woman can let go, and enjoy sex with full abandon, the lovemaking can be much more spontaneous, interesting, and vibrant. Variety is fully available.

**A couple can decide together how
to make their sex life more interesting.**

A couple should determine together what is comfortable for both of them, both physically and emotionally. It's important to have a discussion about why one is uncomfortable, so the other can be more accepting, or the boundaries can be stretched together, gently, lovingly. If one or the other feels pressured to do something that is distasteful or painful, resentments can build up. But if both partners can be flexible enough to at least consider exploring new territory, they may discover something quite wonderful.

Enthusiasm also means taking sex out of the bedroom. Flirt with your husband, play with sexual innuendo, touch him in sexual ways, encourage him to do the same, say sexy things to him. It lets him know you understand him, and you're communicating with him in a language *he* understands. You may like receiving cards with endearing poems, but, remember, sex is most often his vehicle for intimacy. Give him cards and notes that let him know you "want" him. That will be much more meaningful than something poetic. Then, you can let him know how he can communicate his love to you. How to do that will be covered in the chapter on communication, plus the "men's book" at the end of this book.

**The more physical, exciting, and
interesting your relationship, the
more he'll think about you.**

Make him wonder what surprises you're going to come up with next. Try new outfits, maybe even costumes. Almost all men love sexy lingerie, garter belts, and stockings. See if stockings with seams make you feel sexier. Save the stiletto heels for the bedroom and maybe not take them off. A wig that makes you look different can make you feel like a different woman and do things you might not otherwise do. You also get to feed his fantasies of being with someone new. As lame as you might think all this is, it works for a large majority of men.

Men have needs for sexual practices that they think you won't do, so they go to someone else to perform those acts. Sometimes a man assumes his wife won't do those things because he's never asked her, and sometimes she's made it clear that she won't. Men are often berated for their desires—which belittles them, one of the very worst things a woman can do to a man, especially regarding their sexuality. This won't change him, but it will make him keep his desires private. Is that what you want?

If you gently push the boundaries,
you'll create the passion and excitement
that will bring new life to your relationship.

If you're uncomfortable with any aspect of sex, you absolutely must honor and respect your boundaries. But, if you can begin to understand how significant a man's needs are, and remember that you're creating more intimacy with him, you can slowly broaden your attitude, be more flexible, and be more open to all the possibilities for expanding love and passion. The stronger that is, the greater guarantee for an enduring, successful relationship.

I believe that women are actually as sexual, if not

more so, than men. But society has not given women the permission to express themselves sexually. Once they let go of old thoughts and ideas and embrace the sexual being within, they can luxuriate in the ecstasy that comes from two people enjoying each other with full abandon.

A woman who learns to love herself and her body, and embraces her sexuality, is expressing her Feminine Grace and her womanly powers. This kind of woman enjoys sex and the union between herself and her partner. A self-confident woman who loves sex is the most powerful aphrodisiac a man can experience. If you are the most open, available, enthusiastic, and adventuresome lover he's ever dreamed of being with, he's a lot less likely to want to be with anyone else.

Everyone took their seats and Diedra began again. "I hope the tea made you all feel better. So, monogamy. The good news is, most men will be monogamous even when things aren't that good at home. One reason is self-respect. Men are often loyal to the promises they make. They usually know other men who have had affairs and the guilt and work of trying to keep an affair secret. Even though they may sometimes make light of it, they don't really respect another man who cheats, especially if he's got a terrific woman at home. Shame is a factor too. Men have killed themselves rather than face shame for something they've done.

"Another reason is that they don't want to risk their home life. Men like the comforts of marriage and having their children close. Their love for their wife runs deep. For many men, they do not want to put those things in jeopardy.

"Marriage serves many purposes for men. One is that they don't have to endure the pressure of dating and finding someone to have sex with. The biggest reason men give up their fantasies of having sex with many beautiful women is that they find a partner to love, with whom they can have satisfying sex. But you all know how often, in time, sex goes out the window.

"Often, a man in a less-than-thrilling marriage will bury himself in work to avoid feeling the longing that aches in his heart. Remember, if sex is bad at home, he's missing out on his primary source of intimacy. He has to put his energies somewhere, to cope with his disappointment and feelings of rejection.

"Because we know men sometimes wander, it's easy to become jealous; but men need to feel you trust them. It has to do with their stature as men. Jealousy eventually kills love. And it's an unattractive behavior. If you don't trust your partner, why are you with him? Jealousy takes a lot of energy. Trusting does not. Trust allows the relationship to flow and the love to grow. The more a man feels this trust, the less likely he is to violate it. If you don't trust him, you can't respect him. And why would you be with someone you can't respect?

"The best way to insure your husband or boyfriend stays monogamous is—first and foremost—to develop your Feminine Grace so you can, with complete self-assurance, self-respect, and personal choice, understand and accept him as he is; appreciate him, especially for his masculine qualities; don't complain; don't try to change him; stay attractive and interesting; and be enthusiastically available for sex.

"You'll become more than his dream come true. He'll find you irresistible, and fall in love with you all over again."

"It's interesting," Beth offered, "that I've known all that you've said, but somehow the way you explain it makes me understand. I guess knowing doesn't necessarily equal understanding. Thank you."

Diedra took her hand. "I'm happy that you're learning all of this before you marry. You'll get to start off with an advantage over most women. Next week we'll talk about why men need to feel successful, which will make you see even more clearly why men and women are so different."

Men convince themselves that one special woman will be able to fulfill all their erotic expectations, be perpetually sexual and attractive, and satisfy them always. Yes, it's a very tall order, and no, it's not "fair" to women. Of course it's unrealistic…but that's the way it works. (Interesting…as frequently as this "self-deception" is pointed out, especially in the media, it persists just as strongly as ever.) Why? Because of the miraculous and inexplicable magic of love. The adage "love is blind" is the simple and obvious proof. When we love we are transformed; we see the one we love through different eyes, "blind" to imperfections, feeling that yes, this person is different than all the others.

This is why you don't need to fret over looking like a centerfold. A woman's attitude, enthusiasm (again), self-confidence, and openness to sex, her total surrender and genuine passion for a man, will make her, in his eyes, more than "enough." And even more desirable than a centerfold.

It doesn't take much, really, but it's far too important to ignore. It can be done if you want it badly enough.

• • •

4 things you can do:

✓ Write down four things you like and four things you don't like about sex. Determine how you can turn the "don't likes" into "likes." Then, write down what you wish you were more comfortable doing. Try to figure out why you're uncomfortable. Ask yourself if you can possibly give yourself permission to try those things. Finally, write down what you absolutely refuse to do. Determine why you won't.

✓ Now, if you're comfortable enough, talk to your partner about what you've discovered about yourself. Explain to him that you want to bring new life into your physical relationship. He'll most likely support you in your efforts.

✓ Discuss how your attitudes and behavior are affecting his sexual feelings toward you and yours toward him. This can be a touchy conversation, so use your Feminine Grace and remind yourself that the reason you're having the conversation is to expand the love and passion between you and your lover. Another option is to use a therapist or couples counselor to have this discussion.

✓ If you're single, do the exercise; then discuss what you've discovered with a trusted friend. The more you understand yourself, the more freedom you have. The more freedom you have, the happier and more beautiful you'll be. The happier and more beautiful you are, the more desirable and attractive you are to the men you meet. If you want a man to come into your life, you'll definitely improve your odds when you flow with self-love and Feminine Grace.

A note to single women: It's important to guard yourself sexually. When you have sex with a man too soon two things happen. First, you run the risk of becoming

emotionally bonded to him, before you know he's the right man for you. A big mistake.

The second is that men *do* lose respect for you if you go to bed with them too quickly. They admit they will almost always say yes to sex, but they're often disappointed in the woman if they're genuinely interested in her. Yes, it's a double standard, but it serves you in the long run. Wait till you both care enough to think this might be the real thing and you'll start out on firmer ground.

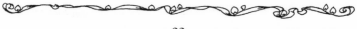

Chapter Seven
Why men need to feel successful.

Secret #6
To a man, failure is "death."

The walk to Diedra's each week had become a favorite time for our three maidens. They got to be girls, chattering away, excited by the changes that were occurring in their lives. And, though they had been friends for many years, the meetings were bringing them closer together. The Settling was a thing of the past because they had hopes and dreams once again, they knew they were actually the strong ones in their relationships with men, and they felt empowered from the choices they were making.

Carol posed a question. "Have you noticed any changes in how you feel about yourself?"

Beth answered first. "I've been thinking about that a lot lately. This Feminine Grace idea has gotten inside of me. I'm thinking differently and naturally doing things in a more beautiful way. All my attitudes are changing."

"Yes, me too," Jenny added. "Choosing how I want to be makes me feel strong.

"The other day I was trying to buy some flowers for my garden and I couldn't get anyone to help me. I was beginning to get agitated. Then I remembered Feminine Grace. So I smiled, which immediately made me feel better, walked around till I found a salesclerk, and, even though I was on the edge of being upset, with as much charm as I could muster, I asked him to help me. I was open, friendly, and appreciated him. And you know what? He couldn't do enough for me. He was really sweet. Then he practically begged to carry everything to my car. It felt great.

"If I'd allowed myself to get mad, the salesman would have been upset, and I would have gone away feeling ugly. I like how Diedra calls it ugly. I took full responsibility for how I was responding, instead of blaming someone else. It's a matter of, 'How do I want to feel when I walk away?' I can be ugly or beautiful; like Diedra says, I get to choose."

"I've been having those same kinds of experiences," Beth said. "What I'm noticing is when I choose to do things with grace I feel completely in charge. Like I'm this superwoman, kind of bigger than life. Does that make sense?"

Carol smiled. "Absolutely. I'm feeling the same thing. I'm less often reacting emotionally to what goes on around me. It's like I'm standing back and watching myself. It gives me time to choose how I want to be. And the best part is I'm feeling more joyful and light."

Arriving at Diedra's cottage, the old woman from the first week opened the door and led them to the back room. Today they were surprised to see Diedra's husband standing next to her.

"Welcome, everyone!" Diedra was beaming. "Do you notice how different it feels to have a man in our presence?"

Everyone nodded. They had all met Michael at different times in the front part of the house, but this was

the first time he'd been in their space. It felt odd.

Michael lifted his arms to make muscles for the women and everyone laughed. "I don't quite know what you're feeling," he said, "but I know how it feels when a woman walks into a room that's considered men's domain. Men and women are different…in some pretty nice ways." He reached over and put his arm around Diedra's waist. "Diedra likes me to come in at this stage and say a few things."

They all took their seats and Michael sat on the arm of Diedra's chair.

"Mostly, I want to thank you for taking this class. Every man who gets to interact with you from now on will enjoy the experience, because you're going to stand out as someone unique and special. We men are aware of how uncomfortable women can be around us, so it's always nice to be with a woman who's comfortable with herself —because that puts us at ease. Plus we enjoy any experience with a woman who's being beautiful.

"We like it when you look us directly in the eye, when you speak clearly and with conviction, and we especially like it when you're happy. A happy woman who's comfortable with herself…well, it's about as attractive as you can be. So, keep up the good work. The men in your lives will be forever grateful. I can't imagine not having this woman in my life." Michael gave Diedra another squeeze and waved good-bye.

Diedra began. "I know you all have stories to tell but I want to get started on an important topic. I'll give you a little extra time during the break to let me know how your week went.

"Today we're going to talk about success. Here's the next Secret." The women read the card.

Secret #6
To a man, failure is "death."

"At their core, men need to feel successful…at everything. If we go back to prehistoric man again, we can get an idea just how important it is. His work was that of a hunter. If he failed, he and his family starved. Today, men still carry that primal drive to succeed. Their instincts tell them that failure is equivalent to death. Women complain that men spend too much time at work, that they're exhausted from the emotional or physical strain, they don't help out at home enough, and that they don't care about their wives and families. Little do they realize that most of the reason men work is to support their families. When she complains, he feels she doesn't appreciate his efforts, so he's demoralized. Eventually he becomes emotionally numb, or he leaves."

"Wow. I see why Thomas has been responding so dramatically to my appreciation," Carol said, closing her eyes. "All the years I've been married, especially since the children arrived—which was also when I quit working—I've been complaining to Thomas that he works too much."

"Carol, it's understandable that you would complain. You want to see him more, you want him to be more available to you and your children, you want his help at home, and you don't want to see him putting so much pressure on himself. When the hunter brought home the kill, everyone could see what he'd accomplished and lavished their thanks and praise on him. It was immediate. What your husband brings home is a little piece of paper with numbers on it. He's often too exhausted to give you the attention you crave—because, remember, you don't have the community of women around you all day—and he rarely feels appreciated. If you work outside of the home, you know what that exhaustion feels like and you know what it's like to not feel appreciated. If he brought home a big slab of meat every day and you knew your survival depended on it, you'd be cheering for him. Because he goes away every day and you don't see him working, you don't see the fruits of his labor directly, you're not able to fully appreciate all that he does."

Diedra let this sink in. "The difference between men and women regarding career is that *a man's job is how he identifies himself as a man*. Women can care greatly about their careers but they're more autonomous from what they do; it's not *who* they are like it is for a man. Overall, women identify more with their relationships: relationships with other women, with their families, their children, and with their romantic partner.

"Much of what it means to be a man has to do with comparing himself to other men. The prehistoric man was part of a team. He hunted with his friends. Everyone knew how good or bad a hunter he was. They played games, honing their skills at teamwork. Their physical strength and talents were compared and judged. Games also helped them create camaraderie. Hunting was a potentially life-threatening activity. They needed to be able to work well together and to count on each other.

"Not every man gets to be the lead hunter, or even in the top ten. So being part of a team helps a man feel part of the whole. If he does his job well, he feels like he fits in. Because most men grow up being part of a team, they're good at supporting each other and they're loyal. In war, they'll give their lives for each other. To be part of a winning team, even though he's not the quarterback, allows a man the opportunity to be a winner, to be successful. If the company has good earnings, or rises in the marketplace, he gets a piece of the rewards by being a part of the team.

"Of course, men are also competitive, for which they're often maligned by women. Men know where they are in the hierarchy. Competition keeps a man sharp, alert, and trying harder. The young man who became part of the hunting team could compete and rise to become number one hunter some day. But today, it's more complicated. A man can lose his job in a flash. The hunter risked his life on occasion, but no one was going to fire him, unless he was a menace to the team.

"Today's man can lose his investments overnight. He feels the pressure of what car he drives, what neighborhood he lives in, how big his house is, what schools his children go to, and what social circle he moves in. Along with all of that is a mountain of debt that he knows he must pay off, often for years to come. These pressures can be a heavy burden, on his ego and on his need to provide for his family. How well he 'succeeds' at these things adds up to how he perceives himself as a man.

"Are you beginning to see how the need for success is in a man's blood?" Diedra asked. "It's *who* he is. We often have those same desires, but it isn't a reflection of who we are as women. Our beauty is the closest thing that compares, but we don't usually lie awake at night worrying about it and it doesn't give us heart attacks."

Beth raised her hand. "I always thought competition and the drive to succeed was selfish and uncaring."

"Competition is both burden and pleasure," Diedra said. "Men need to compete, to spend time together, to succeed. They need to be part of a team and swap stories. Women are always amazed how men remember scores

and plays from a sporting event that took place years earlier." She laughed. "Men can't help it, it's in their blood. Of course, we remember exactly what our prom dress looked like." They all smiled in agreement.

"Men often continue to identify themselves by the glories of their sporting success—sometimes as far back as high school. For many, it was the only time they ever experienced real success. They were praised, appreciated by their classmates and fellow players and got to feel heroic. They cling to those glories as a drowning person clings to a life preserver.

"Encourage your husbands to do things with their male friends. Male bonding is the closest they generally come to being intimate with other men, even if it's just to share a few beers and cheer for their team."

"Well, I resent how much time Brad spends with his friends," Jenny said. "I've told him it's not okay but he does it anyway. I think it's silly and really rude."

"First, I need you to set aside your resentment or you won't hear what I'm saying. There are several elements to your reaction," Diedra responded. "First, you and Brad have lost some respect for each other, which you're now rebuilding, so you're less giving and more easily agitated. I hope you're beginning to realize how much good he gets from being with his friends. When he's with them he rejuvenates his male energy. He comes back to you in better spirits. Most men will admit that they enjoy being with their friends, but there's nothing that compares to being with the woman they love.

"Now that you understand him better you can encourage him to spend time with his men friends, which will make him appreciate you. That turns into him wanting to spend more time with you. You both win.

"You've told us how you complain, and how you

blame him. As you replace those habits with appreciation and affection, he'll transform—as he's already beginning to do—into a more loving, attentive man. Is he really being rude, or are you simply feeling hurt? That's where your feminine intuition comes into play. Only you can know for sure. It can be difficult to be honest with yourself. If you follow the Secrets, you'll be able to work this out. The goal is for you *both* to be happy.

"Although many women have dreams of becoming successful in their careers, most women—at least at some point in their lives—have hopes and dreams about 'happily ever after.' Men's primary dreams are those of being successful in work or making a lot of money. It's so important to them that they measure most of their self-worth against it. Lack of success often triggers a man's mid-life crisis. When he realizes that he's going to fall short of his life goals, he often goes into a tailspin that can last for years, sometimes even cause him to commit suicide.

"Rarely do men share those deep feelings of failure with anyone else. They suffer in silence, often drinking more, using drugs, womanizing, or growing numb to all feelings. Many men divorce and go to a younger woman in their time of crisis. A new lover thinks he's wonderful. More than lost youth—which is certainly a part of it—is the need to feel successful and important. A woman has the power to help him override all other measures of success."

Beth asked, "What if a man just isn't successful? What can a woman do then?"

"Good question, Beth. There's an important role women can play in their husband's lives. They can make them feel successful at home. That way, he can have some part of his life that he feels good about. A woman can let her husband know he's a good father and husband and appreciate how

hard he works. That she appreciates having him in her life. That he's a great lover. That he's wonderful, special, and unique. She becomes terribly important to him then."

Diedra sat back for a moment. "Deeper than that is how good he feels about himself as a man. We've talked about the ways you can help him with that. This may sound like his are the only needs that matter, but this whole conversation is really about both of your needs being met. Your primary sense of self is through all of your relationships—as a mother, a friend, and a wife and lover; his is his success as a man. If you help him feel great about how good a man he is, he'll become that prince we keep talking about, which will help you get your romantic needs met in your relationship.

"I'm telling you what you can do to support a man because I know, as women, you're capable of it. You have the power and the grace to work these miracles. He doesn't. It's simply not in him unless he's one of those rare naturally romantic types.

"The bottom line is, the more successful they feel, the better they feel, and the more energy they have to be with you and love you. If you've become a joyful woman filled with Feminine Grace you can do all these things effortlessly…because they come from love."

There is no loneliness greater
than the loneliness of a failure.
The failure is a stranger in his
own house.
— Eric Hoffer

Men have specific areas in their lives where they can shine. Career is usually the primary source of reward, of feeling successful. A second area is athletic achievement. Many men never give up their glory days. On several occasions, just to test this idea, I've purposefully asked men about their early athletic achievements. They change. They get animated, excited…they come alive and then, as they finish the conversation, they get nostalgic.

You may be married to a man who still has his clippings, trophies—you may have asked him why he hangs on to that old stuff—and scars, and talks about his athletic accomplishments as if they occurred yesterday.

A third area where, actually, you can have the most effect, is how he feels about his masculinity. Your power is far-reaching. He wants to impress you in every way imaginable; he wants to be a great lover for you; he wants to protect you, provide for you, and make you happy. Because of all that, women often see men as pumped-up egomaniacs, strutting around like peacocks. To a degree it's true, but they shouldn't be put down for it. It's simply a primal reaction to women they find attractive, and, more importantly, women they care for. Rather, women should be flattered—unless, of course, a man is being rude and obnoxious. Then, and only then, is it fair to put him in his place. But even then, determine your response through the lens of Feminine Grace. How do you want to feel when you walk away from the encounter? Beautiful or ugly?

Women don't realize how easily they emasculate men.

Women have the power to deflate men. Sometimes they do it purposefully, but often they do it unknowingly. If you're

still reading this book, it's a fair assumption that you like men and are responding positively to the Secrets thus far. If that's the case, you'll be surprised to know how easily you can emasculate a man, and certainly you won't want to do so in the future...ever again.

The *American Heritage Dictionary* defines emasculation as: 1. *To castrate.* 2. *To deprive of strength or vigor; weaken; render effeminate.* Is that anything you would ever want to do to the man you love? Of course not. There's no Feminine Grace in that. But following are some ways in which you may be doing it, albeit unknowingly:

1. You belittle, ridicule, or embarrass him, especially in front of his children, family, friends, or colleagues.
2. You're insensitive when you turn him down for sex.
3. You withhold or give sex as a weapon of control.
4. You let him know you don't need him.
5. You treat him like an incompetent child.
6. You blame him for being overly sexual.
7. You make him feel as if he's a failure, especially by comparing him unfavorably to other men.
8. You demean him sexually by belittling or mocking his lovemaking and romantic skills.
9. You mock or tease him about his body, appearance, clothing, age, intelligence, or especially the size of his penis.
10. You tell male-bashing jokes in front of him.
11. You try to be a better man than he is.

Every time you do any of these things, you whittle away at his masculinity. And each time, he withdraws a little more. Originally, when he was first attracted to you, you made him feel virile and masculine, like Superman. That's why he pursued you. And you thought he was wonderful. But as you got to know him, the illusion of perfection began to lose—as it inevitably does—some of its luster, and you began to see his imperfections. As that happened, you possibly began to say or do one or more of those things on the above list. With each insult, a man withdraws a little and fortifies his defensive walls. If you make a regular habit of it, he'll either tend to strike back at you or begin to shut down completely. Often, the man who isn't interested in you sexually has been emasculated, either by you or society.

Men usually respond to attempts at emasculation with feigned indifference; they tend to avoid reacting visibly because if they make a big deal of it, others might think it's true. But underneath, they're damaged a little, hurt and angry.

There's no equivalent of emasculation for women, so a man's way is to abuse a woman either verbally or physically, or both. WARNING! I am *not* saying that physical or vicious verbal abuse of any woman is her fault. If a man does either or both, the capacity was already there and he's evil for doing it. I *am* saying that to emasculate any man can exacerbate an already volatile situation. Most men are aware of their potential for anger and have a healthy respect for it. If women's emasculation of men angers them enough, most will remove themselves from the situation. The point is, it is by far the worst thing a woman can do to a man, and the quickest way to damage, even destroy, his love. It is the antithesis of everything you're learning to do in this book.

You have the power to make your man feel successful.

The media creates exorbitantly high standards of success by

focusing on the small percentage of men who are heads of corporations, professional athletes, or film and music stars. Advertisements bombard men and their families with all the high image and expensive products that people have come to believe are necessary for a comfortable, happy life. Consequently many men don't feel successful by today's skewed standards. Women can counter much of that pressure by making their partners feel successful at home.

But what if he's not really doing a good job at home? What if he never helps out? What if he ignores the kids? What if he ignores you? If you still care, and want to renew your love, you, and only you, can improve your relationship. As you develop a stronger sense of self and act more from Feminine Grace, you'll be able to use the Twelve Simple Secrets more effectively. Give him time and he should begin to be more attentive to you. As far as helping around the house goes, appreciate him for anything he does. If you've been complaining, stop! It obviously hasn't helped and it's ugly behavior. If he brings an empty glass into the kitchen, appreciate him. And, if it feels right, give him a little kiss, maybe slightly longer than he'd expect. This may feel manipulative, but remember that you're trying to behave with Feminine Grace and that you'll *both* be happier if you can bring him around to becoming your prince.

If he ignores the kids, sit them down and give them a talk about all that he does, how he works hard every day and that no one thanks him. Explain the power of being acknowledged and appreciated. They'll then begin to appreciate him. Teach them to show him respect and to let him know they're glad he's their dad and that he works so hard for them. Teach them how to ask him to help them, talk with them, and play with them. Only the most insensitive man will not be touched. Respect, appreciation, affection, and love can soften even the hardest of hearts.

As John Gray points out in *Men Are from Mars, Women Are from Venus*, men need time to transition from work and the commute to being home. If the family gives him love and doesn't ask for anything until he's settled in, he'll be more open to participating with the family. Remember, men don't focus well on more than one thing at a time. It's a simple matter of understanding. As a happily married man from Seattle put it, "The love that I receive from my family sustains me. It's what life is all about."

• • •

5 things you can do:

✓ Make a list of ten ways you think your husband or boyfriend is successful and all the things he does well. Then remind yourself to appreciate him for each item on your list.

✓ Make a list of five to ten ways you see him as "unsuccessful" and the ways he does not meet your expectations. Ask yourself why you feel that way and if your expectations are realistic and fair. Is it a comparison to someone else? Does he not provide at the level you think he should? Notice how it makes you feel to think these things about the man you've chosen to love and build a life with. Determine how you can turn those thoughts around so you can see him as a successful, wonderful man. Write your discoveries in your binder.

✓ Make a list of at least four ways you have emasculated your husband or boyfriend. If you find yourself doing it again, stop! Ask yourself why you feel the need to strike out that way. Is there anger, resentment, or frustration that

you don't know how to communicate directly? Do you want to hurt him? Or is it just a habit? Write your thoughts in your binder.

✓ If you've been making him feel unsuccessful or emasculated, have a discussion about how you didn't realize you were doing it and how you don't want to hurt him anymore. Let him know you appreciate him. This may be a difficult conversation but it could be one of the most healing conversations the both of you will ever have, especially if you've been together for a long time.

✓ For you to want to make the Secrets work, you've got to feel good about yourself and good about the level of respect and caring you receive from your partner. The above discussion is a good time to bring up how you've been feeling. The most effective way to tell someone something bad about how they've been behaving is to begin with a compliment and appreciation. Then, never say "you," but keep the focus on "I." Point out how you're feeling. Maybe your partner is disrespectful toward you. Tell him how it makes you *feel*. Tell him you sometimes wonder if he cares and how *that* makes you feel. If you focus on your feelings and don't blame him, he'll be more open to what you have to say, less defensive. Begin by saying something like, "I'm sure you don't realize it's going on, but sometimes I feel like..." Then give him a problem to solve by asking him if he has any suggestions for making things better for you. If you don't like his suggestion, acknowledge it with appreciation by saying something like, "That's an interesting idea. I wonder if it might work if... What do you think?" Work through the conversation with an attitude of caring teamwork and eventually, he'll come to be your hero.

Here's a tip. Try to avoid the word *but*. No matter what

follows it, if you say *but,* it negates everything that precedes it. How would you hear this: You're so beautiful, *but* you'd look better if your hair was curlier. Would you focus on the first part of that comment or what followed the *but?* Instead of *but,* say *and.* Feel the difference: You're so beautiful *and* if your hair was curlier, you'd be even more beautiful. The first example causes defensiveness and the second causes openness. This works in all arenas.

When any of the above conversations are complete, appreciate him for listening so attentively, for caring enough to want to make things better, or whatever is appropriate. *You* have the power to control where the conversation goes. Use your Feminine Grace, be clear and concise, and thoughtfully select each word so your meaning gets transmitted correctly. He *will* pay attention because Feminine Grace makes him *want* to please you. But don't forget to be patient. Give it time because you may have some bad habits that need undoing.

Chapter Eight
Why men are driven to make women happy.

Secret #7
If you're not happy, he's a failure.
Secret #8
Men show their love through action.

It was the seventh week of classes as Carol, Beth, and Jenny took their places on the sofa. "Okay, girls, catch me up. How are the Secrets working in your lives?" Diedra leaned back in her chair, ready for the news.

"I must tell you that I was a bit resentful in the beginning of these classes," Carol confessed. "I wanted my relationship to be better, of course, but it seemed so one-sided, like I had to do all the work. But I figured it couldn't get any worse between Thomas and me, so I went along.

"Now that I've been doing what you say and using the Secrets I can see how it's really up to me, but he's following along, just as you said he would. Not only has it been easy, it's been fun.

"He seems to be getting more relaxed with me and I'm beginning to feel his love more. I don't mean like

fireworks; that's not us. It's like he's content and happy. He's gentle with me, and thoughtful. There's no tension, no disharmony like there used to be. I find I'm softer, rarely agitated, and everyone around me is more pleasant. Don't get me wrong, there *have* been times when I've gotten angry, but I made myself understood through Feminine Grace and not by losing control. I've felt empowered, rather than disappointed in myself. Each time it's happened, I've been able to be heard, so I can make my point. Being the kind of woman you're teaching us to be is definitely a more powerful way to be. Another thing is that I don't have so many expectations. I have a more realistic picture of Thomas, so I don't get as upset as I used to."

"The concept of Feminine Grace is the key," Jenny agreed. "I'm making smarter decisions and interacting with people in a more centered, confident way. I'm not letting my emotions take over. The other day Brad bought some stupid new golf club for two hundred and fifty dollars and I got angry. Instead of saying anything to Brad, I called Beth and vented. When I calmed down, I went to Brad and told him that I was upset that he bought something so expensive without talking it over with me. I stayed calm, though, and we ended up having an open, respectful conversation. Together we decided we need to tell each other when we want to spend more than two hundred dollars on something. Before these classes, that would have been a totally different conversation. We both would have gotten angry, said things we'd be sorry about, and not resolved the problem. With each passing week I've felt more in charge of my life."

Diedra smiled. "None of you have serious relationship problems to contend with, so the Secrets are working fairly quickly. Most relationships simply get bogged down

in The Settling. You settle for ordinary when you could be getting exceptional. The irritations, resentments, and hurt feelings can slow down the process, but with patience—as long as the desire to reignite the love is still there—the relationship can improve dramatically.

"When the problems are more severe, sometimes people are so hurt and defensive that they can't overcome the damage that's been done. That's when Feminine Grace and intuition can help a woman gather her strength and make the decision to leave a situation she knows isn't going to improve. It's scary, but women do it every day and move on to better lives."

"Beth, what's been happening with *you?*"

"Well, I'm mostly trying to act with more Feminine Grace. Because I'm choosing how I am, I feel stronger than I used to. I'm marveling at how empowering it is to become aware of my feminine side. Thinking it makes me *become* it. And I'm having lots of fun. I love the attention I'm getting from men. It feels like they see me as a more complete person. They're more respectful and they seem genuinely interested in me. And the man I'm seeing is wonderfully attentive."

"You should all be proud. You've been very brave. You've taken charge of your lives on every level. Today I'm going to share two Secrets with you. The first is: If you're not happy, he's a failure." Diedra put the card with the Secret in front of them.

Secret #7
If you're not happy, he's a failure.

"Last week," Diedra said, "we talked about how important success is to a man. If the ancient hunter was successful at his job, he brought his 'kill' home for his mate. That's how he made her happy. And if he was successful among his peers, her pride made him feel good. He equated his success to her being happy.

"Men today aren't that much different. If you're happy, he feels successful, whether or not he had anything to do with it. If he feels successful, he feels good about himself. When he feels good about himself, especially if you're part of the reason he's feeling good, you're more attractive, more beautiful, and more important to him. You become a catalyst for his good feelings. When he connects feeling good to you, he's going to be more attentive and caring.

"But—and I want you to hear this—*he* should not be responsible for making you happy. That's *your* job. If you need an outside source to make you happy, then you're going to be constantly disappointed. It's those expectations Carol was talking about. Loving yourself and connecting to the universal source of love is a direct link to happiness. Happiness is not a destination but a way of traveling. It can become your usual frame of mind if you're willing to cultivate it. How you react to the people around you, how you react to situations that come up in your life, and how happy you are is entirely *your* responsibility."

"Diedra," Jenny said, "I've been struggling with what you're saying, but now I've got to speak up. When someone is mean or rude to me, I'm going to respond to them by getting rude or worse. They asked for it; it's *their* fault I get mad."

"I'm sorry, Jenny, but how you react is up to *you*. Yes, they may trigger your anger but you can *choose* whether or not you lose control and get angry. You have the choice to take a moment, gather yourself, then respond as a powerful

woman who's in control of herself and the situation. Then you get to make your point, and in return you get to be beautiful. *That's real power.* You can rant and rave and let your emotions fly when you're alone or with a trusted friend. You don't want to hold those in, but you don't want to be out of control in the presence of the person you're angry at because you'll give away all of your power. You can let someone know you're angry *and* still stay in control."

"I don't see how I could possibly do that," Jenny said. "I don't think it's good to hold anger in."

"I'm not saying to hold it in. Here's an example of what I mean: Let's say that you have a dinner date with Brad. He's supposed to be home at six-thirty, so he can get cleaned up for your seven-thirty reservation. You've been looking forward to it, so you put on a dress you know he likes and do your hair. You're feeling particularly good.

"It's six-forty-five, he's not home yet, and he hasn't called. You're beginning to get irritated. At five to seven, you begin to get angry. You hear his car coming up the drive; then he comes in the door. How are you going to react?"

"First, I'd let him know how inconsiderate and rude he was," Jenny replied. "Then I'd probably raise my voice, let him know how much trouble I'd gone to to be ready on time, how disappointed I was, and make him call the restaurant to tell them we'd be late."

"Okay, how would *he* react to all to that?"

Jenny thought for a moment. "He'd get all huffy, not take any responsibility, not apologize, and tell me he didn't want to go out at all."

"So, Jenny, what would you gain?" Diedra asked.

"I'd get to let him know how I felt. Hopefully I'd get him to think twice before he did that again."

Diedra smiled. "How about if I make up a different scenario? You're ready to go to dinner and he's late. You choose not to take it personally, assuming there were circumstances you are as yet unaware of. You decide to call the restaurant and tell them to make the reservation for eight. You find that book you've been meaning to get to, and sit in the living room to wait. He shows up at five to seven. He walks in, you look up and say, 'Hi, where have you been?' He apologizes, 'I'm sorry, I got a last minute phone call; then there was traffic. I'll hurry and get ready.' You say, 'I changed the reservation to eight, so relax. I'll wait here and read.' He says, 'Thanks. You're terrific.'

"Now you're at dinner. You're enjoying yourself, but you need to let him know that you were not happy that he was late. You could say, 'You know, Brad, I was looking forward to dinner all day. It was fun getting ready. Like a real date. And this evening has been wonderful. When you were late though, I almost got mad. But I decided I didn't want to ruin our evening, so I changed the reservation, got my book out, and waited. When you're late, I feel like I don't matter. Do you have any ideas?' Remember, men like to solve problems, so if you let him come up with a solution that will make you happy, you both win. He's going to be more understanding—and less defensive. It's very powerful. Then he would probably say something like, 'You're absolutely right. Next time, how about I call you the moment I know I'm going to be running late? And thanks for being so understanding.'

"Could you imagine doing it that way, and having him respond like that?"

"Yes...and it would be such a nicer way to do it. It almost makes me want to have a problem come up so I can try this." Jenny laughed. "I really see your point."

Diedra nodded. "It's a matter of being in control of your emotions, your actions, and your communication. If you get angry and make someone wrong, they're going to get defensive. It takes concentrated practice, but with work, you can become a master at enhancing all your relationships. The better you get at choosing how you react and respond, the happier you'll be. Trust me on this. When you're happy, he's happy. Your relationship then has more room for love to grow."

The Woman-Soul leadeth us
Upward and on!
– Johann Wolfgang von Goethe

"We want to make you happy. Just tell us how." Men say this over and over in my seminars and in private interviews, but women don't realize men really do mean it or how important it is to them.

"There's nothing more attractive than a happy woman. I can't help myself—I'm drawn to her like a magnet." Fred, a real estate developer, echoes what men across the country have told me. Men want the women they're involved with to be happy, but when women complain and want more and more, the men get frustrated and worn out from the burden of trying to make them happy.

Yes, men want you to be happy. But happiness comes from within. If you want your relationship—and, actually, your entire life—to improve, becoming a shining light of happiness is one of the best things you can do. If you're generally happy:

1. You're less likely to become irritated at the challenges that you deal with each day.

2. You're more pleasant to be with.
3. You make others feel good because happiness rubs off.

When you're happy, you're in a state of choice, rather than reaction. You can be graceful and tough, or graceful and soft, depending on the situation.

You can learn to be happy.

Wanting to be happy and knowing how are not inclusive. There are many things you can do to improve your level of happiness, but, for now, here are several "tricks" you can use whenever you find yourself not feeling happy.

First, develop an *inner* smile. Close your eyes, allow a soft smile to settle on your face, and then turn it inward, at yourself. Notice how calm you feel. Now, let your face turn into a mild frown. Feel the difference? Make it a project to carry an inner smile all the time. With conscious practice, you can make an inner smile your habit.

Second, put an outer smile on your face. Let your teeth show; sit up straight. Then, frown and let your shoulders drop. Notice the contrast in how you feel. Everywhere you go, smile. Smile just a little, then look in the mirror. Do you look like you're smiling? If not, make it just big enough that you look happy, but not so big that people think you're crazy. Smiling changes your outlook, how you see the entire world. If you don't believe me, just try it.

Finally, try this: Begin to laugh. Laugh out loud. Keep doing it until you feel so silly that you actually start laughing for real. Now notice how you feel. This, like nothing else, *is* a magic potion.

Whenever you choose, you can change your state with a big smile or by laughing out loud. Try to find the humor

in each situation. Most things can become funny with time, so why not see the humor now? Problems will look and feel different if you're feeling good. You can handle them with a more level head, with more grace. You'll stay happier and feel a whole lot better about yourself, and you know what?…so will everyone else.

"Now I have a second Secret to give you." Diedra picked up the next card. "This one will help you better appreciate your husband's love."

Secret #8
Men show their love through action.

"This is so funny," Carol said. "Since the 'magic' of the Secrets has begun to take effect, Thomas has been fixing things around the house and he even took my car to be washed this weekend. I wondered what was going on."

Diedra laughed. "Men are outward, action-oriented. They solve problems and make things happen by using their masculine traits and abilities. They give of themselves through their actions. It's about needing to be successful hunters. The way the hunter showed his love was to bring home the kill. He had to solve the problem of survival; he took action by hunting; and when he brought meat home to his mate, he was successful. He did it for her, and he got to show he cared. It worked for them. Isn't it interesting that we still use the term 'bringing home the bacon?' This stuff is very primal.

"Today, because we've added romance to the equation,

men are often at a loss as to what to do. Romance isn't about solving a problem or using their masculine traits. It's certainly not about survival. But it *is* about a goal, which is to win you. Even though men aren't real clear about what women want, they still keep trying.

"Men usually think romance is about getting a woman ready for sex—his goal. Whereas, women see romance as a way for a man to show his love, that he cares. Women like romance simply because they like romance; it makes their hearts sing. When a man shows his love regularly, in little ways that makes a woman feel beautiful, cherished, and adored, she's more open to his sexual advances. Many men have missed this point and missed out on a lot of loving.

"Remember that for most men—being action-oriented and emotionally shut down—sex, sexual flirting, and touching is their outlet for intimacy. It's a way to *love* through *action*. But women know that men can have sex without caring for a woman so they don't always accept sex as love. And when they're being sexual, most men aren't thinking love. They admit they enjoy sex more when they love their partner, but sex isn't usually as intertwined with love—in the moment of lovemaking—as it is for women."

"Diedra, I want Brad to *tell* me he loves me. I don't really feel his love when he does things for me, or to me. Not that it isn't nice." Jenny frowned.

"Words and emotions are almost one and the same for us. When women feel emotions, they want to talk about them because it expands the experience. Most men can't relate to a woman's need to talk about what she's feeling. And because men are so busy doing, achieving, and being action-oriented, we feel like they don't love us. We need to hear the words and they don't often think to say them because their focus is outward, not inward. When they do verbalize their feelings, they're frequently uncomfortable about doing so. If you discount the things they *do* to show you their love, they feel they can't win. And when they can't win, what happens?"

"They shut down and back away." Beth sighed. "I had no idea how different men really are. There are so many adjustments I'm having to make."

"There's something you should be careful of," Diedra warned. "Pay closer attention to what a man *does* than what he *says*. Many women have been fooled by a man's words because that's what she wants to hear. If he tells you how much he wants to see you, but isn't showing up, then he probably isn't that interested."

"I understand. What you're saying about men *doing* things to show their love makes sense, but why do they *quit* doing those romantic things that they know we like so much? Like sending flowers?"

"Good question. When men are focused on achieving a goal, they stick with it until it's achieved or they've given up. For a lot of men, sending flowers is something they do because they know women like it. But it's not a masculine action. Probably the most masculine part of it is that they get to show you they can afford to buy flowers for you. They do it because they're trying to win you over and they enjoy making you happy. *You're* the goal. They're the hunters; you're the hunted. When a man knows he's 'bagged' you, then he goes on to the next goal, which—for the hunter—was providing for his mate. If you're only dating, and he feels he's accomplished his goal of winning you over—or having sex—he goes back to focusing on work. But because he's not providing for you, you're not the beneficiary of the results. And if he's not sure how he feels about you, sometimes he loses interest. That's why so many relationship experts say to play hard-to-get. I don't like games and manipulation, but there's some truth to it. I recommend you don't have sex with a man until you both are clear that you're wanting to create a long-term relationship."

"Yes, I've discovered that I get attached too soon when I have sex too early. I've learned to wait. And I don't like games either," Beth offered, "but I like it when I'm being 'hunted' because the guy is so attentive. What should I do to avoid playing games *and* keep his interest?"

"Well, he's the hunter, so remember that you're giving him pleasure by staying somewhat illusive and mysterious, out of reach. Don't be the first to tell him you love him; don't tell him his work is done, because—unless you're simply looking for someone to have fun with—it isn't. Until you feel secure that he's not going anywhere, he still has work to do to achieve his goal, *if* his goal is a permanent relationship with you.

"Don't give away every detail about yourself too soon. He'll ask you what he wants to know. Usually it has to do with what you do, how you think, and what you know, which will be mostly outward things.

"The subtle shades and nuances of your inner, emotional self are not always that interesting to a man. In fact, it can turn him off. If he asks about that part of you, then you can tell him, if you're comfortable with it, but don't go into things like how close you were to insanity the last time you became an emotional heap. That scares men, a lot. Stay beautiful and feminine. Save your less-than-graceful moments for your closest friends. They won't judge you or turn away.

"And men absolutely don't want to know about your past relationships. They may ask, but they would rather

not hear much detail. And never, ever blame the new man for what another man did to you. They hate that and it's unfair and disrespectful to them as individuals.

"We women like to talk, and we often talk about things that men aren't interested in or shouldn't be hearing. In the beginning of a relationship—and actually after you're married—do you really want the man to know what you go through to look as attractive as you do? The coloring, plucking, curling, clipping, and polishing? Of course not. That's part of the mystery. It's the same for your deep, dark secrets. It's none of his business and he would rather think this sparkly person sitting by him is always that way. He *knows* that's not the case but he prefers to see you as you are, in that moment he's admiring you.

"Men worry about women being too emotional. They don't understand it, they can't relate, and they don't know what to do when a woman is crying or being what men call 'irrational.' When you're being emotional, go to your girlfriends. Don't burden a new man with it. At least not at first. Don't give him problems he can't solve. Practice Feminine Grace. Be in charge of what you say, how you say it, and how emotional you get. Be the intelligent, wise woman that you are. Be someone he's fascinated with, someone he has regard for, and appreciates. Be honest, be yourself, but enjoy the benefits of being a fully empowered woman.

"Men are fascinated by women because they know they'll never figure them out. And they don't really want to. They want you in their lives, but they don't want you to be a burden. Feminine Grace gives you strength and power enough to step away from needing to show him how equal you are. Your self-confidence and self-comfort can let your femininity shine forth. After all, that's why you like having a man around, isn't it? So you can enjoy being a woman? When you do that, he gets to enjoy being a man.

"So, appreciate the actions he takes to show you he cares. Accept them as tributes of love. Explain to him how much you love all the things he does for you—even list them—and when he *also* tells you he loves you, tell him it's like putting the cherry on top of the ice cream sundae. Tell him it makes you feel beautiful, womanly, and special. When he sees that smile on your face, and that look in your eyes, he'll want to do it more. If you complain that 'You never tell me you love me,' you've just told him that all the things he does, including going to work every day, don't count. Plus, as I've pointed out, complaining is *always* ugly. When *you* go to work you aren't doing it because you love him. When he brings home that piece of paper, his paycheck, it's equivalent to the hunter bringing home a deer. Let him know how much you appreciate his efforts and he'll be more open to doing the romantic things you like."

"What you're teaching us is making so much sense." Carol smiled. "I feel like the mystery of what men are about is clearing up. Thank you, Diedra."

"This is truly my pleasure. I can see you all feeling more powerful and softer at the same time. That's good. Next week we're going to talk about how and why men are willing to continue to face rejection. You'll find it to be revealing. Now, go home and practice what you're learning and have fun."

7 things you can do:
✓ In your effort to become a happier woman, ask yourself

if you're a positive or negative person. Do you focus on what's *wrong* with the world and the people around you? No one likes to be around a negative person, except another negative person. Live by the adage: *If you can't say something nice, don't say anything at all.* If you *are* negative, it might take some time to notice because it's a difficult thing to admit. Just pay attention and you'll see some patterns emerge. Avoid being critical of others. It makes others unhappy, which is bound to come back to you. Wouldn't you prefer to spread feelings of love and harmony? Look for the positive and you'll develop a new habit and a new, more attractive way of being.

✓ Learn to love your body. How do you feel about your body, really? Are your self-criticisms unreasonable? There are few women who can stand naked in front of a mirror and say they love every inch of their bodies, not wanting to make at least some changes. The point is, do you focus on the imperfections? If so, you'll be self-conscious and not as nice to be around. Besides, a perfect body would be boring and *so* much trouble to maintain. As novelist Duane Unkefer wrote, "Women don't know how beautiful they don't have to be."

If a man says he loves your body just as it is, believe him, and don't ever, *ever* respond to his compliments with a *put-down of yourself*...ever...on any subject. When you do it you neutralize and discount his compliment and maybe even embarrass him and you might not get another. Receive a compliment with a "Thank you" and a smile. To be even more gracious, embellish it with something like, "How sweet [or kind, or flattering] you are to say so."

If you're not happy with some part of your body, can you do something about it? Do you need to lose weight? If so, it's probably affecting your level of happiness. To lose weight you need to change your eating habits—no dieting allowed—and begin to exercise. Both will give you a greater sense of well-being, make you feel more confident, and allow you to wear more attractive clothes.

✓ Do you like your clothes? Are they in good repair? Are they flattering? Make those repairs, throw away anything that doesn't make you feel good, and invest in a few quality items that make you feel terrific. Get a friend to help you go through your closet and help you shop.

✓ Replace your negative beliefs with empowering beliefs. Affirmations work if they come from your heart. Look at the beliefs you have about your appearance, your abilities, your education, etc., and write them down. Then sit quietly and close your eyes. When you're relaxed, create new beliefs that state how and what you want to be. Write them down and repeat them out loud. When you have negative thoughts about yourself turn them into something empowering and self-loving.

✓ Make a list of four activities that make you happy. Would you like to sign up for pottery, or dancing, or go swimming? Then do it. Take the time for yourself and the pay-off will be a happier, more contented you.

✓ William James said, "Act as if you are, and you shall be." Pretend to be happy, confident, outgoing, and fun, and eventually you'll develop the habit of being that way. It works like magic, but you have to press forward, work through your resistance and fears, and be patient—because it takes time. Your happiness is at stake, so don't give up.

✓ Take workshops or seminars, read books, or—if you're comfortable with it—do some therapy in private or in a group, or create a group of women friends so you can support each other. Make self-improvement a priority. After all, if *you* don't, who will?

Chapter Nine
Why men are willing to face rejection.

Secret #9
Men take risks to survive.

Our three friends took their places on the down-filled cushions of the now-familiar sofa. Their teacher beamed with affection for her students.

"Next week we're going to talk about commitment, but right now we'll discuss how rejection is a part of every man's life. As little boys they feel the sting of rejection when they aren't selected first or second to be on the team. And what about those boys who don't get chosen at all? For some, it haunts them for the rest of their lives.

"As they get older, they face rejection from females, which for most males is the worst of all: when they ask a girl to dance, when they ask a girl on a date, every time they try to steal a kiss. As they move to each level of intimacy with a new female, they continue to risk possible rejection.

"Men face rejection when they confess their love for

the first time and when they propose to a woman. Then, after marriage, if they occasionally get turned down, they risk rejection each time they move toward making love to, or showing physical affection for, their wives. When a woman turns a man down, for any reason, his manhood and his masculinity are being rejected.

"When they apply for jobs they risk rejection, and then experience it if they lose their jobs. Of course, women lose their jobs too, but, remember, their job isn't a reflection of who they are the way it is for men. Salesmen endure the most rejection, a constant part of their daily life.

"But men are amazingly resilient. They keep sticking their necks out, willing to be rejected, humiliated, or embarrassed. So why do they do it? Survival and enculturation. Survival kept the hunter from giving up. Even though many times he came home empty-handed, facing humiliation, he had no choice but to persevere. Peer pressure adds to the drive to risk rejection. Taking risks is part of being a man and taking calculated risks is part of their problem-solving skills.

"Seeking a mate had to do with survival of his genes. At the very least, he needed a wife to create a family. But, as we've discussed, he also needed an outlet for his emotional side—to feel whole and to express his humanity.

"In our culture, and most others, men naturally assume the responsibility of pursuing women. The drive for sex, procreation, intimacy, and love are all very strong, so—like the hunter of ancient times—the modern man perseveres. Men are taught to stick to the job at hand, to set goals and complete them, to ignore pain and discomfort, to be tough, and to never give up. Facing rejection is facing risk. Rejection is simply part of what it means to be a man. Here's Secret Number Nine."

Secret #9
Men take risks to survive.

"Just because men are willing to face rejection doesn't mean it isn't frightening. But, because they've been taught since they were boys that they should push through the bad feelings, most often they do. But to do so, they must continue to defend themselves against the emotional pain, denying it, out of touch with it, which keeps them distant from others, in particular, us.

"Have you noticed yourselves softening toward the men in your lives? Are you more aware of how their hearts ache, how hungry they are to connect and feel deeply, how isolated and lonely they are? And are you now aware of how important you are to their emotional well-being?"

"Of course we are." As Carol spoke, the others nodded their agreement. "I'm amazed how little of my husband I saw before these classes. It's like he's become three-dimensional, and at the center is this heart that I couldn't see before. I feel how much love he has to give and how he wants to receive love back. And I can see the soft, vulnerable person hidden within that hardened exterior. I'm sorry for all the times I've rejected him, and I want to make it so he'll open up more and be more loving. It's a privilege to know these Secrets about him."

"Well, what about *us*?" Beth asked. "I face rejection all the time."

"Yes, of course you do, Beth, but one of the most important points I'm trying to make in these classes is how hard it is for men to not have anyone to share their feelings with. If you can understand what goes on inside of them, you can be a better partner and friend to a man. Probably the greatest experience of rejection is being passed over by

a man. But would you rather risk being passed over, or risk asking a man for a date? Which do you think would be the most humiliating and painful way of being rejected?"

"I see your point," Beth agreed. "The more I learn, the more I'm glad to be a woman."

"Good; that's one of the most important things I want you to learn.

"Carol, you were saying what a privilege it is to be able to see into your husband's heart and soul. You may be the first to ever see into that private place of his. If you respect and appreciate him, stay open to his loving, and let him make you happy, he'll open his heart even more. The gift to you will be more love."

"Diedra, I'm so happy to be learning your Secrets." Jenny smiled. "My relationship with Brad is getting better and I can see how it will continue to improve. He's become so much more loving and attentive. I'm finally getting what I've wanted from my relationship all along."

"I'm pleased at the progress all of you have made. Love is truly what makes life worth living. When a man loves a woman enough to want to marry her, he'll make a lot of sacrifices. Next week we'll talk about those sacrifices and why men are willing to make them. You'll be surprised."

Husbands are like fires,
They go out if unattended.
– Zsa Zsa Gabor

Imagine how the men in the scenarios below might feel.
    1.— "Not tonight, honey, I'm exhausted."

After receiving her conciliatory kiss on the cheek, Ted rolls over, hiding the humiliation of rejection.

2.— "Hey Dan, guess what? I've been promoted to assistant manager. Isn't that great?"

Dan's smile and congratulations, which accompany a slap on his co-worker's back, hide his disappointment. Dan thought *he* was going to get that promotion.

3.— "Would you care to dance?"

James works up his courage to ask a woman to dance and, in three seconds, her "No, thank you" discourages him to the point that he vows to quit going to singles' functions.

4.— With tear-stained eyes, Cindy rushes past her daddy.

"Mommy, I fell down. Would you kiss it and make it all better?"

Cindy's father understands, but he's hurt that Cindy doesn't choose to go to him more often.

5.— "Legal custody goes to Martha Thomson. Roger Thomson will have visitation every other weekend."

Weeks later, the judge's words still sting. Missing the daily contact of his children, Roger faces another night alone in his apartment.

Men say that rejection—especially from a woman—is the worst thing they have to endure. But because it's their job in society to make the first moves with women, they will risk rejection if they're interested enough.

**A woman's rejection is a
rejection of him as a man.**

Warren Farrell, in *The Myth of Male Power*, says there are more than one hundred opportunities for rejection from first eye contact to intercourse. Maybe that's why men try to move to intercourse so quickly, to get the possibilities of rejection over with. It's also why men make women objects. It's less hurtful to be rejected by an object than a flesh-and-blood woman they may be interested in.

"There have been a lot of women I wish I'd approached, but it was just too scary. Funny how a little woman can scare a big man," Dan, a computer salesman, lamented to me during an interview. Many men say that they don't follow through on most of their opportunities to meet women because the fear of rejection is too great. How sad, since most women talk about all the men they hoped would make a move, but never did.

Married men speak about sexual rejection from their wives in solemn tones. Each time it hurts, and they *do* take it personally. A husband, married twenty-six years, expressed his sadness to the group in a workshop. "I feel like some lecherous villain when I want to have sex with my wife. You'd think she'd be flattered. It hurts every time she says no." Men know how to desensitize themselves, but what wife, if she gave it any thought at all, would want to add to her husband's emotional isolation and add to his defensiveness? If you've ever been sexually rejected, you know how humiliating it can be.

Rejection in the outside world is always going to be there. But you can bolster him by not rejecting him at home. You can assure your partner so he feels renewed, strong and powerful, and able to face the daily rejections outside of your relationship. No doubt you've faced rejection in the workplace, but it doesn't reflect on who you are as a woman like it does for a man. As discussed in earlier chapters, he *is* his work.

If he wants to touch you in sexual ways, why not be

open to him and be thankful he's attracted to you? If he wants to make love with you, and you don't want to, know that no matter what you say, it's a sensitive subject. Be cautious of his ego and his feelings when you feel the need to turn him down. Unless you have a good reason, why would you want to turn down the man you love, the man you have chosen to be your mate? If you're not attracted to him, what might be going on?

Resentment, more than anything else, destroys love and desire.

Resentment is one of the biggest killers of sexual desire. It builds up over time and often goes unnoticed because it gets repressed. Maybe he's gotten out of shape; maybe he's not nice to you. If you still care and want to enhance the love you have for him, give the Twelve Simple Secrets a few months to work. After you read the chapter on communication, you'll be better equipped to solve a variety of problems that might be getting in the way of strengthening your love for each other.

If you make your partner feel good at home, he's better able to withstand the onslaught of rejection that he faces each day. You'll be an important part of his well-being, which in turn will make him want to be loving and helpful to you. It may seem like a small thing to you, but to him it can make all the difference.

What if he's not interested in you or turns *you* down? The same applies for him. If he has resentments and hurts, he's going to need some time. Are you negative, complaining, never happy? If so, you're not attractive to anyone, especially him.

Are you feeling as beautiful as you could? Have you

been taking care of yourself? Is your weight where you'd like it to be? Are you opening up to him sexually? Don't forget that he can't help himself. Love can get him past a lot, but if you let yourself go, he's going to lose some interest—the same as you lose interest if *he* lets *himself* go. Have you gotten around to purchasing some sexy new lingerie? Making love is a two-way street and you can both do things to make love grow. Often, all that's lacking is better communication, more sensitivity, and respect.

• • •

3 things you can do:

✓ If you find yourself rejecting your partner's physical advances, make an inventory of why that might be. Write at least six things that come to mind. If hurts and resentments come up, write them down too. Are there things about his appearance or hygiene that could be improved? Is he an insensitive lover? Can the problems be resolved? Do you need to talk to your partner about them? Or would therapy be in order? How important is your relationship to you? You must decide, and then take the proper steps to rectify the situation.

✓ If you're not involved with anyone, think about the times you've rejected a man's interests. Make a vow to be more polite and caring in the future. When you're not interested in a man's advances, smile and say something like, "I'm flattered but I'm not available at this time." That gives a man an opportunity to not take it personally. He can make up what his ego needs to feel okay. If he's being rude, that's a different story and your intention should be to stay in your power using Feminine Grace. If you're rude or ugly, he might deserve it, but he just might tell

other men. Something to consider.

✓ If you're interested in a man, give him strong, obvious signals that will give him the go-ahead. Pat Allen, author of *Getting to "I Do,"* says to make eye contact for five seconds and smile. Try it sometime. Five seconds can be a very long time. Most women look away and the man thinks she's not interested. Remember, men take calculated risks, and they're driven to succeed. Much is at stake, and if he doesn't at least get a smile, most men will not take the next step. Smiling. Lingering eye contact. Glancing his way often. This is enough to give any man the signal that he won't be rejected.

Rejection is one of the most sensitive subjects for a man and anything you do to alleviate his fears and discomfort is a kind and caring gesture. Do it all with Feminine Grace and you can't go wrong.

Your Notes

_____

_____

_____

_____

_____

_____

_____

_____

_____

_____

_____

_____

_____

Chapter Ten
Why men are so cautious about commitment.

Secret #10
Men lose when they commit.

You know that man I met last month?" Beth asked her friends as they walked the path to Diedra's house. "Well, he's been acting more differently toward me than any other man I've met: He's more respectful, calls me when he says he will, shows up on time, and showers me with compliments and occasional gifts.

"I've been using the listening skills that Diedra taught us and he's been sharing things he says he's never told anyone before. We've made an emotional connection that seems deeper than even some long-term relationships I've been in. I think it's different with him because I knew so much about his inner self even before we met...you know, because I know the Secrets."

"I know what you mean," Jenny agreed. "It's like men have become a brand-new species; they seem that different. I can see that before these classes I kept a wall between me and pretty much all men, except Brad, of course...well, even

Brad to a certain degree…Wow, I never realized."

"What do you mean?" Asked Carol.

"I mean I can see how I also put up a wall between Brad and me. Like I didn't completely trust him. I'm thinking out loud here. It's like…because I didn't feel I understood him, there was a kind of caution, a kind of distrust. Do you know what I mean?"

"Yes, I think so," Carol concurred, "though I hadn't thought about it before. Because we never knew much about what went on in a man's heart and head, it felt like they were holding back. And that's bound to create mistrust. Now that we have greater understanding, we can see how it's more a matter of conditioning that's kept them so private, not secretiveness. How did we get so lucky to learn this stuff? Thank you, Ginger, wherever you are."

They laughed together, the bond of friendship ever deepening. Diedra welcomed them at the door.

"Come on in, ladies. We've got lots to talk about."

After they took their usual seats, Diedra began. "Today, we're going to talk about commitment: why men want it, why they're hesitant to go into a committed relationship with a woman, and why they sometimes avoid it altogether. When we're done, you'll have a clearer picture of what it means to a man and, I think, a new appreciation for them when they *do* commit.

"Let's look at the hunter's life. He wanted 'marriage' because he was driven to procreate and because he needed a helpmate. His mate did the gathering, gardening, made tools for household use, cooked, bore and cared for his children, cared for their parents, and kept peace within the community. He also became an accepted, adult member of his community when he took a mate and had children. And of course there was his need for affection

and intimacy. A mate was pretty much a necessity.

"Today, men get married to get those same needs met. Often, when younger men marry for the first time, they're driven by a primal need to procreate. Some are aware of it, some are not. Creating a family gives him stature, allowing him to become a responsible man in his community, a grown-up. Social and family pressures have a lot to do with it, and it's just assumed that he'll settle down and marry. A wife and family give him stability after years of restless adolescence.

"A key word in that description is 'responsible.' A responsible person is someone who takes care of their obligations. A wife and children are huge responsibilities."

"Wait a minute," Jenny exclaimed. "I work just as hard as Brad, and actually I bring in almost as much money, so I think the responsibility is equal."

"I understand your point," Diedra said, "but when you were engaged, it's likely that after your friends shared your enthusiasm, one of them asked, 'Are you going to continue to work?' When Brad announced to his buddies that he was getting married, that question wouldn't even enter their minds. Yes, you both work, but, in our culture, it's assumed that you're *choosing* to work. He doesn't feel he has a choice. If you mutually decided that he was going to become a house husband, how do you think people would judge him?"

Jenny's face softened. "I never thought of it that way."

"What I'm talking about," Diedra continued, "is the sense of *responsibility* that men accept when they choose to marry, especially if they're intending to create a family. It's a very big decision for them. When we put men down for being afraid of commitment, it's not so much fear as caution. You need to understand how big a decision it is.

"In our culture, because of the societal acceptance—by

men *and* women—that 'of course' he's going to work, men are seen as success objects. Women complain that they're seen as sex objects—and rightfully so—but men have every reason to complain as well. Interestingly, most men can't help but show off their success and most women can't help but try to be attractive."

"I'm afraid I'm guilty of seeing men as success objects," Beth offered. "I want to marry a professional man. It's not just about money, although that's part of it. It has to do with compatibility, shared interests, level of education, and lifestyle. What a man does tells a lot right away."

"I'm not saying it's a bad thing," Diedra said, easing Beth's defensiveness. "I just want you to see what a man is taking on when he commits to marrying a woman. It will help you better appreciate his role. And if you're planning to have children, realize how serious a responsibility that is. Now, let me give you Secret Number Ten."

Secret #10
Men lose when they commit.

"Sometimes, when a man chooses to marry, he gives up his personal dreams. He'll maybe choose the higher paying job rather than the job that would be more meaningful to him. Ask a man what he'd rather be doing if money were not part of the equation, and—if you can get him to be really honest—he's likely to say something that will surprise you. Often a man gives up his dreams: dreams of being a bachelor and dreams of the work he desires. Not only is he giving that up, but, if marriage and family have been *your* priority, you're getting *your* dreams fulfilled.

"This next point is so important it almost qualifies as a Secret. We've talked about the power you gain through

Feminine Grace. If power means having control over your life—which is how I mean it—then men who marry actually have less power than women. Society doesn't allow men the choices that it does women. Just more of how wonderful it is to be women. Are you getting this?"

All three women nodded.

"Besides the financial responsibility," Diedra continued, "there's the drive—which can become a responsibility and burden—to make his wife happy, something we've already talked about. Part of giving up his youth and bachelor freedoms is giving up the traditional fantasy of having sex with a variety of beautiful women. Remember our discussion of monogamy: What he hopes to get in return for giving that up is intimacy and a steady sex partner who loves him.

"Other fears that men have are that when they marry they'll lose the freedom of how much time they can spend with their male friends, they'll lose their privacy, and they'll lose their alone time."

"So what can we do about this?" Carol frowned.

"Regarding loss of privacy, what will help is to trust your husbands and remember that they're not so much secretive as they are *conditioned to be private*. Then build in time to be alone. It's good for everyone and it helps bring romance back. If you're together all the time, and *expected* to be, you can get weary of each other. If women understand and appreciate what men give up in return for what they hope to gain, harmony and love can grow.

"Financially, women can take a more conscious role in their contribution. Until children enter the picture, it would help if women let their husbands know that they're financial partners. The cultural belief that men *have* to work and women *choose* to work will probably always be there,

because of raising children, but it will ease a man's burden some if the wife lets him know she's aware of this inequity.

"Another thing that women do is complain when a man works long hours, especially when there are children. She wants more time with him, wants the children to see their dad more, wants him to help with the children and household, and needs his adult companionship. But women must not forget how important success is to a man and that he's working for two or more people. It's his way of showing love. Of course this should be talked about, but in a noncomplaining way. Not only do men hope to get love and intimacy when they marry, they also want understanding and emotional security. If you can ease his feelings of responsibility, he can soften in every aspect of his life."

Beth sighed. "This isn't sounding very encouraging."

"I know, and this next point doesn't help. When a man chooses to marry, it means he loves the woman a great deal. Men don't generally have a lot of fantasies about marriage. They take things for their surface value. He hopes she'll stay the woman he fell in love with, that she'll stay beautiful, that she'll continue to think he's wonderful, that she'll continue to be enthusiastic about sex, that his emotional and intimacy needs will be met, and that he'll continue to love her. But how often does that happen?"

"Oh, boy." Carol slumped in her seat. "I see your point, all too clearly. Mostly, we change on every count. We often let ourselves go, and not only do we not think he's wonderful but we become hyper-aware of his imperfections, we frequently complain, and, especially when the kids arrive, we lose our interest in sex. And we give them such a hard time for being commitment-phobes."

Beth's forehead wrinkled. "I'm embarrassed. I feel like I've only been seeing men as potential husbands. I've

forgotten to see them as men. No wonder they're so squeamish about getting involved."

"Yes, men know that most women have a hidden agenda—sometimes even from themselves—of getting married, being taken care of, and looking for financial security. You can see how a man might want a prenuptial agreement. It's not just about protecting their assets. They want to know a woman loves them for who they are, not for their wallets.

"We talked about men's burden of having to initiate each phase of a relationship. They say they'd love women to initiate more, but then they're on guard against the possibility that she's just a gold digger. It makes it tough for anyone to get something started.

"Another thing that keeps men guarded is that they know women have a long list of expectations about how men should be. I think men can actually be more pure with their love. He just wants her to be the woman he fell in love with and to think he's wonderful and not want to change him. Men don't have nearly the agenda going that women do. Usually, their agenda—which is easy to spot—is trying to get a woman to have sex with them."

They all laughed.

Instead of getting married again,
I'm going to find a woman I don't
like and give her a house.

– Lewis Grizzard

In *Why Men Are the Way They Are*, Warren Farrell says most men's primary fantasy is having sex with lots of

beautiful women, while most women's primary fantasy is to be married and have children.

Men don't want the women they marry to change.

Men have trepidation about marriage because, even though they may love a woman dearly, they're aware that:

- Most women's income drops after marriage because she often quits or works part-time once children arrive.
- Women gain an average of fifteen pounds after marriage.
- Devotion, intimacy, and sex diminish.
- Women lose the respect they felt for their husband prior to marriage. And respect is an absolute must if he is to continue loving a woman.

You may know this colloquial observation: *Women marry men hoping they'll change, but they never do, and men marry women hoping they'll never change, and they always do.* There's a cartoon in *Playboy* magazine that says it all: The svelte, gorgeous bride, holding an overflowing plate of *hors d'oeuvres*, is saying to the groom, "Let's eat, dear. I've been dieting for years."

A bachelor I once interviewed was honest when he said, "Every time I see a married man with a sloppy, overweight wife my resistance to commitment is strengthened, because *I see myself in that husband's shoes.*"

However unrealistic it may be, it's a man's nature to hope that the woman will somehow continue to be attractive to him. And when a woman forgets that and lets herself go, you have the perfect circumstance for the man to seek extramarital sex. It happens all the time. "Maybe

it's just an excuse, but when my wife gained weight after our second child, she just wasn't appealing anymore," Joe, a tax accountant explained. "I love her, but I need to be with someone who turns me on."

A man is *always* conscious of how his partner looks to other people. He wants to feel proud of his partner and if this isn't the case he secretly feels embarrassed, even humiliated.

There's a process I call "compensation"; a man loves a woman for a variety of reasons and often he reasons that his woman may not be as attractive as he might wish, but she has other virtues that compensate for this particular shortcoming, e.g., she may not be glamorous, but she has great legs or wonderful breasts or beautiful hair or a great sense of humor.

If a woman (and this works for both genders, of course) neglects herself in some ways, then this "balance" of compensation is upset...and the man begins to feel not only "cheated" but trapped. Add children, and higher demands on his income, and the downward spiral develops.

The nightmare of prospective grooms is that they will find themselves trapped with a wife who has abandoned her femininity and glamour, with kids that demand time, energy, and increased expense, so that he becomes nothing more than a working drudge responsible for supporting everyone. "I know she's busy with the kids and the house, but I sure would enjoy her more if she put a little effort into looking nice for me," James, from Chicago, shared in an online interview. Most men are conscientious enough to endure all this and they can't/won't abandon their wives and children because (a) they love them and (b) they have some sense of fairness and responsibility.

In light of all of that, it's amazing that men and women

get married at all, and that any marriage is ever successful.

Success—definitely a relative term—in marriage is a great deal more than just longevity. If the woman changes in ways that make her less attractive—lets herself go, complains, is never satisfied or happy, or is no longer interested in sex—he often leaves. Not necessarily by way of divorce, but by shutting down emotionally, burying himself in work, and sometimes seeking other sexual partners to fulfill his need for intimacy, understanding, and acceptance.

Some men avoid marriage altogether: some because they married when they were young and had painful divorces; some because they're narcissistic and aren't interested or able to care for another; some because they don't have to give up anything to get what they need from women—companionship, sex, intimacy; some because they don't want to give up any of their freedoms; and some because they're afraid to open their hearts enough to let another person get that close.

Most men like being married.

But men do marry, every day. And because they live longer and healthier lives than do their unmarried counterparts, marriage seems to suit them. Overall, men gain more than they lose. And if the marriage is good, all the better. Love is in short supply for most men, which makes the risk and responsibility seem more than worthwhile.

"There's one more thing I want to talk to you about. Men are not the only ones who give themselves away when

they marry. Many women lose their spirit, their fire. They worry about losing their husband and often change themselves to ensure a successful marriage. Many women have a predetermined idea of what a wife is and unknowingly slip into a different persona when they become one.

"Think back to when you were single. Are you different now? Are you as happy, free-spirited, and enthusiastic now? If you've given away part of who you are, Feminine Grace can help you recapture the glorious woman you once were."

"Diedra, I'm inspired." Beth beamed. "I'm loving being a woman more than I thought I could. Thank you."

• • •

4 things you can do if you're married:

✓ Let your husband know how much you appreciate the way he works to take care of you and your children. Even if he isn't a gift giver, make a list of ten things he does that are ongoing gifts to you and your children. Explain to him what you've learned about the inequity of his *having* to work, while you get to *choose* to work, and create a plan whereby you both feel even more like partners.

✓ If you've ever complained about his long hours or that he doesn't give you gifts, apologize and explain to him what you've been learning, that you understand how wonderful his contribution is. Explain to him how it makes you feel when he's away and what receiving thoughtful gifts means to you.

✓ Have a talk with him about his choice of work. Find out if he's following his heart's dream. This is such a foreign idea for most men that you may not be able to get him to even look at that part of himself. Be gentle and use the listening skills you've been practicing. If it turns out that he'd be

happier doing something else, talk about how you could make that happen. It may mean that you have to live in a smaller house and have less disposable income, but since you now know what his work means to him, wouldn't you rather your husband was happy in his work? There are serious considerations that go along with this discussion, so be prepared.

✓ The discussion that should go hand-in-hand with this is to look at what *you're* doing to fulfill *your* heart's dream. It could be a different kind of work, or it might be pursuing some creative outlet. Create a comfortable setting and enjoy what could be a heart-warming talk.

4 things you can do if you're single:
✓ Write down your thoughts about how you see men as success objects. Make a list of six ways those thoughts interfere with your successful interaction with men.

✓ If you're talking about marriage, have a discussion about the work inequity, and talk about how you can be better partners in your financial well-being, especially if you're going to have children together.

✓ Have a heart-to-heart discussion about doing the kind of work that fits both of your dreams. Be clear why you've each chosen the work you do. You don't have to follow your heart's dream but when you're clear why you *choose* to do otherwise, you have more power and will be less likely to resent the work. Remember, *power is how much control you have over your life.*

✓ If you're just beginning to date, allow him to pay and give him lots of appreciation and even tell him that his generosity makes you feel womanly. See his paying as a constant gift to you. To pay him back, prepare him nice meals occasionally. He'll appreciate your thoughtfulness.

Chapter Eleven
Why men need concise communication.

Secret #11
To be heard, you must speak his language.

Diedra was beaming. The women had just shared the changes that were coming over the men in their lives, how their love was blossoming once again, and, most important, what had been happening within each of them.

"Great news, you three! Didn't I promise you magic?"

"The Settling is a thing of the past," Carol exclaimed, "and what you've taught us has definitely created magic for Thomas and me. Beth and Jenny and I have been sharing with other women how the Twelve Simple Secrets have changed our lives. We've shown them by example that they don't have to settle for ordinary and how easy it is to make significant changes in their relationships."

"Thank you," said Diedra. "Several have contacted me. I just wish all women could know the Secrets."

Beth spoke next. "What I'm finding is how wonderful it feels to be so conscious of the gifts of being a woman. I feel like a big part of me was asleep before. I can see how

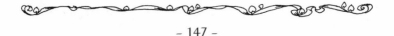

disempowering the Settling can be."

"I'm happy for you, Beth." Diedra smiled. "You've discovered the real secret of being happy: liking who you are and expressing your uniqueness.

"We have only one more lesson after this. You've been incorporating the Secrets into your lives and you've seen the results. Next week we're going to talk about intuition and how to use it to get even better results, but right now we're going to focus on communication. Even though we've already talked about it, I want to fill in any gaps so you can be heard and understood by the men in your lives and get more of what you want.

"Men and women are quite different in the way they speak as well as the way they listen. Let's begin with the Secret for this lesson."

Secret #11
To be heard, you must speak his language.

"First we'll talk about how differently men and women communicate. For women, feelings and words are totally interconnected. When we feel an emotion, we want to express it with words. We experience great pleasure and comfort when we discuss what we're feeling, as well as why, so we seek opportunities to do so. We've learned how bonding it can be when we share what's going on inside us.

"As we've already discussed, most men have limited access to their feelings, and when they do get emotional, they generally want to be alone. Then, after they've made sense of it—*if* they make sense of it—they might tell someone about it, but usually they'll keep it to themselves. Often, even the wife is unaware when her husband is going through an emotional experience; she only notices that he's more quiet and distant than usual. More often than not, he'll shove his feelings aside by involving himself in some activity and not acknowledging them at all. When you use the Secrets in your relationship, as you've already noticed, the trust level rises, allowing your partner to feel safer, and more likely to express his inner thoughts and turmoils. Of course it's not going to happen with all men, but it seems to be working that way with *your* partners.

"Men are often uncomfortable when feelings are being expressed—by anyone. They don't understand them and they can't relate, so they feel somewhat helpless because they don't know what to do to solve what they perceive as a problem. When you need to express your emotions to your husband, try to give him a more logical explanation than you might otherwise. Tell him what you're feeling and whether or not you need help in solving your problem. He'll be relieved to know what to do and he'll be more supportive.

"Another difference between men and women is that women love the details of life and enjoy talking about them: clothing, personal grooming, interior design, home, cooking, children, what makes people tick. These things hold a fascination for women that most men can't fathom. Men are usually more interested in the bigger picture, the bottom line, and solving problems. They're generally bored with most of what women like to talk about, so they'll be grateful if you don't give them too much."

Carol laughed. "Now I understand why Thomas is always saying, 'get to the point.'

"Yes, Brad always says, 'Jenny, what are you trying to say?' It's like we're speaking two different languages."

"You're getting it," Diedra said. "Because we women get so much pleasure out of talking about anything and

everything, it's important to make time to talk to other women. Otherwise, our need gets pent up and we want to tell it all to our partners. More often than not, they're overwhelmed and you're hurt because they're not really interested. Haven't you experienced your partner's eyes glazing over in the middle of one of your monologues and then you notice he's only half-listening?"

All three women nodded in unison. "I had that happen the other night," Beth offered. "Steven, the man I'm seeing, called and asked what I'd done that day. I gave him a blow-by-blow description and when I started telling him how I'd done a bunch of ironing I'd been meaning to get to, I could tell his attention had wandered. Looking back, I can hardly blame him."

"Give them an overview of what you want to talk about," Diedra offered, "with just the outcome and only a few details in between. How do you feel when he talks about business or sports or whatever subject he's interested in but you find boring? It's the same for him. Go ahead and discuss this with him and explain how much pleasure you get out of talking about the little things. Tell him you understand it can be boring for him, but that you want to share some of it with him. Don't expect him to be very different, but there will be greater understanding between you.

"You can create balance by asking him questions about his favorite subjects. Ask him why he likes something, how it makes him feel—but don't expect too much detail—and show genuine interest. After all, this is part of who this man is, and don't you want to know about him? Learn a little about his favorite interests so you can speak intelligently. He'll be very appreciative and find you more fascinating."

"Actually," Jenny said, "I did that just this week. I read

an article in the sports section that caught my attention. That night I asked Brad to clarify something I didn't understand. He got so excited. It was the first time we ever had fun talking about sports."

"That's a good point, Jenny. Asking men questions about a subject that you don't understand can really light a man up. Be truly interested and you'll learn something. Not only about the subject, but about your man. It shows you care and he'll notice.

"Let's talk about gossip. It's a myth that men don't gossip. They do, but generally about different subjects than most women do. Women prefer to talk about people they know, although—contrary to popular belief—it's not *always* malicious. Most gossip between women is simply sharing information, nothing harmful. Men generally talk about sports figures, politicians, business leaders, and sometimes entertainment celebrities. When they *do* talk about people they know, it's not generally that derogatory. Men are usually disapproving of women's gossip, particularly if it's harmful. Use Feminine Grace as your filter. After all, is mean gossip *ever* attractive?" Diedra waited.

Beth shook her head. "Of course not. With Feminine Grace as a filter, it's easy to tell."

Diedra winked her approval. "Here's a *big* difference between men and women: Men tend to take words literally. Consequently, men are careful to choose just the right words to express their intended message. And they're judicious, rarely using superfluous words. We women tend to talk for the sheer pleasure of talking, of connecting with another. And often, because we're in the habit of not planning what we say, we get ourselves in trouble with the men in our lives. The best example is when we're angry we often say things like 'never' and 'always.' That drives men crazy and can be quite harmful."

"I don't understand," Jenny questioned. "Give us an example."

"Here's a good one: 'You never tell me you love me!' Does that sound familiar? When a man hears that, he thinks that's what you mean. No matter how seldom he says those words, 'never' doesn't fit. It hurts him because it discounts the times he does tell you he loves you. Does that help?"

"That's what I was afraid you meant." Jenny dropped her head in mock shame. "Just this weekend I was angry at Brad for not hosing down the driveway like I'd asked him to. I told him, 'You never help around here. Why do I have to do everything?' Well, as you can imagine, he stomped off and I didn't see him all afternoon. I can see how mean that sounded to him. The truth is, he helps a lot. How can I mend this one?"

"Well, fortunately, you can. One thing you can do is pick a time when you know he'll be open to talking. Ask him if it's a good time and, if not, find out when a better time will be. I mentioned this before: Don't *ever* say, 'We've got to talk.' That strikes fear into every man. Men don't usually say it, but can you imagine how you'd feel if your husband said that to you?" Diedra laughed. "Pretty scary stuff.

"Once you sit down together, explain what I just told you about how men take words literally. Tell him how women talk for the sheer pleasure of connecting with another person, how sometimes they don't think and the meaning of their words often comes out in ways that are not intended. Explain to him that *of course* you're aware of all the ways he helps around the house—enumerate them for him—and apologize for hurting him. Then vow not to do it again, and if you do, ask him to stop you as it occurs. You can come up with an agreed-on signal. Then, restate what you *really* meant."

Jenny rolled her eyes. "Diedra, I don't know if I can control myself when I'm angry."

"Well, if you remember Feminine Grace, it will short-circuit your feelings of anger. If you stick with it, Feminine Grace will become a habit and color all of your actions. You'll find yourself getting angry less often. You'll begin to experience a moment of calm when you can choose to communicate in a more poised, graceful way. Remember, when you're being feminine, your husband is powerfully affected by you and stays the man who wants to cherish you and make you happy. It's really your *only* position of power with him—or any man."

"Diedra?" Carol asked. "How can we get a man to listen to us?"

"I remember you asked that same question a few weeks ago. It really depends on the importance of the subject. If you're just chit-chatting, don't give him too many details. Don't talk about subjects that you know will bore him, and get to the bottom line fairly quickly. It's a matter of respecting your listener, a good idea no matter who you're speaking to. On the occasion that he's not paying attention, you'll be less likely to take it personally because you understand him better.

"If it's an important subject that requires his undivided attention, say something like, 'I've got a problem I need some help with; when's a good time I can have your full attention?' This wording invites his interest. It isn't as likely to scare him off, either. Remember, he likes to solve problems, especially for you, because then he can make you happy and gets to be your hero. As you

explain the problem, use thinking words rather than feeling words, even to the point that you ask him what he thinks about something, rather than how he feels. Try to put yourself in his place and choose your words with precision, words that he can relate to, words that sound logical. You know, 'Just the facts, ma'am.' Then ask him for some suggestions. Give him a problem to solve."

"Please, Diedra, give us an example," Beth suggested.

Diedra thought for a moment. "Let's say you needed to tell your date that it was upsetting to you that he didn't introduce you to the couple you ran into at the movies. Rather than saying, 'It hurt my feelings that you didn't introduce me,' a better way would be to say, 'When you didn't introduce me to your friends, I felt like I didn't matter and that maybe you were ashamed to be seen with me. I doubt that's what was going on, but that's how I felt. Does that make sense?' Asking a man 'if that makes sense' gives him the opportunity to ask for clarification and involves him in a deeper mode of listening. When you explain yourself clearly, he understands what you mean, and can apologize without feeling he has to defend his actions.

"Which brings me to blaming. We've already talked about it so I think you understand that when anyone accuses someone, the other person's defenses go up—and listening stops. Everything from then on is about protection and counterattacks, and can turn what could have been a constructive, healing, and even loving conversation into a fight. Blaming *never* works.

"Let me tell you about what I call the *I, Not You Principle*. When you start a sentence with *you* you're most likely blaming or criticizing. If you start with *I* you can describe the problem by telling him how you *feel*. That way, it becomes a problem he can solve. He won't want to

solve your problem if he's defensive. He might solve it, but only to get out of trouble, to get you off his back, but not because of feelings of love for you.

"Ladies, are you seeing that all we've been learning in these classes is how you can get more of what you want from your relationships with men? It's not about giving your power away to him, it's about taking it back and using it to its full potential."

"Absolutely!" the women agreed.

"Sometimes," Diedra continued, "you simply need to express yourself about something that has nothing to do with him. If you don't want advice, simply tell him you just need him to listen. If it's appropriate, you might ask him to hold you, which gives him something to do. He then feels more in control. Remember, if you're unhappy he feels responsible and helpless. Most men simply don't know what to do, which makes them uncomfortable. Is this making sense?" Diedra leaned back.

"Well, yes," Carol was hesitant, "it makes sense. But I question my ability to think that clearly in the moment."

"These kinds of changes won't happen overnight. It takes practice. Explain to your husband what you're trying to do and, believe me, he'll support you in your efforts. In fact, he'll love you for it. And you can't change who you are, so having a sense of humor with him about your need to talk will make it fun."

Let your speech be always with grace, seasoned with salt, that ye may know how ye ought to answer every man.
— St. Paul, Colossians, 4:6

Most problems on this planet boil down to bad communication. The only way we can get to know someone, and thus understand them, is via clear communication—either verbal, visual, or written. We cannot read each other's minds, but how often do we get our feelings hurt, how often do we get angry, how often do we misinterpret the meaning of someone's actions or words, or lack of same, because we expected them to just "know?"

It's amazing how often, when I've been coaching women on improving their relationships, that I hear them say, "If he loved me, he'd know," or "If he loved me, I shouldn't have to ask." Men *don't* know. To men, women are a total mystery and often they complain, along the lines of what a ski instructor told me, "My girlfriend gets so offended if I don't do things a certain way. But I can't relate to most of what she wants. I'm always guessing and hoping I won't get into too much trouble if I guess wrong. It's a lot of pressure." Can you hear how unfair that is? Give them clear, specific instructions about what you want. They want to do it right. Remember, they need to be successful.

Talking is a pleasurable way for women to connect with others.

In *Men Are from Mars, Women Are from Venus*, John Gray has given us a great gift by pointing out how women like to talk just to be talking. It's an activity as much as it is a means of communication. And explaining to us how men need to "go to their caves" has given men more permission to be themselves.

In ancient times, women who lived communally spent most of their time with other women. To pass the time they talked about all the varied things that made up their lives:

other people, household details, the little things that created beauty and pleasure, and the men and children in their lives.

The men were mostly focused on hunting and solving problems such as finding water, protecting women and children, securing shelter, making weapons and tools, etc. They had to be clear and concise because everyone's lives depended on it.

If you slow down and plan more carefully, and use more precise language, and keep a sense of humor, men will understand you better. This will cause less frustration and misunderstanding, and the outcome will be more harmony. You get more of what you want, and so does he.

A part of good communication is being able to read between the lines. The next chapter, our final, explains how developing and using your intuition will help you use the Secrets to their full capacity. You can become a magnificent woman, fully empowered, molding your relationship so your heart sings...because you're happy and well loved. That is your destiny, yours for the taking. But, as you've already discovered, it won't happen on its own. Feminine Grace will allow you to create the love you both long to know. What a powerful gift you hold in your hands...and what an exciting path lies before you.

• • •

4 things you can do:
Have a conversation about communication with your husband or boyfriend.
✓ Discuss with each other:
1. How it feels when each is being listened to.
2. How it feels when the other is half-listening.
3. How you can bring up areas of discontent without it

accelerating to an argument. (Don't forget Feminine Grace.)

4. What would be a mutually agreed-upon signal to stop a conversation before it gets out of hand. Use some kind of time-out signal.

✓ Have a discussion to discover your individual communication styles. Find out:

1. What each of you needs from the other to feel heard.

2. If you each get enough talking time, and, if not, what can be done so you do.

3. How to improve your verbal interactions so you both feel more fulfilled and closer as a couple.

✓ As you become more aware of your communication styles, vow to work together to improve how you speak to each other so you both get your needs met. Vow also to push beyond your comfort zone so you can speak with more ease about subjects you've avoided in the past. Maybe you haven't been able to ask for what you want. Maybe he hasn't been able to say no to you. Maybe you need to let him know how he's been hurting you. Maybe the sexual side of your relationship could improve with better communication. Make it a project that you can work on together. It's guaranteed to bring you closer because you'll both become more open to each other. It can be very sweet.

✓ Continue to learn more about better communication. Read books, take classes, do therapy. Whatever you do to further your ability to communicate well with your partner will only enhance your relationship.

Improving your communication skills, developing ways to be better understood, and using language to appreciate each other and pleasure each other will be the most important thing you will ever do together. It could make the difference between divorce or ever-flourishing love.

Chapter Twelve
Feminine Grace and Intuition:
Without them the
Twelve Simple Secrets won't work.

Secret #12
A man wants to be with a woman
who makes him feel like a man.

The cottage sat peacefully on the edge of the enchanted forest, its garden alive with color. Did the Twelve Simple Secrets really come from the Wise Woman of the North Forest, or was Diedra responsible?

"You can never go back, you know." Diedra spoke softly as she poured tea for the three women. "You can never go back to not understanding men and not realizing the power of your femininity. Life will never be the same for you." She sat back in her chair and smiled.

Carol looked to the others for agreement. "I think I can speak for all of us when I say we would never want to go back to not knowing what you've taught us."

"Thank you, Diedra, for the gift of the Secrets." Beth took the hands of her two friends who sat beside her on the

sofa. "And thank you, Carol and Jenny, for being such perfect friends." The women took turns exchanging hugs.

"You know," Diedra said, "it's wonderful that you've shared these classes together. It's essential for a woman to have at least one friend she can call when she needs coaching, a friend who understands the Secrets and what she's trying to achieve. Supporting each other will help you develop your poise, your grace, and be successful at making the changes in your relationship that you seek.

"As I said the first week, the key to what you want is Feminine Grace. But there's another component that we've only touched on and that's your intuition. Intuition coupled with Feminine Grace is an unbeatable combination."

"Do you mean like a hunch?" Jenny asked.

"Well, that's certainly part of it, but it's much more than that. It's a *knowing* deep inside of you. How often have you said to yourself, 'I *knew* that's what he'd say'…or 'I *knew* it was going to turn out that way. Why didn't I *listen?*' " All three women nodded in agreement.

"It's that gut feeling you get sometimes," Diedra went on. "There's an innate wisdom within each of us that gets covered over by fears, expectations, culture, society, family, 'shoulds,' self-doubt, and mind chatter. Too often, we ignore that inner voice, what I call your Wise Self. Carol mentioned she felt she already knew what I've been teaching. You all know this stuff. You're the kind of women for whom relationships are of uppermost importance. When you learn to listen to your Wise Self, you'll get better at making the right choices in your life. Especially regarding your relationship. *But you must learn to trust it.*

"There are many men that you interact with. Your partner, of course, but also brothers, fathers, bosses, co-workers, and men in businesses you frequent. We've

been discussing men in generalities. *But each man is unique and the Secrets must be applied individually.* That's where your intuition will serve you. Some men are not as shut down emotionally, some are not as driven to make you happy, some are not as success-oriented, and some are not as sexual. *You* must determine the most effective ways to interact with each man you encounter.

"Feminine Grace is the fuel that energizes your actions and men's reactions to you. Intuition is what you use to interpret each individual situation. There are universal truths that we've talked about. Most people respond to appreciation, respect, and caring. That's basic nature. Most everyone's responses are automatic, but, frequently, with each man in your life, an individual determination has to be made. That's when you must consciously decide what to do or how to react. Learning to trust your Wise Self will help you find your answers. What's your gut telling you to do? Sometimes it tells you to do nothing, to wait and get coaching from a friend.

"When we get emotional we tend to respond that very moment. Fear especially makes us react on the spot. Your body will tell you if it's fear. You might have a knot or butterflies in your stomach, your breathing could become shallow, you may experience tension in your neck, your shoulders, or your chest. Without fear, your body is calm. Even though a situation sometimes feels like life or death, if you sense you're going into an automatic reaction, it's best to wait."

"Yes, but how do we do that when we're in the middle of something with someone?" Jenny asked.

"Tell them you need to think things over before you make a decision. Or tell them you don't want to do or say something you'll be sorry for and that you need to take a moment. Or tell them you care about them and want to do the right thing. Use the term 'I know you'll understand.' How can they argue with that? Take the necessary time to move into grace, to check in with your Wise Self, to get coaching or support from a friend, or to ask for guidance from someone who is better informed. Sometimes you just need time for the answer to come to you. What you don't want to do is something you'll be sorry for later. Am I making sense?"

"Yes, of course you are," Beth offered. "It's like when I met a man a few weeks ago. You all know I'm getting to know a pretty special guy, but we haven't made any commitments to each other yet. Well, this other man I met was very attractive and seemed nice, but I hesitated when he asked me out. I was surprised at the hesitation so I decided to give myself a few moments to think about what was going on. Instead of answering immediately, I stalled by saying, 'Well, that's an interesting offer. I'm flattered.' I flirted a bit more while I pondered my feelings. Finally, I trusted my hesitation and said, 'You know, you seem like a terrific guy. Right now, though, I'm not available. But thank you.' It was hard to do that because he was so attractive and charming. But something told me it wasn't a good idea. I guess that was my intuition."

"Absolutely. That's exactly what I'm talking about. And you were gracious in your response. You left him with his dignity. You put it in such a way that he could make up whatever he needed for his ego to feel okay. Like maybe another time you might have been available. Very good, Beth." Diedra gestured her approval.

"When you're gracious and poised, how can anyone treat you with anything less than respect and dignity? That doesn't mean you can't be strong when you need to be. As your self-respect and self-confidence grow, you'll be better equipped to handle even the toughest situations with the power of your Feminine Grace. You own the world when you come from that position. Self-respect helps you go for what you deserve and decline what you know isn't right. When you behave with that kind of grace and confidence, men will be attracted to you. You'll stand out as uniquely as a red rose in a field of dandelions. And that, ladies, brings me to our final Secret."

Secret #12
A man wants to be with a woman who makes him feel like a man.

"Your Feminine Grace makes you beautiful. Your self-comfort and your joy make you shine. Your uniqueness will stand out and men will be attracted to your femininity. They'll instinctively know you're not a hostile enemy and that you actually like men. Men crave respect and honor. Being a man is primary to their self-image. Being around women like you will allow almost any man the opportunity to feel good about being a man.

"Of course, not all men have earned the right to be honored, but almost anyone you treat well will behave better. We're all the same. *Assume* someone is good and they're more likely to *be* good. You, like no other, may be able to get the grouch at the corner market to be sweet to you. Wouldn't that be a more empowering way to be…in *all* situations?"

"Diedra," Carol said gently, "I'm so grateful to you. I have such a different perception of who I am now. I feel I'm bigger, like I matter more. And I like being in charge of what goes on in my life." Carol began to laugh. "This is

crazy, but…I'm beginning to feel a little bit like a queen, at least with Thomas."

"Oh Carol, I like that." Diedra grinned. "In a way, you are a queen. Because you have sovereignty over your domain by being more in charge of every aspect of your life. And in a way, you're in charge of everyone around you, because the power of Feminine Grace, which is so hard to find today, affects the people with whom you interact. You've already experienced it. People respond positively, especially men, to that power, but don't ever abuse it. If you do, you lose your grace and you become a very unappealing person. So it's self-correcting, like magic."

"Diedra," Beth asked, "I want to continue to improve and grow, but this is our last lesson. What's next for us?"

"Because you three are so close, I haven't needed to talk about it, but I always recommend that women create a support group. A network of like-minded women who wish to incorporate the Twelve Simple Secrets into their lives. Out of context, some of the Secrets may not sit well with other women. You need to be around women who will support you. Most women don't understand that their *femininity* is a woman's *power base*. They think they have to be like men to be powerful, that they need to be tough. Consequently, they tend to resent men, which causes them to *give their power away*. You need to be with other women who know that's not the case, women who know that poise, grace, and beauty is strength. When you're beautiful in everything you do, you're a powerful force that can't be ignored, a force to be respected and honored.

"Continue to remind yourselves of each Secret. Focus on one or two per week, rotating through them, over and over. Look for ways to enhance all your relationships, especially the one with yourself, from whence your beauty emanates."

"Diedra," Beth asked, "would you go over the Twelve Secrets with us? Just as a reminder."

"I'd be happy to. I've got the cards right here."

Secret #1: The key to what you want is Feminine Grace.

Secret #2: Men need to feel understood and accepted for who they are.

Secret #3: You are his only source of intimacy.

Secret #4: Sex is the only way most men know how to be intimate.

Secret #5: Men have high hopes for monogamy.

Secret #6: To a man, failure is "death."

Secret #7: If you're not happy, he's a failure.

Secret #8: Men show their love through action.

Secret #9: Men take risks to survive.

Secret #10: Men lose when they commit.

Secret #11: To be heard, you must speak his language.

Secret #12: A man wants to be with a woman who makes him feel like a man.

"Thank you, Diedra," Beth said, "I'd forgotten how much we'd learned. I can see how it would be good to review each Secret once in a while."

A friend is a person with whom
I may be sincere. Before him,
I may think aloud.
– Ralph Waldo Emerson

The feminist movement taught women that they had to

compete with men, and be more like men, if they were going to create equality. But men and women can never be equal because they're too different. To try to create equality has only caused strife. Women can move forward by being the best women they can be. They actually *lose* power when they try to be like men.

Yes, there are inequities in the workforce. Women sometimes get paid less than men for the same jobs. Yes, there seems to be a "glass ceiling" in the corporate world. Many men in power don't want to let women into the "hunter's circle." Knowing what you now understand about men, you can hardly blame them. One of the costs that came out of the feminist movement was a great deal of animosity between men and women. Animosity that continues to grow.

So, because the feminist movement seems—in many cases—contrary to some of the ideas in this book, you may feel like you're going against popular beliefs to follow the Twelve Simple Secrets. In many ways, love and romance are an old-fashioned idea, scorned by many women. But remember the popularity of the movie, *Pretty Woman*? When Edward offered Vivian a life of luxury with an apartment in New York, and all the money she could want, her response was, "No." When Edward asked, "Vivian, what do you want?" she said what many women are too embarrassed to say, "I want the fairy tale." It really is okay to want the fairy tale and the Twelve Simple Secrets can give you a chance to have at least a piece of it.

So, ideally, if you can organize a support group of five or more women to meet once a week you'll find your Feminine Grace growing more rapidly, and your power with men as well. You can phone each other for coaching when you need it, lean on each other for support, and grapple with the barriers that interfere with your development of self-love, self-confidence, and self-comfort. Because they can give you feedback, being part of a group will help you develop your sense of beauty and learn to trust your intuition. Often, we can see in others what we cannot see in ourselves.

"One of the problems with generalizations," Diedra continued, "is that they keep us from seeing the individuality of the man. When you're interacting with your husband or boyfriend you need to see who he really is and respond accordingly. Look for, and enjoy, those qualities that make him unique.

"When you focus on, and appreciate, all of who he is as a man, you can make him feel better than he's ever felt in his life. It's that powerful. That's when your intuition will serve you well. The generalizations let you see into his general makeup as a man, but your intuition and feminine strength of understanding people will assist you in knowing how to bring the very best out in the man in your life.

"Of course, some men are not worth your time. You have to let your intuition guide you. How many women do you know who continue to pick men who are wrong for them? They're ignoring the signals to beware. As a woman's self-respect and self-confidence grow, she's more able to hear and heed the warnings of her Wise Self. She's able to make smarter choices. Obviously it would be best to say no when we first meet a man who's bad for us. It would save a lot of heartache. Sadly, it's often not till after the fact that we realize we didn't heed the warnings, the red flags. We often say, 'I knew better. Why didn't I listen?' Which brings me to another point.

"This may be a little difficult to embrace, but I believe that some of the things we do, especially those that don't seem to be very good for us, are really opportunities that we create so we can learn some kind of lesson. Maybe your big lesson in life is to learn to stand up for yourself. So you keep choosing men who want to control you. But eventually—hopefully—you gather the strength to stand up to one of them, gain your footing, and begin your path to self-love and self-confidence, thus allowing the opportunity to choose a man who *is* good for you. Or maybe you need to learn to accept others as they are, so you find yourself with a man who resists your efforts to change and control him.

"Life is about learning and growing. The more we learn, the more we grow, and the more capacity we have to love because we understand more. Loving yourself has to come first and Feminine Grace throws open the door to self-love. *You can love others only to the degree that you love yourself.*"

Beth frowned. "I sure wish I'd known the Secrets earlier. I've made so many mistakes in my life."

Diedra leaned forward and held Beth's hands. "There's no such thing as a mistake, or even a failure, as long as you learn the lesson hidden within the experience."

Tears filled Beth's eyes. "I just wish I could go back and do things over."

"I understand, Beth. But you can turn your mistakes and failures into gold. Think about an experience from the past and find out what you were supposed to learn. Maybe you changed your behavior because you became a little bit wiser. When you mine the lessons from past experiences, you'll transform them into opportunities to grow. Then

they're no longer failures and mistakes.

"This leads me into another area that I'd almost forgotten to discuss with you. First, let me ask you a question. How many of you would prefer to avoid *all* heartache and crisis?"

Naturally, three hands went up.

"How many of you think heartache and crisis are inevitable?"

Again, three hands were raised.

"So we agree that problems will arise in all of our lives. I'm going to tell you something that will *almost* make you look forward to the bumps along the way. If you look at all heartache and crisis as an *opportunities to learn and grow*, then you're better equipped to get through them. Let your Wise Self become a Witness Self. If a part of you can step back and watch yourself go through the crisis, but at the same time give yourself full permission to feel all your feelings, you'll come out of the crisis a better, wiser, richer person."

"I've never thought about it that way," Carol exclaimed. "What an interesting way to look at it! I remember a time when I felt like I was watching myself. I was heartbroken over some guy in college that had broken up with me. I was throwing things around my room, ranting and raving, but I also talked to myself, saying things like, 'Carol, what on earth are you doing? You're better off without that guy.' Then I went right back to crying. I didn't know to search for the lesson, though. I suppose I could go back there now and learn something, couldn't I?"

"You sure could. That voice that spoke to you was your Wise Self, your Witness Self that's always watching over you. It's your intuition. It's there all the time, available to you whenever you need some self-guidance. It can be developed by paying attention and trusting it.

"Well, ladies, you've now received all of the Secrets. What I've taught you *is* simple *and* effective. When you become the very best you can be, and not only allow but encourage men to be men, magic will happen...a lot. That's as simple as it gets. The power to create that magic rests in your hands. It *will not* happen otherwise. If you want it, you *can* make it happen.

Diedra sat still for a few moments, smiling. "My dear friends, thank you for trusting me by coming here every week. You are truly magnificent women and I know you will continue to blossom like that red rose among the dandelions. Support each other, develop your Feminine Grace, incorporate the Twelve Simple Secrets into your lives, and you'll be amazed at what you will create. And most importantly, you'll be happier in everything you do and spread love wherever you go. Please come visit me often and let me know how your lives are unfolding."

Diedra stood and hugged Carol, then Jenny, and finally sweet Beth. They knew they would never forget this woman filled with grace and love, and that her Twelve Simple Secrets would color the rest of their lives. They said their good-byes and walked through the colorful garden onto the road. Heading back to the village they turned in unison to look one more time at the cottage on the edge of the enchanted forest.

Their hearts swelled with gratitude. They knew The Settling was gone from their lives and what lay before them was a life filled with hope. They knew their blossoming Feminine Grace would transport them to ever-deepening love, joy, passion, and a more fulfilling life. Already the men in their lives were responding to the changes that the Twelve Simple Secrets had helped bring about and they were excited at all the possibilities that lay before them.

Arm in arm, with joy lighting up their faces, our fair maidens walked back to their lives as new women, beautiful women, happy women.

The End

6 things you can do:

✓ Form a support group of women who want to incorporate the Twelve Simple Secrets into their lives and who want to develop their Feminine Grace. Read a chapter or two—either on your own time, or in the group—then discuss what you learned. If you can't find anyone to meet with, go to the Feminine Grace web site and list your name and contact information or look at the growing list to see if there are other women in your area who would like to form a group. The web site address is: www.femininegrace.com or www.menmadeeasy.com. If there's no one in your area, then find at least one woman with whom to form an email relationship.

✓ Do the exercises at the end of each chapter. If you pair up with someone in your group—or a trusted friend if you don't have a group—it will help to have someone to work with, to call for coaching as you incorporate the ideas into your life, and to talk with throughout the week.

✓ To help you get the most out of the exercises, order the *MEN MADE EASY Workbook* so you can be more organized and proactive in your efforts to develop your Feminine Grace and improve your relationship.

✓ Make a list of regrets, mistakes, failures, heartaches, and crises that you have experienced in your life. Look at

each one and discover the lesson in it. Write down what you learned. Now turn it into gold by incorporating the learning into who you are so your life is better, richer, and fuller. Discover how you can be a better person so you are happier and more fulfilled.

✓ Tell other women about this book. As more women learn the Twelve Simple Secrets, the mistrust and resentment that stands between men and women will begin to dissolve. *Everyone* will benefit. You can help by sharing with others. Be a shining example of grace, poise, and beauty by expanding your Feminine Grace into every aspect of your life. Be beautiful in everything you do and you will affect everyone with whom you interact.

✓ Finally, don't take life too seriously. Hold in your heart that you are here to learn to love and be loved. Be happy, joyful, caring, creative, and filled with the thrill of being alive. You will then be a gift to everyone you meet…and more importantly, to yourself.

Why not turn your life into a fairy tale come true? You now have the ability to be a magnificent and beautiful women, fully empowered to transform your and your partner's life into a fairy tale filled with love, romance, and joy. Trust your intuition, trust your heart, and trust in love.

A Special Bonus

Now that you've read an entire book about *him*, have him read the next eight pages. It's *his* book about *you*. When asked, the men said their book should be very short, with lots of white space. They'll learn Twelve Secrets about how to make you a happier, more loving woman. Which is exactly what they want.

How to Make Her Happy

A Quick Guide For Guys

What *you* should know about *her*.

▼◆▼

Yes, it's true that most men don't read or talk about relationships, but your lady love just read an entire book about what makes you tick and how to make you a happier man. Maybe you've already noticed she's treating you...differently. So, to level the playing field, she wants you to read just these *few* pages so you can make her a happier woman. Does that sound fair?

Following are Twelve Simple Secrets that *you* should know about *her.* When you're done reading them you'll have a better grip on what to do to make her smile a little brighter.

▼▼▼▼▼▼▼▼▼▼▼▼▼▼▼▼▼▼▼▼▼▼▼▼▼▼▼▼

❖ How to Make Her Happy ❖

Secret #1
Romance is the key to sex.

Romance is routine maintenance—yeah, like your car—to keep things running smoothly. Remember all those romantic things you did to win her in the first place? *Keep doing them* now and then. If you let her know often that you care, she stays open and responsive to your sexual overtures.

Romance is all the little things you do to let her know you care. Call her just to say hi. Buy her a gift "just because." (Remember, it isn't the *cost* of the gift, it's the *thought*.) And flowers, even the smallest bouquet, *always* work. How about mailing a card or leaving a note where she'll find it? Or planning a special outing, or arranging for a baby-sitter so you can take her to the movies? Anything that lets her know you've been thinking about her melts her heart. For her, romance and sex go hand-in-hand. If you want more *sex*, give her more *romance*.

Secret #2
For her, sex takes time.

Okay, your romantic efforts have paid off and she's in the mood for sex. When asked what sex advice they'd give to men, women almost always say, "Tell them to SLOW DOWN!"

Think of sex as a slow, sensuous dance. Be gentle, seductive. (Rent the movie *Don Juan deMarco* and listen to how he talks about women and making love.) Explore her entire body. You both may be surprised what you find. Hold her like you never want to let her go. And give her lots of long, slow kisses. (Women often complain that men don't kiss enough.)

What you're doing is warming her up. You wouldn't take a Ferrari that's been sitting in your garage for a week, start it, and immediately run it up to 100 mph, would you? Well, think of her as a Ferrari.

Oh, and don't roll over and fall asleep immediately after sex. Women really hate this; they need to be held and they love a little pillow talk afterward, so stay awake for at least a few minutes. Then, better yet, fall asleep holding her.

Secret #3
Talking is the way she connects with you.

Women talk for the sheer pleasure of talking. It's how they connect to people. Because your woman has read this book she understands that a lot of what she talks about—all those little details—is boring to you. So, she's going to be more selective about what she says to you. But if you *give her your full attention* when she *does* talk to you, it becomes one of those romantic gestures. Got it?

And you know how she's always trying to get you to be "more intimate"? If you listen to her more, she'll think you *are* being more intimate. All you have to do is look at her and pay attention; she'll think she's died and gone to heaven. It's *that* important to her, and that simple.

Secret #4
She needs to hear you say you care.

For her to really *feel* your love, you need to tell her in words. Of course, she wants to hear you say "I love you," but anything you say to let her know you care and appreciate her will earn you major points: "You're wonderful, do you know that?" "I'm so lucky to have you." "Do you know how much

I love you?" *Big* points on *that* one. Whenever you say these things, look into her eyes and mean it. Remember this, you *cannot* tell her you love her too often. This definitely wins you points on the romance chart.

And, how often have you heard one of your buddies, who's gotten a divorce, say, "I never realized how much she did to make my life comfortable."

Secret #5
She needs to hear she's attractive.

In today's culture, because of what they are taught as girls, and because of what they read in magazines and see on TV and in films, women get insecure about how they look and whether they're sexually appealing. So, tell her regularly—and let her know you mean it—that she's sexy and beautiful.

Compliment her on a new dress, the color she's wearing, or how her hair looks. Tell her she has soft skin, how much she turns you on, how pretty her breasts are. The more *beautiful* she feels, the *sexier* she'll feel. This should pay off big time in the bedroom.

Secret #6
Her feelings need to be honored.

Her feelings are as important to her as your work (or maybe sports) is to you. That's why she likes to talk about them. She needs you to acknowledge what's going on for her when she's being emotional. Don't try to tell her that what she's feeling is "wrong" and don't try to fix the problem unless she asks you to. And never tell her "not to feel" her emotions. A sure-fire winner: ask her, "What are

you feeling?" Then sit down and listen.

She understands that you get kind of uncomfortable when she's being emotional, but if you just let her express herself and listen with your full attention, she'll think you're the most sensitive man on the planet.

Secret #7
Making up is hard to do.

When you fight with your partner, are you often surprised that it turned into a bigger event than it should have? If she's like most women, she tends to get going with her emotions and lets everything spill out. She doesn't mean a lot of what she says. Do your best to pay attention, let her vent, but don't let the words get to you. The best way to stop her in her tracks is to admit that you were being stubborn, insensitive, inconsiderate, and hurtful. The more conciliatory you are, the more she'll be stopped in her tracks. If you make the first move to make up and offer no resistance, she can't keep fighting with you. Someone has to take charge so it doesn't escalate, and because she's lost in her emotions, it's going to have to be you. Be willing to look at her complaint and see where you may have been insensitive to her needs.

If you both vow to *never go to bed mad*, you'll be making love instead of war.

Secret #8
She likes to be pampered.

Your woman naturally does for others. She appreciates the value of nurturing but all too often doesn't take the time to care for herself. You can score big time if once in a while you run a bubble bath for her, take her on a special trip or

plan a romantic dinner, give her a gift certificate from her favorite shop or a trip to a day spa. Talk about getting a woman "in the mood." Wahoo!

Sure, she appreciates that you change the oil in her car, but it doesn't really tell her you love her, even though that may be what you mean. To pamper her just remember, *personal* luxuries.

Secret #9
She needs your respect.

Throughout history, and in many cultures even today, women have been second-class citizens, looked down on as less able in every category. Only recently have we begun to consider women *worthy* of respect. To be the open, loving woman you want, she needs you to honor her as a person and appreciate her contributions as a capable person. Don't treat her as a child. Don't judge or criticize her. Don't ignore her or take her for granted. Don't be rude. Treat her like a lady at all times and she'll treat *you* with the respect that you expect and enjoy.

Secret #10
She needs to feel secure.

Your lady has a deep biological need to feel secure, to have a man provide for her and protect her. Financial security is obviously important, but even more than that, she needs to know you're *there for her*. That's one of the reasons she needs to hear you say, "I love you."

What really helps is to give her ongoing affection and the reassurance of physical contact. If you do this every day, several times a day, you'll give her the security she

needs. Hold her hand, put your arm around her, hug her, touch her in gentle and reassuring ways. The more secure she feels, the happier she'll be. When she's happy, she's open to you.

Secret #11
She needs your time and attention.

Does she ever try to talk to you when you're reading the newspaper? Or walk in front of the TV in the middle of the play-offs? Does she complain that she never sees you, never has time to talk with you, or that you don't even know she's alive? If so, it's a plea for your attention. She knows how focused you can be when you're working, but she feels left out. It's part of that security thing.

What to do? Set aside time now and then to focus on *her.* Let her know she's important enough to devote yourself to her *completely* and she'll be less likely to feel ignored. The rewards will far outweigh the effort.

Secret #12
She wants a man who
makes her feel like a woman.

She chose you because of your masculine qualities. Qualities that make her feel more womanly. In your presence, she feels protected, provided for, and loved. Be masculine, but do it with sensuality and sensitivity. Be hungry for her, be passionate, be strong, but be tender, as if she were a delicate flower. And, yes, open the car door for her, carry heavy things for her, pull out her chair. The feminist movement did a lot of damage to romance but if your woman has been reading this book, she's not into

feminism, she's into love and romance. That means you. Be chivalrous, be gallant, be thoughtful, and win her heart...over and over again.

Make her feel beautiful, make her feel desirable, make her feel special and important, and you'll make her feel like a woman—as only a man can do.

Yes, It's That Simple!

So there it is in a nutshell. Twelve Simple Secrets that could very well change your life forever. You can never know for sure what's going on with a woman, but you can certainly make everything a lot nicer—for both of you—by following the advice you've just read.

Men complain that women nag, criticize, try to change them, are never satisfied, are too emotional and unpredictable. If you follow these Secrets and make them a habit, that irritating behavior should pretty much disappear. If it comes back, consider it a barometer of how you're doing. Then get the Secrets out and read them again.

The way to be a great lover is to be a romantic lover. When you focus on romance, she'll respond to you like never before. And she'll feel like she's the luckiest woman alive.

▼ ◆ ▼

If you're really serious about becoming more romantic, you can subscribe to The RoMANtic, a newsletter—written by a man for men—filled with hundreds of tips for fun and creative romance. Subscribe by sending $15 to Michael Webb,P.O. Box 1567-MM, Cary, NC 27512 or going to his website: www.theromantic.com.